Film and Cinema Spectatorship

Film and Cinema Spectatorship
Melodrama and Mimesis

Jan Campbell

polity

First published in 2005 by Polity Press

Polity Press
65 Bridge Street
Cambridge CB2 1UR, UK

Polity Press
350 Main Street
Malden, MA 02148, USA

ISBN: 0 7456 2929 6
ISBN: 0 7456 2930 X (paperback)

A catalogue record for this book is available from the British Library.

Typeset in 10.5 on 12 pt Sabon
by SNP Best-set Typesetter Ltd, Hong Kong
Printed and bound in Great Britain by MPG Books Ltd, Bodmin, Cornwall

Every effort has been made to trace all copyright holders, but if any have been inadvertently overlooked the publishers will be pleased to include any necessary credits in any subsequent reprint or edition.

For further information on Polity, visit our website: www.polity.co.uk

Contents

List of Illustrations

Acknowledgements

For many years now, I have taught film studies and psychoanalysis within the academy. I have also worked clinically as a psychoanalytic psychotherapist. This book is an attempt to think through psycho-analysis and film studies in a way which opens both out to the embod-ied and disembodied dreaming, or mimesis, which is at stake whether we are watching films or, indeed, immersed in the therapeutic trans-ference. This is, of course, a book about film spectatorship where I bring psychoanalysis and phenomenology together in a re-reading of film theory. Psychoanalysis has become increasingly unfashionable in academic thinking because it is seen to deliver a deterministic and ahistorical narrative of subjectivity and the unconscious.

The argument mobilized in this book is an attempt to dissolve psy-choanalysis as a discrete discipline or a master narrative. There is no certain interpretation of the unconscious, only ways of understand-ing our experience within, and out of, lived time. When we watch film we can delineate between the dream in our head and dreaming the world. However, to do so is to inhabit a hysterical split which delivers a certainty of theory and subjectivity, but obscures a more radical dissolution of the self and the spectator. One of the premisses of this book is that the sexual-difference spectator of film theory is a hysterical spectator: a spectator who can't inhabit lived time because she or he has not learnt how to lose it. Film experience, though, is not just hysterical, pure presence, it can also be a lived, lost and embodied time – whether that is characterized by Walter Benjamin's film traveller of the optical unconscious or by François Roustang's vision of the astonished existence that lies as a possible outcome of the therapeutic encounter.

I want to thank:

My editor Andrea Drugan for all her help

Erica Carter, Anita Rupprecht and Debbie Parsons for insightful comments and editing skills with the script

Steve Pile for fascinating conversations about hysteria, dreaming and ghosts

Pam Howard – much love – I would not have survived my training without you!

Prue Green for sharing friendship and intellectual/clinical conversation

Noreen O'Connor for clinical supervision and for discussions on psychoanalytic phenomenology

Adam Phillips for supervision and intellectual conversation and for showing me how to make therapy up

Esmé Campbell for sharing love, humour and the highs and lows of adolescence

J. – thank you for everything!

Mike Van Duuren for your love and support and for being there.

Finally, I want to acknowledge all my friends and colleagues who worked with me at the department of Cultural Studies at the University of Birmingham from 1998 until its shameful closure in 2002.

Acknowledgements are also due to Ann Gray, Stuart Hanson, Jorge Larrain, Mark Erickson, Helen Wood, Frank Webster, Nuala Killeen, Beth Edgington, Michael Green, David Parker, Clive Harris, Marie Walsh and Yvonne Jacobs.

In memory of my father – Lawrence Blight – I will miss you.

Introduction

So much of film theory has been about language, and it is time now to focus on the body. Such a role, incorporating the real of the spectator, has arguably been introduced with the increasing preoccupation with cinema going and cinema audiences. However, an emphasis on empirical audience studies and their social context is inadequate in explaining the phenomenological experience of the spectator, or indeed to account for the embodied and disembodied identification and mimesis that move between spectator and film.

This book re-reads film theory and spectatorship through a concept of phenomenological mimesis. Phenomenology is a philosophical movement which provides a detailed description of lived experience and emphasizes the continuous lived experience, intertwined between mind and reality. In this book I emphasize a phenomenological reading of psychoanalysis and unconscious experience where there is no Oedipal division between the imaginary and the real: they are fluidly connected.[1]

Mimesis means the imitation of nature and human behaviour. Mimesis has, since Plato's *Republic*, constructed a truthful relation between referent and sign, between the self and the world, between nature and image. For the psychoanalyst Jacques Lacan, this is the fiction of the paternal phallus, although this does not stop him from setting up this paternal law as an immutable symbolic order. Walter Benjamin draws on Aristotle's notion of mimesis to describe a more creative imitation or copy of human behaviour and nature. Rather than rooting his ideas in a mimesis of platonic form, Benjamin elaborates them as material practice and behaviour. Freud sees mimesis as hysterical identification and repetition. In this book I describe film spectatorship as a phenomenological mimesis which is (1) an imaginary hysterical identification and (2) a more social, creative dreaming with which we can reconstruct experience.

This book begins with a questioning of the psychic and textual account of identification mobilized in psychoanalytic film studies, otherwise known as Apparatus or Screen theory. In this Lacanian and Althusserian account the cinematic apparatus and text are determining, focusing on the image as an identification with sexual difference, which is replicated in the spectator. This spectator identifies Oedipally; 'his' textual and sexual identification of difference is symbolically distinct from affectual response. In this book film spectatorship is read as a mode of the imaginary rather than the symbolic; a phenomenological imaginary which moves between the text and the spectator. This imaginary mode performs the body, oscillating between disembodied, hysterical dreaming and a more embodied, social mimesis. Filmic identification is, therefore, mimetic in a bodily sense. There is no pre-Oedipal point of trauma or the real before we identify with the representational text, only the shock, thrill and pleasure of a mimetic desire that is always already identified, like Freud's death drive, with the film or the imaginary of the other.

Arguing that the railway can be seen as paradigm for the early film spectator, Lynne Kirby maps how the hysteria of shocked railway travellers suffering from 'Railway Spine' (concussion of the spine resulting from a railway accident) doubles as the hysteria of the shocked early film spectator. Both railway traveller and film spectator are assaulted by the new urban environment of modernity, ushering them into a new space-time configuration where space and distance become shrunk into time, as 'both railroad and cinema demanded a new obedience to a new authority of movement and scheduling'.[2] The hysterical trauma of the early film spectator is illustrated by Uncle Josh's exaggerated, frightened and funny parody of the Lumière spectator, panicking before the oncoming train in the cinema.[3] But this hysterical, bodily and melodramatic response is not simply the traumatic assault of a cinematic apparatus and image on the shocked spectator. The cinematic apparatus and filmic image are, after all, only a sum of what we have hysterically projected into them. Therefore, there is no trauma or hysteria before the point of Oedipal textual identification, just hysterical identification and projection from the beginning, as a mimesis that rolls between primordial and socialized states of being. Cinema and psychoanalysis began together and their simultaneous roots in nineteenth-century modernism are crucially interwoven with the figure of the hysteric. In this sense cinema and psychoanalysis can be seen to historicize each other as they are intrinsically and hysterically bound to each other.

This book argues for film spectatorship as a phenomenological mimesis which moves between Oedipal hysteria and a more social and embodied place within time. Such an account entails bringing together psychoanalytic and phenomenological concepts of mimesis. Or, in other words it means bringing together Freud's and Benjamin's notions of the unconscious and dreaming. Whereas Freud's dreaming wants to ward off time and preserve it, Benjamin in contrast wants to capture time and mark it by 'the dynamite of a tenth of a second'.[4] The filmic tradition that fetishizes and wards off time, preserving the privatized, Oedipal imaginary of Freud by elevating it to a linguistic level, is encapsulated by Apparatus theory. Alternatively, Walter Benjamin's phenomenological dreaming on the streets, his social and bodily optical unconscious, is taken up in the more historical tradition associated with thinkers like Miriam Hansen and Tom Gunning. As Thomas Elsaesser has noted, Hansen, together with other film critics writing in the late 1980s in *New German Critique*, such as Getrud Koch and Heide Schüpmann, has sought to marry German film theory (Béla Balázs, Rudolf Arnheim and Siegfried Kracauer) with Marxist theories of the Frankfurt School, such as Benjamin's. The social theory of the 1920s drew on the concept of 'distraction' to define what was seen as the phenomenological experience of the new white-collar workers with the emergent society of mass media. While Benjamin attributed 'distraction' to the montage of film forms, Kracauer used the term to sum up a largely alienated fetishization of film and society by mass audiences within Weimar culture, and, later, to ground his theories of realist film.[5]

With the exhaustion of Screen theory in the 1980s and the oppositional move to empirical film studies in the 1990s, psychoanalysis has become fixed – some would say left behind – within the textual universalism of Screen or Apparatus theory. The alternative, historical, film tradition, associated with *New German Critique*, developed to include, as well as Hansen and Gunning, thinkers such as Vanessa Schwartz, Anne Friedberg and Leo Charney. These critics have focused on the emergence of film within the sensory urban environment of modernity. David Bordwell has termed the scholarship associated with these thinkers, the 'modernity thesis'.[6] Critical of what he sees as a causal relation between modernity and films in this body of work – Benjamin's idea that film corresponds to deep changes in the perceptual apparatus – Bordwell suggests the cognitive idea of a perception of modern life. Shocks of a modern, urban environment are not, for Bordwell, causal of a particular change in the apparatus of psychic perception. Instead, people adjust to the tempo of modern life through habits and skills which are cognitively acquired. Cognitive perception, for Bordwell, rather like Oedipal psycho-analysis for Freud, remains a timeless and universal structure or mindset, undisturbed by the vicissitudes of history. Ben Singer endorses Bordwell's argument and yet remains sceptical of how it can provide an adequate account 'of the experiential consequences of modernity'. What we need, according to Singer, is to follow Benjamin's insights and develop a physiological account of the history of perception and film.[7]

Bringing together a physiology and the psychology of perception of film within modernity entails a rethinking of psychoanalysis in relation to the critical work of Benjamin and Kracauer. Rather than taking Benjamin and Kracauer as film thinkers whose work applies solely to specific historical periods, this book utilizes them as thinkers of a social and optical unconscious whose dreaming is located within social time, and not out of it on the privatized couch. Like Freud, Kracauer and Benjamin both theorize a mimesis of desire and sub-jectivity that moves between melancholia and mourning. Unlike Freud, however, their dreaming refuses to stay on the couch, in the family or within the mimetic hysterical rivalry of sexual difference. Instead, their distraction and dreaming move out into public space, into what Michael Taussig calls the 'mimetic faculty of modernity'.[8] Whereas Freud places the Oedipal complex and the art of repression as the resolution of our rivalrous mimetic death drives, Taussig, René Girard and Jean-Michel Oughourlian profess the need to move beyond mimesis as repression, rivalry or obstacle and submit to the mimetic process.[9] For Girard and Oughourlian, only peaceful sub-mission to the mimetic model enables the route out of hysterical rivalry and neurosis. In Taussig's view, it is the self-awareness of the mimetic process, enabled by mimetic excess that allows us to re-member, like Benjamin's profane illumination, a more embodied and experiential relation to history. Like Benjamin, Taussig describes the mimetic power of the filmic camera not to just mime reality, but also to cut the image, slice it open to time and, through montage, make the free associations that Freud tells us are so important in overcoming repression or disassociation in the analytic session.

Benjamin's filmic unconscious, his dreaming on the streets, describes the ability of film to open up the fetish of the commodity, to transform the aura of tradition through a re-embodiment of mimesis, a mimesis that can creatively recollect experience and connect it to the past, so projecting into the future. Mimesis, as

Benjamin notes with reference to Freud's essay 'Beyond the Pleasure Principle', is a hysterical repetition that defends against the shocks and traumas of the modern world, but it is also a way of reconstructing experience. If the film camera's profane illumination in capturing time, or cutting through its fetishization, is its ability to free-associate, move and reconfigure space-time, then this ability is also a capacity to acknowledge and connect with the double, and work creatively with it. The double within film manifests itself as melodrama and as hysteria. Following Peter Brooks, I argue for melodrama and hysteria within film as interchangeable terms, but rather than being located simply in the text, I argue for them as mimetic structures of the imaginary, a melodramatic mimesis that also organizes film spectatorship. Just as the melodramatic and hysterical imaginary organizes the analytic transference and our psychic dream space, so it figures as a mimesis that rolls between film spectator and text, between the film in our head and the film as a more social representational space. Recognition of the double or other within film and psychoanalysis is precisely the mimetic awareness of its status as our psychic and social unconscious. The Oedipal complex only makes sense in this scenario, as Borch-Jacobsen has so lucidly pointed out, as a hysterical relation between rivalrous doubles. Like analysis, film is an arena of space-time where the subject/spectator moves in and out of lived time, oscillating between hysterical disembodied mimesis, or a privatized dreaming that has become narcissistic retreat, to a more social embodied dreaming where the double is accepted and time can be lived, allowed to pass and be remembered.

The strategy in this book, to re-member the heritage of cinema and psychoanalysis, is to re-read the dominant, critical film texts and films that have constructed ideas of the spectator in relation to different (film) traditions. In addressing the accusation that this book simply reads symptomatic texts I want to foreground the methodological difficulty in film studies in addressing both history and theory simultaneously. In many ways this book makes no pretence to be a historicization of film in that it does not contextualize and compare film theory and filmic texts within a specific period. On another level, this book is a theoretical attempt to map the historical tracks of psychoanalysis and cinema, whose history lies in their primary mimetic relation with each other. Tracking this heritage is a re-reading of established film criticisms and film texts that have hitherto been subjected to Oedipal interpretations within film theory. Key to this history of psychoanalysis and cinema is a mimesis which moves between hysteria and social memory/mourning.

Beyond the pre-Oedipal/Oedipal film binary

My re-reading of the history of film theory rejects the familiar distinction that equates early cinema with the pre-Oedipal and classical
cinema with Oedipal narrative. This traditional reading of film theory
ends by defining early film as performative and embodied in contrast
with the narrative turn of classical cinema. However, this book
refuses an Oedipal/pre-Oedipal distinction, and argues for film spectatorship as a mimesis of disembodiment and embodiment. Following from this, a central methodological argument is a reading of
melodrama, which both develops and contrasts with the Freudian
meaning elaborated by Peter Brooks. For Brooks, melodrama is
situated as a bodily excess that is repressed, returning to destabilize
the narrative (realist) authority of the text. As Linda Williams and
Christine Gledhill both suggest, melodrama is not a marginal or
discrete genre, located say within women's film or attributed to specific historical periods. Instead, it is a dominant organizing modality
of film.[10] In this book melodrama and hysteria become the pivotal
ways of understanding spectatorship, in terms of a mimesis which is
peculiar to specific historical moments. Re-reading specific film texts
and criticisms from the earlier moments of film theory and history is
then a key strategy in what follows, and melodrama is central in the
location and selection of texts that reflect filmic debates on early
cinema, modernism and the sexual, textual difference of Apparatus
theory. Although the last chapters do move to a later focus on cultural studies, stars, postmodernity and aesthetics, it is the reworking
of Oedipal, narrative film theory that underpins the structure of this
project. If the Oedipal complex is hysterical – and I will argue that
it is – then hysteria and melodrama become the key terms with which
we understand the film spectator in early classical and contemporary
accounts of film spectatorship.

In this book I read psychoanalysis and phenomenological film
theory through each other, but it is important here to spell out
what exactly I mean by a phenomenological conceptualization of
hysteria, melodrama, mimesis and of course the cinematic imaginary.
I am not so much wresting them from an Oedipal interpretation
as turning that Oedipal interpretation into its hysterical mimetic
double through a phenomenological understanding of cinema and the
unconscious.

Melodrama and mimesis

Raymond Bellour is the film critic most famous for making the
analogy between cinema and hypnosis. Arguing for the regressive
hypnotic powers of cinema, Bellour suggests that there are

> Two ways of living the look that remains the spectator's, that person
> who has not really been hypnotised: the identifying look and the look
> of fascination, one heading towards life and the other towards death
> (this distinction is Lacan's: between that which he calls 'the instant of
> seeing' and the 'fascinum').[11]

Bellour is making a distinction between hypnosis as Freud initially
viewed it, as a vehicle for increasing consciousness, and hypnosis as
a fatal fascination. For Lacan, movement away from a fatal, hypnotic
transference entails the analyst taking up the symbolic place of
language and the law. François Roustang is critical of the ideal
Lacanian analyst who insists on being Nobody or the phallic law.
This is because this nobody law, who in fact represents everything –
all certainty and knowledge – confronts the hysteric with an absence.
In the face of this absence the hysteric continues to repeat her same
old gestures in the imaginary of the Other.[12] Thus blocked from
following new paths, the hysteric is always in a dependency and necessary opposition to the phallic law of psychoanalysis, knowledge
and reason. Historically, as Foucault showed us, the hysteric is
produced in relation to this figure of science and moral reason with
the birth of the clinic. Madness began its career as mental illness
at the end of the eighteenth century, an origin that gave birth simultaneously to the mimetic and symbiotic roles of, on the one hand, the
scientific doctor/psychoanalyst/psychiatrist steeped in the Enlightenment mores of rationality and irrationality, and, on the other, the
hysterical and psychotic patient, whose supposed regression to an
instinctual and primitive level creates infantile dependence on her
physician's knowledge and scientific expertise. Oedipus and hysteria
are simply two sides of the same coin.

The psychoanalytic session is in a sense a melodrama: a mimetic
hypnosis where the hysteric dramatizes the conflict of hearth and
home in a domestic enslavement to an essentially private theatre. In
thrall to the authority and imaginary of the Oedipal psychoanalyst,
the hysteric forgets, or chooses not to remember, that 'she' is a product
of his scientific law. The hysteric wants to disrupt his phallic law
of reason and language, but only so, in the event of his destruction,
she can set another analyst in his place. In order to therapeutically

cure the hysteric, one cannot take up a position of law and resist her, neither can one collapse and agree with her. Instead, one has to open up the rivalrous mimetic melodrama of hysteric versus Oedipal law to a more embodied mimesis. Such mimesis is where the hysteric can access a more intersubjective phenomenology, where melodrama can abandon fascinated suffering to enter the possibilities of lived time and social memory. Winnicott describes this sense of being in time as the creative transitional space, where affects are integrated and the infant or adult can exist alone in the presence of an 'other'. The hysteric is not capable of this and lives in a melodramatic world where power relations substitute for less destructive co-existence.

The split melodramatic world of the hysteric is emblematic of modernity. Although, as Christine Gledhill has noted, there has been a common misconception that equates realism with the novel and melodrama with theatre, their relationship has been much more enmeshed. Cinema, indeed, combined 'pictorial sensationalism' and 'photographic realism' in ways which solved limitations of both novel and stage. It became the realization of the melodramatic imagination.[13] Peter Brooks charts how melodrama arose with bourgeois capitalism as a crisis of modernity. The loss of traditional, sacred forms of cultural organization and the rise of individualism led to a 'moral occult' where ethics and morality become staged as a personal and psychic concern. Melodrama's inheritance from a popular tradition meant that it exerted a force on the repressive principle of post-Enlightenment reason. But if melodrama put pressure on the dominant rationality of modernity, a symbolic which wants to grasp and understand the world, it also dramatized the moral conflicts and made public what had hitherto been private and unseen. Brook's use of Freudian psychoanalysis is brought to bear, here, where the Oedipal conflicts of the family are not liberated through melodrama, but socially externalized and staged.

Historically the terms of realism have changed, and as they have, so the ground for melodrama changes. The repressive Victorian bourgeois, male subject is met with the suffering, hysterical femininity of the 'Angel in the House'. And the realist hero of the classical American Hollywood movie is matched by the melodramatic, struggling mother of the woman's film. Thomas Elsaesser traces the origins of melodrama to two historical traditions: a public and popular tradition evolving into nineteenth-century spectacle, and a more individual figure of interior thought and feeling developed in French romantic drama with links to the bourgeois novel.[14] It is this latter tradition that, in Elsaesser's view, leads most directly to the 1940s and 1950s domestic, family melodramas. He notes that the melodrama is a 'historically, socially conditioned mode of experience'.[15] Now I want to emphasize this. Elsaesser correlates melodrama with Freud's dream-work, whereas Brooks and Geoffrey Nowell-Smith explicitly link melodrama with Freud's concepts of hysteria and a return of the repressed. However, there remains a contradiction between representing melodrama as a repression of psychic structures, or perceiving it as a mode of experience and an externalization of those psychic structures. Peter Brooks writes, 'Melodrama exteriorises conflict and psychic structures, producing . . . What we might call the "melodrama of psychology" '.[16]

This notion of melodrama as an externalization of the unconscious contradicts Freud's meta-psychology and Oedipal complex arrived at in *The Interpretation of Dreams* (1901), where Freud makes a clear Oedipal demarcation between an interior unconscious world and external reality. Melodrama has been linked by Brooks and Nowell-Smith to the notion of hysteria as a bodily excess that disrupts and accounts for the point in a text where realist conventions break down. This model constructs neurosis as the mental repression of bodily affects. If melodrama is tied to a purely Oedipal notion of hysteria, as the return of the repressed, then it is hard to see how this notion of hysteria equates to either an external structure or a mode of experience. Freud carefully described hysteria as a conversion symptom derived from the repression of an *idea* or a *wish*. Freud, though, was never consistent and his early work maps a phenomenological tracking of the hysteric, which he abandoned in a move announced with the famous Oedipal moment in *Interpretation of Dreams*, where he announces the meta-psychological split between neuro-physiology and psychoanalysis. Oedipal psychoanalysis is predicated on a split between the material and symbolic; it structures a division between the internal mental world and an outer physical one. A phenomenological approach to the unconscious makes no such division between unconscious and conscious. We can see this difference within the early debates between Freud and Jung. Quarrelling over the status of the unconscious, Freud wanted Jung to adhere to his meta-psychological theory of the psyche, whereas Jung persisted in describing a phenomenological unconscious of surface effects.

What would it mean then to understand hysteria and melodrama phenomenologically, according to Freud's earlier thinking? Laura Mulvey has written on melodrama's role in the development of contemporary film theory.[17] In this piece she maps the differing trends of melodrama that have contributed to the influence of that genre in contemporary film theory. In tracing debates around Hollywood melodrama, Mulvey is interested in the role of melodrama in film criticism, particularly for the development of feminist film theory and psychoanalysis.

Mulvey argues for the hysterical *mise-en-scène* of melodrama as 'a gallery of collective fantasy', the collective myths and fantasies that culture represses. She relates Freud's early lecture on hysteria where he describes hysterical symptoms as mnemic symbols of past traumatic experiences. Freud links hysterical symptoms to the mnemic symbols of the past that adorn large cities such as London, such as the Monument of the Fire of London. The melancholic Londoners, who stop and weep at the past destruction of London by fire, fail to acknowledge its present, rebuilt, glory. In similar vein the hysterics behave like these 'unpractical Londoners', in weeping over past traumas.[18] Mulvey writes:

> The images and stories of popular cinema can function like collective mnemic symbols, and allow 'ordinary people', us, to stop and wonder or weep, desire or shudder, momentarily touching 'unspeakable' but shared psychic structures. We are licensed to respond, in Freud's terms, 'neurotically'.[19]

Proceeding to apply an Oedipal interpretation to two of Sirk's famous melodramas *Magnificent Obsession* and *Imitation of Life*, Mulvey concludes with a discussion of how the psychic process of obsession works in *Magnificent Obsession* to exclude and subordinate all social and economic factors to the central Oedipal love story, and how in *Imitation of Life*, the performance and masquerade of commodified white femininity serves to abject black womanhood, obliterating questions of race and class.

I want to re-evaluate Mulvey's piece, replacing her Oedipal reading of melodrama with a phenomenological one. Freud's early phenomenological tracking of the hysteric when he was still in accordance (in differing ways) with Charcot and Jung, saw the unconscious as a 'twilight' state of disassociation and splitting. Such a model of the unconscious was based on the psyche as analogous to neurophysiology. This is the unconscious that Freud still adheres to in his 'Five Lectures', where he makes the analogy between hysterical symptoms and the mnemic symbols and monuments of London's past. What is striking about Freud's account, here, is that he attributes hysteria to a melancholic dwelling in the past, a melancholia that is an escape or flight from the present. This model of hysteria accords with Jung's early thinking and is quite different from the subsequent moves Freud makes in formulating an Oedipal meta-psychology. In this early understanding there is no disjunction between the psyche and the social. The hysteric is described as suffering from hypnotic absences, occupying a double consciousness that for Freud doubles as the collective neurotic fantasies of 'unpractical Londoners'. In Freud's later Oedipal model the hysterical symptom is a repressed, converted wish or idea. Within the earlier phenomenological understanding, however, hysteria is an altered experiential and neurotic state.

Comprehending hysteria and melodrama as phenomenological allows us to move the historical debate on psychoanalysis and cinema. Instead of reading hysteria and melodrama as a return of the repressed, an excess that can put pressure on the dominant reality principle, we can see hysteria and melodrama as a doubling and splitting of consciousness. Melodrama and hysteria are a 'mode of experience' to quote Elsaesser, historically and socially determined: a melodrama that exists intersubjectively between people. Melodrama and hysteria thus become located between the psyche and the social; they exist not as an internal repressed mental imaginary, but as a private *and* social imaginary.

If we go back to Mulvey's essay on melodrama and film theory, it is perfectly possible to read her Oedipal interpretation of Sirk's *Magnificent Obsession* and *Imitation of Life* in terms of a hysterical mimesis. In *Magnificent Obsession* we can see how the central Oedipal love story in the film is in fact a story of the deathly imaginary and mimetic rivalry that exists between father and son. The younger man at the beginning of this film accidentally kills off the symbolic father figure, who is a doctor, through careless driving. Subsequently, he trains in the dead doctor's shoes and romantically wins his widow. Mulvey notes how this story fails to 'subordinate illicit desire to the law'.[20] Likewise, in *Imitation of Life*, the performative masquerade of the white heroine, Lora, is a hysterical mimesis of idealized femininity, projecting categories of race and class onto the abject, bodily sexuality of her black servant Annie. My point, here, is that I don't disagree with Mulvey's reading, except for one vital exception: there is no Oedipal, symbolic operating in either of these texts – the Oedipal in this melodramatic cinema is completely imaginary and hysterical.

As Foucault suggests, the hysteric and the Oedipal doctor were born as doubles of each other. Similarly, we can see the historical construction of realism and melodrama, not as an (Oedipal) return of the repressed, which marginalizes melodrama to a pre-Oedipal arena, but rather as the split and divided face of modernity, a mimesis where Oedipus and the hysteric, realism and melodrama are constant doubles of each other. Cinema is historically Oedipal, melodramatic *and* hysterical.

Drawing on the work of Luce Irigaray and Bertolt Brecht, Elin Diamond suggests a feminist mimicry as a more embodied and performative spectator of theatre which can subvert classical mimesis or realism.[21] In Raymond Bellour's theory the regressed spectator in the darkened womb/cinema is sent back to states of symbiotic regression. As Diamond comments, this is very different from the Brechtian notion of active distancing and reception where the spectator cognitively revises the stage or filmic meaning.[22] How, then, does a spectator move between hysterical regression to a more cognitive dialectical reading of the cinematic image? Diamond rightly sees the solution to this problem as resting with a more embodied notion of mimesis. I want, therefore, to develop Diamond's argument for a performative mimesis from stage to screen, by elaborating it within a (more) phenomenological reading of hysteria and melodrama.

Realism and melodrama as mimetic doubles

Drawing on Ibsenite realism at the end of the nineteenth century, Diamond reveals how the hysterics of Ibsen's plays, hysterics that perform on the stage and in the audience, ground the platonic truths of nineteenth-century realism and science, granting them legitimacy through the characterization of the fallen woman of popular melodrama as a hysteric. These plays also stage realism as a form of hysteria. Hysteria undoes realism and it does so through its bodily figurations of melodrama.

Freud and Breuer's *Studies in Hysteria* was published in 1895, and was translated into English in 1909. Coinciding with the rise of feminism and the 'new woman' in England and America, Freud's hysteric manifested herself time and time again in the melodrama of Ibsen's plays. Popular melodrama displayed the hysterical woman as both suffering and degenerate. The strife of domestic melodramas mirrored the social upheaval of the day caused by the increasing forces within society that were moving towards the emancipation of women. Melodrama, as Bernard Shaw depicted, elaborated the most sadomasochistic fantasies of the audience with the binary polarizations of innocence and evil, hero and victim, before resolving them with an unbelievable family romance at the end.

As Diamond documents, realism of the nineteenth century was hysterical and melodramatic, and these melodramas that staged the hysteric also translate into the hysterical melodramas investigated by Freud and literally staged as a *mise-en-scène* by Charcot in his famous Sâlpetrière. As I will discuss later, early cinema was intricately interwoven with the figure of the hysteric and Charcot's clinic. Charcot's induction of hysterical fits that were staged and photographed only to reveal the scientist's curative powers, welds early cinema, science, hysteria and melodrama ineluctably together. Whereas realism is a mimesis that claims a stable truth referent, hysteria mimetically destabilizes that truth system. Just as realism can be deconstructed to reveal hysteria and melodrama as its mimetic other, so can the Freudian analyst, purveyor of truth and science, be shown to display the melodramatic hysteric – as its double. Freud analyses one of Ibsen's plays on female hysteria, *Rosmersholm* (1887), and interprets the new woman or hysteric in the play, Rebecca West, finding in Ibsen's work the literary equivalent of the analytic session.[23] Freud detects in Rebecca the Oedipal taboo of repressed desire for the father, but in Freud and Breuer's *Studies in Hysteria* it is not Oedipal repression but a doubling or splitting of consciousness that Freud discovers, the hypnoid or twilight states that are accompanied by the conversion, or displacement, of an earlier traumatic event into bodily or somatic symptoms.

Jung was critical of Freud's early trauma theory of hysteria, arguing that the twilight states of the hysteric were in fact a retreat into infantile and regressed fantasies or complexes. Such fantasies enabled the hysteric to escape from the conflicts of reality. In two case histories written at the time, by Freud and Jung, we can compare their very different interpretations of the hysterical dilemma. Freud's more famous case of Elizabeth Von R. is a story of a young woman whose hysteria and somatic conversions are finally traced back by Freud to the repressed trauma as erotic desire, not for her father, but for her sister's husband. In Jung's more anonymous case history, the young woman is in love with her best friend's husband. On leaving a farewell party for her sister/rival who is off to a health resort, the young woman in question suffers from a hysterical attack. This attack is brought on by the sound of galloping horses behind her, horses which remind the patient of an earlier trauma witnessing bolting horses as a child.

Now, Jung is unconvinced by this hysteric's reminiscences and argues against Freud's trauma theory. Jung describes how the young woman's hysterical attacks are not due to repressed traumatic memories. On the contrary, the fright with horses is 'stage managed', with the result of the young woman's being taken back to her sister's house with the now-alone brother-in-law – her unconscious object of desire. This is not a conscious desire, nevertheless it is a peculiar staging of hysteria, 'so that the mise en scène appears almost exactly like a reality'. Hysterical pains are, according to Jung from a psychological point of view, just as real as those due to organic causes, 'and yet they are stage managed'.[24]

Jung's theory of hysteria is phenomenological: he sees the hysteric's melodrama as a stage-managing of the past in order to evade the present. In Freud's early 'Five Lectures', he is in agreement with Jung: hysteria is a melodrama that defends against time by rooting everything in a causal past. Why, then, did Freud move away from these ideas? Perhaps his own hysterical collapse in the face of his father's death meant that Freud's own melancholic defence against time can be seen to manifest itself in his theory, or melodrama, of the Oedipal complex?

The cinematic imaginary – disembodied and embodied mimesis

Freud's paper 'Mourning and Melancholia' can provide a model for the movement between hysterical mimesis and a more embodied, social identification with the filmic image. In this paper Freud describes how melancholic and narcissistic identification in early object choice is a cannibalistic incorporation where loss, hate and love of the other is indistinguishable from the loss, hate and love one feels for oneself. This melancholia is similar to and 'paves the way' to an understanding of hysterical identification.[25] Freud wonders what leads from melancholia to mourning, from a mimesis where the self is the object diminished, to an identification where the world is the object, and subject, of loss.[26] He notices, but does not know why it is the case, that within mourning the object becomes a historical object. In mourning it is the world that is lost (and therefore re-presented), whereas in melancholia the self only is diminished, and access to the historical lost object is denied.

Melancholic and hysterical mimesis constitute a disembodied imaginary for the film spectator, whereas a more embodied spectatorship of mourning enables a reconfiguration of the lost historical, filmic object. We can locate these two forms of mimesis as film spectatorship within the work of Walter Benjamin and Siegfried Kracauer. Benjamin's phenomenological and experiential imaginary brings together (as Susan Buck-Morss demonstrates) a dialectical understanding of the dream-world and mimesis.[27] Melancholic memory and identification are operative in Benjamin's sleeping, dreaming collective: the frozen wish images of the Arcades and the metropolis. But these melancholic, paralysed and indeed idealized identifications are the very images which can be opened up through a more dialectical process of mourning and re-memory.

Benjamin's thesis on mimesis and film maps how hysterical dreaming and identification with film can move to a more social and embodied reconfiguration. For Benjamin the dream-world (of Arcades) was a collective one, not individual, thus staking out the crucial difference between his work and that of Freudian psychoanalysis or surrealism. Capitalism was the collective dream-state, from which Benjamin saw the possibility of historical awakening through the mimesis and dialectical reading of the image world of profane illuminations. But Benjamin did not see this awakening as some essential truth or reality, rather he saw it as the historical awakening and transformation from one dream-state to another, the difference being that in the latter dream-world, memory, childhood and the profane illumination are mobilized to historicize the (unconscious) imagination.

Benjamin opens up Freud's concept of the individual repressed unconscious through his twin concepts of the dialectical image and the profane illumination. The dialectical image is where the forgotten past is re-membered as a moment or flash in the present.[28] Such awakening is processed through the dialectical image as *an activity of reading*. Closely tied to this idea of the dialectical image is Benjamin's notion of the body image-space. This surrealist image is then an embodied expression of the real which Benjamin entitles 'profane illumination'.[29] Both the dialectical image and the profane illumination operate dialogically between past and present.

For Benjamin, the reflective reading and ethnography of the profane illumination is key to a theory of experience which in turn can frame the cinema. Film is not just a vehicle of ideological coercion, but also becomes a practice of redemptive criticism. Benjamin's famous essay on the cinema 'The Work of Art in the Age of Mechanical Reproduction' sketches how the technical reproducibility of art in the modern age, particularly the aesthetics of photography and film, has marked an important historical change in the privileged status of art.[30] Whereas art has traditionally been allied with an aura of uniqueness and cultural authority, the onset of mass technological reproduction in the modernist moment destroys that sense of authentic aura. Benjamin aligns art with unique aura and technical reproduction with the masses. His artwork essay describes how traditional modes of experience can be transformed and redeemed through the active reading of the cinematic image, thus producing a more secularized and popularized aura. Important to Benjamin's conception of reading is the mimetic faculty of language. Although for Benjamin the mimetic aspect of language is closely tied to the semiotic, it is distinguished by its bodily and physiognomic properties. Mimesis, in this account, becomes the bodily and magical parts of language which

re-play and re-member nature and the physical world in a fluid relationship of similarity and sameness.

Film, then, mimes the reified world in the same way as the debris
of the Paris Arcades or the surrealist object. This process is described
by Benjamin as an 'optical unconscious', where the camera can
reclaim lost shared experiences. The 'optical unconscious' is first
defined by Benjamin in his 1931 essay, 'A Small History of Photography', where he suggests that the viewer of a photographed subject,
however careful the photographer might be, always searches the
picture for traces of the real. The spectator searches

> for the tiny spark of contingency, of the Here and Now, with which
> reality has so to speak seared the subject, to find the inconspicuous
> spot where in the immediacy of that long-forgotten moment the future
> subsists so eloquently, that we, looking back might rediscover it.[31]

Whereas the human eye corresponds to consciousness, the camera
corresponds to a second space – the unconscious. The optical unconscious of film thus reveals 'the physiognomic aspect of visual worlds'
found in small objects and in our everyday dreams.[32] Film can release
us from the urbanized and mechanical environment that imprisons
us. Through its apperception of the world 'we calmly and adventur-
ously go travelling'.[33]

Siegfried Kracauer was a colleague of Benjamin's who shared many
of his ideas of an optical unconscious. Kracauer also identifies two
movements of a melancholic (hysterical) immersion in the filmic
image, and a more mournful identification where the film image is
experientially re-membered. Kracauer frames a spectator who moves
towards the film and mimetically identifies in a limitless journey. This
film spectator mimetically identifies with the filmic and cultural
objects that are intersubjectively apprehended. Consciousness is
lowered; Kracauer cites an unnamed Frenchwoman saying 'but in the
cinema I dissolve into all things and beings', and this dissolution of
consciousness into the film phenomena that beckons the subject also
activates the bodily senses.[34] What is described is a dreaming process,
where the spectator projects his unconscious experience into the
object, disappearing and travelling with it.

> So he drifts towards and into the objects – much like the legendary
> Chinese painter who, longing for the peace of the landscape he had
> created, moved into it, walked towards the faraway mountains sug-
> gested by his brush strokes, and disappeared into them never to be seen
> again.[35]

As Kracauer suggests, the 'material existence' manifest in the film 'launches the moviegoer into unending pursuits', but the dreaming process is not just limited to the dissolution of subjectivity by the film; there is a second movement where the image becomes detached from the object and is elaborated on within an imaginative reverie.[36] This imaginative daydreaming and free association in terms of the film image, mobilizes memories for the spectator from the past, moving the spectator beyond 'the orbit of that image' – the here and now of the film – to an imaginative re-memory.

For Kracauer, these 'apparently opposite movements of film are well-nigh inseparable from each other' and together construct a stream of consciousness whose fantasies and thoughts 'still bear the imprint of the bodily sensations from which they issue'.[37] Kracauer's work paints a scenario of the spectator whose consciousness dissolves into a material identification with the film, disintegrating the subject only to set him travelling, not just in relation to the film objects, but also to the re-memories of subjectivity and history that are imaginatively yielded by the filmic image. Melancholic escape into the image is mixed inseparably with imaginative and mournful re-memory.[38]

Now, Benjamin's concept of an 'optical unconscious' is very different from Freud's notion of the unconscious in many respects. The major difference, and it is one which I am going to elaborate on in terms of film theory, is that Benjamin's 'optical unconscious' is based in a phenomenological account of perception, whereas Freud and Lacan's unconscious signify a mental imaginary. In phenomenology there is no division between social and psychic identification, between language and the body or indeed between the film experience and everyday life. The so-called pre-Oedipal baby and child is always a cultural one, where language and the body are inextricably mixed. It is through this more phenomenological understanding of psychoanalysis that philosophers such as Luce Irigaray have challenged the Oedipal psychoanalysis of Freud and Lacan.[39]

Lacanian psychoanalysis has stressed the Oedipal scene of language as a phallic law – a linguistic knowledge that has been used within film studies to explain and deconstruct the masculine nature of a cinematic apparatus, and the consequent phallic construction of a textual film spectator. However, the feminist film criticism that espouses Lacanian theory has failed to recognize, or to take up fruitfully, Luce Irigaray's phenomenological stance. In line with Anglo-American feminist debates this film theory has often misread her through a post-structuralist tradition, whereas Irigaray's debt lies not with Lacan, but with Levinas, Heidegger and Merleau-Ponty.[40]

A phenomenological cinematic imaginary

We can, therefore, bring psychoanalysis and phenomenology together through a reading of the (cinematic) imaginary. Merleau-Ponty and Luce Irigaray have challenged and displaced Lacan's mental and linguistic imaginary with a more embodied account. Lacan's theory of the imaginary is synonymous with the ego. He depicts this imaginary in his account of 'the mirror stage' as a developmental stage where the small, unintegrated infant sees its bodily image reflected in a mirror, and then misrecognizes that reflection, seeing itself as unitary and whole, rather than fragmented.[41] Merleau-Ponty sees this mirror stage differently. Instead of the total body image in the mirror being a fiction, he sees it as a necessary stage for the child in working out a spatial intersubjectivity. Whereas for Lacan the imaginary is a mental counterpart of a linguistic symbolic separated from the bodily real, for Merleau-Ponty the imaginary is embodied. Merleau-Ponty, unlike Lacan, sees the subject as present in a primordial, perceptive, sensual being before the reflective self appears. The imaginary is not a narcissistic illusion covering primary fragmentation, but a stage where the perceptual relations between self and other, or self and object, are dialectically put into play. In Merleau-Ponty's view the image in the mirror is other; the child knows that what he sees is not where he experiences himself introceptively.[42]

In Lacan's account the perceptual 'I' becomes social through the rupture and lack of the phallic symbolic. Merleau-Ponty's primary and embodied self–other relations, as Vivian Sobchack points out, are not necessarily rivalrous, but can be 'co-operative figures constituted against the ground of the primordial experience of the body-being-in-the-world'. The young infant is therefore centred but intertwined with objects in the world; there is no integrated subject, here, that is boundaried from the social.[43] Luce Irigaray is much influenced by Merleau-Ponty's account of intersubjectivity. But she takes issue with what she sees as its masculine imaginary. In Irigaray's view, Merleau-Ponty ignores the question of flesh and embodiment between two, privileging sight, making vision complete the aesthesiological body. She asks,

> Must my aesthesiological body be completed by vision? Why completed? Why vision? Does it represent the sense which is the most capable of completing? The most unveiling/revealing? That which covers? Especially gaps, depths, abysses? That which finishes, finishes me in relation to the other? In particular the other who is touching and being touched.[44]

For Irigaray, Merleau-Ponty makes the intersubjective relationship between the infant and mother reversible through vision, thus locating it as a pre-Oedipal and masculine imaginary because it does not acknowledge the symbolic and sexually differentiated status of the mother's body.[45] Irigaray's argument for a more embodied imaginary questions the complicity between language, knowledge and a metaphysical privileging of sight and vision. She questions the Freudian and Oedipal analytic practice, for its continual desire to know and deconstruct, where light is always subordinated to sound and bodily flesh colours have to make way for interpretative rules and linguistic language. This language in its voyeuristic urge to know will decentre and fragment the subject but will do little to give back to the client the necessary powers of imagination to re-synthesize, to psychically explore and integrate a 'sense' of self. She asks, 'Why is there such a desire to know? Knowledge alone cannot constitute the unity of the subject; in fact it tends to splinter the subject, or even force its obedience to some absolute cause.'[46]

Instead of an interminable analysis where the subject is continually deconstructed by language, but in the process suffers sensory deprivation, Irigaray suggests a form of analysis that can give the subject back his or her perceptual balance within space-time. Her proposal is to paint. She writes,

> The point about painting is to *spatialize* perception and *make time simultaneous*, to quote Klee. This is also the point about dreaming. The analyst should direct his or her attention not only to the repetition of former images and their possible interpretation, but also to the subject's ability to paint, to make time simultaneous, to build bridges, establish perspectives between present-past-future.[47]

This notion of unconscious creativity and painting is very different from an Oedipal scenario, where the voyeuristic gaze of the other represses the body. In this Oedipal framework the imaginary goes to war with the real and we are left with the symptoms: hysteria, obsession, psychosis. But within a more embodied imaginary, the imagination works in harmony with the senses, enabling creative work for the subject and providing them not just with a harmonious relation to space and time, but also a situated perception and identity within history.

Although Irigaray criticizes Merleau-Ponty for his 'masculine' privilege of vision, her work is obviously indebted to the way he counters the Lacanian imaginary by bringing the body back into the reversable, intersubjective gaze of the mirror. So whereas an Oedipal account of the symbolic and imaginary splits language from the body, a bodily and phenomenological imaginary connects the body and material objects with language. This more phenomenological under-standing of the imaginary does not automatically place a split between the unconscious and conscious, but sees the relationship between real and imaginary as more fluid. The unconscious, then, becomes what Jung calls a 'negative borderline concept', an experi-ence that we are not aware of because it has become split off and disassociated.

A phenomenological imaginary thus reverses the perception between embodiment and the social that exists within Oedipal psy-choanalysis. The latter account views the pre-Oedipal child in terms of a symbiotic, instinctual excess of the body. However, within a phe-nomenological imaginary the infant is seen *as disembodied* when merged symbiotically with the mother because it participates only in terms of the other's dominant imaginary.[48] Hysteria is a good example of this distinction between an Oedipal and a phenomenological imag-inary. In an Oedipal scenario hysteria becomes an excessive bodily and symbiotic relating, often characterizing a mother–daughter rela-tionship that has failed to achieve symbolic, paternal triangulation and mediation. If we understand the hysteric's dilemma phenomeno-logically, her symbiotic connection to the mother renders her disem-bodied, as she has no access to an imaginary that is creatively mediated, or any sense of herself as separate. The hysteric then performs and masquerades the body, precisely because she cannot psychically integrate or 'own' it.

Oedipal psychoanalysis polarizes being pre-Oedipally in the body (and out of culture) or being Oedipally in language (and separated from the maternal body). Within phenomenological psychoanalysis you are always within language and culture, and your libidinal expe-riences are on a continuum of being psychically embodied and hence performed and brought to life within language, or they are disasso-ciated. Here, bodily symptoms perform and 'speak' precisely because they have lost contact with the psychic mental world. In terms of the analytic session this means that the imaginary is not simply an uncon-scious negativity of murderous maternal identification that has to be escaped/repressed through a privileged phallic symbolic. Instead, the imaginary is a world of embodied or disembodied objects and images which can be creatively elaborated on within an intersubjective trans-ference to become, as Merleau-Ponty would put it, a gestural sense or language.

Merleau-Ponty has written one lecture on film, entitled 'The Film and the New Psychology'.[49] In this piece, he links his philosophy of perception to a Gestalt psychology that is critical of classical psychology's focus on the primacy of intelligence and the idea.[50] Origins of subjectivity and meaning do not rest with a pure intelligence, instead they are located in a material situation, where we are 'thrown into the world and attached to it by a natural bond'.[51] Film for Merleau-Ponty provides a heightened sense of our embodied and intersubjective relation with the world and its objects.[52] So although films tell a story, the film means nothing on its own, and rather takes on meaning within an embodied, and intersubjective, situation, accomplishing a perception, which reproduces our way of being in everyday life.[53]

Vivian Sobchack's remarkable book *The Address of the Eye: A Phenomenology of Film Experience* takes Merleau-Ponty's phenomenology of perception and weaves a new theory of film experience around it. For Sobchack, the cinematic apparatus is an 'intentional technology'.[54] Film is a lived, intersubjective body which accomplishes a perception between us and the world. This expression is analogous to the act of human perception.[55]

She writes:

> film's body will be considered also as the film's means of perceptually engaging and expressing a world not only for us but also for itself. Thus, the film's body will be considered as a *direct means* of having and expressing a world-given to us as a technologically mediated consciousness of experience, but given to itself, through the praxis of its existentially functional body, as the immediate experience of consciousness.[56]

How can film be intentionally conscious, as an existential body in its own right? Surely, the intersubjective dynamic that Merleau-Ponty outlines emphasizes the agency of the spectator, not the apparatus. To argue for film as an existential body in its own right gives too much weight to the cinematic apparatus and not enough to what we project into it. Sobchack argues that film experience is historically variable and subject to change, according to changing dominant technologies. Whereas realism (industrial capitalism) brings a fixed objective representation of the world with photography, and postmodernism (multinational capitalism) heralds our abstracted, fragmented and disembodied consumption of the new, it is only the modernist moment (monopoly capitalism) which provides us with a truly embodied experience of the cinematic technology and apparatus as an intentional consciousness.

Sobchack situates the experience of the viewer or spectator through a changing representative and cinematic apparatus. For

Merleau-Ponty, the dialectics of embodied perception means that we only find in film images and objects what we have already projected into them. Now this projection and our embodied experience are undoubtedly affected, as Sobchack notes, by changing technologies.[57] However, it is our embodied projection into the filmic body and image which transforms technological representation into a lived relation, imagining and re-membering film in relation to history and everyday life. Thomas Elsaesser notes how digital imaging in television and the media reveals how truth claims or proof of the photographic image in the age of celluloid never did reside in the indexical relation of the moving image to the real. Digital imaging is used in newspapers and films but it does not affect claims to authenticity; what does alter our beliefs in the moving image is the degree of trust 'invested in a given mode of representation'.[58] A trust that is reliant on complex discursive, political and institutional conventions. This trust or projection into a given mode of representation is our embodied and disembodied projection into a filmic space of objects, a space which operates as a private and social world.

This book examines a phenomenological mimesis of film spectatorship. Oedipal sexuality cannot explain how we move from a hysterical identification with the film text to a more social dreaming because it is quintessentially part of that hysterical, melancholic imaginary. The film spectator mapped in this book moves between disembodied, hysterical mimesis and a more social dreaming where the relation between viewer and film text becomes reconfigured and embodied.

Part I

Sexual Difference, Film Spectatorship and the Text

Introduction to Part I

This book follows a chronology of film theory and spectatorship, rather than a linear film history. The history of film theory is not linear; in Walter Benjamin's sense it is a lived history, which means that it moves backwards and forwards in time. Addressing the textual film spectator, the first three chapters are focused in relation to the debates on feminist film theory and sexual difference which originated with the famous journal *Screen* in the 1970s. Chapter 1 centres on a re-reading of sexual-difference arguments in relation to the film *Mildred Pierce*, a film that has been the focus of much feminist film critique. Chapter 2 turns to a historicization of these arguments through an examination of Weimar cinema. The final chapter in this section brings these arguments within a more contemporary setting in relation to the film *Boys Don't Cry*.

This introduction will sketch some of the central debates that were crucial to feminist film theory and the textual spectator, specifically apparatus theory, melodrama and what is known as classical film theory. Screen theory used psychoanalytic concepts of sexual difference as a key to understanding how the cinema, as both institution and apparatus, constructs us as sexual and textual spectators. This post-structuralist framework posits the spectator or 'subject' as discursively constructed, meaning that the 'subject' or spectator is not a real person, but a discursive position constructed by the cinematic apparatus. Hence, the name Apparatus theory, that is used alternately with Screen theory.

Apparatus theory

The use of Lacanian psychoanalysis in 1970s film Apparatus theory developed out of a tradition of structuralist and post-structuralist thinking. Louis Althusser's essay 'Ideology and Ideological State Apparatuses (Notes Toward an Investigation)' was the influential (structuralist) text used to understand the nature of ideological representation in film,[1] while Roland Barthes' book *S/Z* (a semiotic reading of the novella *Sarrasine* by Honoré de Balzac) became the definitive post-structuralist origin of textual analysis in 1970s film theory. Althusser's work was used to explain how cinema as an ideological institution interpellates us and creates us as ideological 'subjects'; Barthes' writing was a detailed deconstruction of the operation of ideology within narrative.[2] Jean Louis Baudry, Christian Metz and Laura Mulvey were film critics associated with *Screen*, who went on to develop Althusser's work in conjunction with Lacan's, explaining how cinema works as an institutional apparatus.[3] Their emphasis was on the structural function of the cinematic institution as a dominant ideology that interpellates us, and constructs us as subjects through mechanisms of Oedipal desire, fantasy and pleasure. Lacan's theory of the mirror stage and the subsequent relation between the imaginary and the symbolic were central ideas to Apparatus theory and to an understanding of how cinema ideologically shapes cinema spectators.

Lacan's mirror stage is an account of a narcissistic imaginary. The imaginary can be understood as the first structuring event for Lacan's illusory self, located in the 'mirror stage' where the young child, previously unintegrated and fragmented, identifies its body image reflected in a mirror.[4] However, this reflection is a mis-recognition, a deluded fantasy of selfhood and mastery, which hides the narcissistic fragmentation of unconscious or psychic life. Although this narcissistic imaginary structures all relations between self and other – in other words all social life – it is only access to the social, phallic and symbolic order of language that can give birth to the individual as a sexual self-knowledgeable subject within culture.

Baudry, Metz and Mulvey all elaborate Lacan's ideas of imaginary identification and mis-recognition in terms of the cinema spectator. Mulvey's seminal essay 'Visual Pleasure and Narrative Cinema' focuses on the Lacanian and Freudian ideas of identification, voyeurism and fetishism. She argues that the appeal and pleasure of mainstream Hollywood films is due to the ideological desires already implanted in the spectator which are further reinforced by the dominant, patriarchal ideology of the cinematic apparatus. Using Freud's Oedipal theory, Mulvey describes how the cinema constructs woman as object of the male gaze, a patriarchal look which is the dominant structure of cinema and society. Within this hegemonic system of visual representation, the spectator is positioned to identify with dominant representations of sexual difference within the text. The cinematic look controls the image of the woman voyeuristically, but it also fetishizes that image, thereby disavowing castration and the real difference that the woman signifies. Whereas pleasurable voyeuristic looking is scopophilic and actively/sadistically objectifies the image, there is also a second pleasurable looking that Mulvey explores which focuses on narcissistic identification.

The narcissistic pleasure of cinematic spectatorship is associated with the idea of the Lacanian imaginary: the identification and mis-recognition in front of the screen/mirror. Just as the infant recognizes and mis-recognizes an image of himself in the mirror, so the cinema offers the spectator an endless imaginary landscape of narcissistic, ideal identifications.

> Hence it is a birth of the long love affair/despair between image and self-image which has found such intensity of expression in film and such joyous recognition in the cinema audience. Quite apart from the extraneous similarities between screen and mirror (the framing of the human form in its surroundings, for instance), the cinema has structures of fascination strong enough to allow temporary loss of the ego while simultaneously reinforcing the ego. The sense of forgetting the world as the ego has subsequently come to perceive it (I forgot who I am and where I was) is nostalgically reminiscent of that pre-subjective moment of recognition.[5]

Despite the obvious centrality of the imaginary in Mulvey's reading, her arguments, along with those of Baudry and Metz, concentrate on the representative, textual structures of cinema that correspond to the structures of Lacanian linguistic desire. This emphasis on Oedipal desire and representation has to be seen as part of the larger political movement in the 1970s that sought to marry Marxism and psychoanalysis through recourse to structuralist thinkers such as Althusser and Lacan. These apparatus thinkers, particularly Mulvey, wanted to deconstruct the ideological hegemony of classical cinema. However, the effect of these debates was to pose a monolithic picture of patriarchal cinema, rendering the spectator as a passive victim to ideology and the apparatus.

Key points

- The textual spectator is associated with debates from feminist film theory, Apparatus theory, or 1970s Screen theory.
- Apparatus theory developed out of a tradition of structuralist and post-structuralist thinking and used Lacanian psychoanalysis and Althusser's concept of ideology to conceptualize a discursively constructed film spectator.
- This discursive 'subject' or spectator was ideologically constructed through the cinematic apparatus and was not the real audience or film spectator.

Melodrama

The use of semiotic, Lacanian notions of sexual difference by Screen theory enabled feminist film critics to break with the realist mainstream film narrative of classical Hollywood film, by foregrounding the ideological construction of the spectator. Crucial to feminist film theory was the genre of melodrama. As classical Hollywood film prioritized realist representation and repressed melodrama as a bodily textual excess, then a focus on melodrama and sexual difference became a key way for feminist film critics to deconstruct the masculine structures of cinema.

Melodrama has been theorized by Peter Brooks and Thomas Elsaesser as disruptive of classical systems, and Rick Altman has stated that melodrama is an excess to the text that systematically disrupts the dominant narrative.[6] Melodrama has been defined by Brooks as a response to the 'loss of tragic vision', a vision exemplified by pre-modern and pre-industrial society. The development of bourgeois society and the nuclear family led to a vacuum within the public sphere which an emotional pathos, namely melodrama, began to fill. Characterized by emotional extremity and moral polarity, dramatic plots of good and evil and heightened expression, melodrama has been analysed as an aesthetic experience that gives rise to emotion in the spectator.[7] Whereas Elsaesser and Altman focus on the bourgeois ideology of melodrama, feminist film critics such as Mary Ann Doanne, E. Ann Kaplan and Linda Williams have focused on the women's film and its specific female address. Melodrama in film has historically been associated with the nineteenth century, the melodramatic imagination and a hysterical pre-Oedipal discourse that puts 'pressure', as Rick Altman would say, on the dominant paradigm of the classical, narrative spectator.[8] The pressure of melo-drama, its excess, has also been understood in terms of a popular and emotional aesthetic that actually grounds the spectator within the narrative of ideological realism or verisimilitude of mainstream film.

Melodrama and Freud have been long-term bed-fellows within film theory, stemming from Peter Brooks's seminal study, *The Melodramatic Imagination*. Brooks explores melodrama as a modern mode developing out of a loss of pre-Enlightenment values and cultural forms. Desacralization of society occurring between the Rennaissance and the Enlightenment periods led to a post-sacred bourgeois society where ethics and meaning were increasingly located within the personal and individual everyday lives. The 'traditional sacred' was replaced by melodrama as a 'moral occult', a set of moral and spiritual values that were played out but also repressed by surface reality. Melodrama, then, was a meeting between the psychic and the ideological or social, a marriage that was far from harmonious. On the one hand, bourgeois society was involved with a reality principle and rationalism that operated through mechanisms of repression at a psychic and social level. On the other hand, however, there were personal demands that could not be contained by the social order and that necessarily put pressure on it, hence the melodramatic struggle between good and evil, or Jekyll and Hyde. Brooks turns to Freudian psychoanalysis to explain how melodrama is a hysterical discourse which breaks the repression of the reality principle to express the unrepresentable in language. For Brooks, melodrama is the gestural, visual, musical excess – a 'text of muteness' that is performed through pantomime and spectacle. The dramatic polarizations and reversals of melodramatic plot present the repressed psychic forces and moral imperatives within society.[9]

Following Brooks, film theorists have also associated melodrama with a Freudian narrative of the return of the repressed. Geoffrey Nowell-Smith discusses melodrama as a kind of Freudian conversion hysteria, where emotional elements that cannot be integrated into the narrative return as an excess of bodily symptoms within the text.[10] In this model, Oedipal narrative represses the feminine body as hys-terical. In feminist film theory the woman spectator is denied access to male pleasures in gazing, and the women characters in Hollywood cinema are read as absence, lack or ground to a male system of rep-resentation that denies women their subjectivity. Classical Hollywood film narratives thus repress women. The return of the hysterical feminine via melodrama has been construed positively by feminist critics in relation to women-addressed melodramas of the 1930s. In these melodramas the woman is portrayed as an idealized, sacrificial and noble figure, whose emotional excess displays both suffering and courage and can be identified by female spectators. On the other, more negative, side, Hollywood films of the 1940s saw the rise of the film noir, and a more masculine framing, where the female hysteric is portrayed as deadly and dangerously sexual. Rick Altman and Thomas Elsaesser both perceive melodrama as putting 'pressure' on dominant systems of classical cinema. For Elsaesser, melodrama is a mode of experience and for Altman it is part of a textual dialectic, operating with the dominant realist narrative. Both Altman and Elsaesser liken the movement of melodrama in film to Freud's analysis of the dream-work with its codes of condensation, displacement and symbolization.

One of the problems with this insistence on mapping melodrama in relation to a Freudian model of the return of the repressed is the textual model we are left with. In Freud's Oedipal drama, narrative represses the hysterical body, leaving us with a predominantly textual understanding of the bodily excesses of melodrama. This Freudian theory of linguistic representation, as Borch-Jacobsen notes, leaves the subject 'in a position of exteriority (subjacence) with respect to representation'.[11] But the dream is not just a textual representation or spectacle that is staged for the subject; it is also an experience of lived experience and history located in sleeping and waking life.

If the hysterical and melodramatic body that puts 'pressure' onto the classical film text is a mode of experience (Elsaesser) that dialogically interacts with the classical Hollywood text (Altman), then this bodily and figural melodramatic excess cannot be understood in terms of theories of textual representation. Neither can it, for that matter, be understood as textual codes of primary and secondary mental elaboration, as in Freud's dream. As the first chapter will discuss, it is a phenomenological reading of melodrama, rather than one that posits it as a return of the repressed, which is most able to illustrate the dreaming and experience associated with film.

Classical film theory

Both feminist (psychoanalytic) film theory and classical Hollywood film theory have in different ways positioned an Oedipal split between the real and the imaginary and between text and spectator. In feminist film theory this split is the founding phallic and linguistic split of an Oedipal unconscious: a split which divides the textual spectator from the real and thereby constructs a theory of identification that focuses on textual, ideological meaning, evacuating the historical experiences of real audiences and spectators. Classical Hollywood film, as realist mainstream film narrative, also contains similar Oedipal repressions or divisions between language and experience, narrative and the body, text and spectator.

Classical Hollywood film has been defined as a realist narrative of representation, which represses bodily melodramatic excess. In its classical form, Hollywood was at its most predominant in the first half of the twentieth century. Representing bourgeois values, the classical Hollywood film developed out of the nineteenth-century classical and popular novel, but its roots in theatrical melodrama and spectacle conflict with the more transparent mimesis of social reality that the more bourgeois style of the classical novel and film aspired to. This contradiction between so-called classical Hollywood cinema and its more embodied and hysterical underbelly of melodrama has been the focus for much feminist film critique. Within this account of the contradiction between classical realist cinema and melodrama, there is an Oedipal hierarchy; classical film realism is a narrative mode which represses melodrama into a pre-Oedipal arena, as bodily textual excess.

Classical film theory can be broadly divided into two main trajectories, one narrative and one empirical, which lead to very different frameworks for the spectator. First is the realist trajectory of classical cinema associated with 1950s French film criticism, especially André Bazin. Bazin suggested that the 'myth of total cinema' which arose in the minds of the first film-makers was the idea of creating a perfect illusion of reality. It was not as some people have believed that Bazin actually saw film as a transparent medium reflecting the world, he simply valued the technology and style of films that created an illusion of reality.[12] For Bazin, the essence of such classical Hollywood films then became located in films by William Wyler, John Ford and Orson Welles. Critical of montage and emphasizing the deep focus shot and the realism inherent to the image, Bazin influenced the Cahiers du Cinéma collective. But within the context of the politics of May 1968 this collective moved to critique cinematic realism and to emphasize the ideological construction and basis of such realism. This paved the way to the semiotic tradition of post-structuralist apparatus film theory, the Marxist-psychoanalytical tradition that culminates in a re-reading of classical film theory through feminist film theory. Bazin has, however, been erroneously misread in terms of a tradition of realist representation, especially by semiotic film theory. Colin McCabe's famous essay on realism and cinema, where he locates the classical filmic text in terms of the nineteenth-century novel does little to illuminate the kind of filmic realism that

Bazin was exploring.[13] This realism, as Dudley Andrews discusses, was a much more phenomenological realism concerned with the aesthetics of the image. As this phenomenology has been lost in the listing of Bazin under classical realist cinema, so Bazin's work becomes conjoined within a narrative and textual account.

This narrative tradition becomes in turn separated from the second account of classical film theory: the empirical formulations of the classical film spectator arising from the work of Bordwell, Staiger and Thompson in the 1980s.[14] Critical of the rather fixed and homogeneous ideological claims of textual spectatorship, David Bordwell, Janet Staiger and Kristin Thompson argued that the theoretical tradition of classical film theory has ignored the historical specificity of Hollywood. In place of ideological thematics, Bordwell, Staiger and Thompson proposed a more empirically based formalism, where Hollywood cinema was analysed in terms of group practice and stylistic practices. For them, this classical style and mode of production of Hollywood films remained a constant paradigm between 1917 and 1960 across differing historical periods, genres, studios and technological workmanship.[15] Refusing psychoanalytical theories of ideological and textual spectatorship, Bordwell argues for an empirically located real spectator that can be understood through the lens of perception and cognitive psychology. Countering what he sees as the textual accounts of a passive spectator duped by ideology, Bordwell emphasizes the active perception of the spectator. In Bordwell's view, film texts don't position the spectator; instead they offer cues that in cognitive psychology terms are perceived and picked up by viewers. Sensory information that is cognitively perceived is then organized in relation to psychological patterns or schemas held by the viewer, who consequently produces specific expectations and executes certain operations in relation to the film text.[16] As several film critics have noted, this theory of spectatorship remains as ahistorical as the more psychoanalytical film theories, because the cognitive perception of the viewer is deemed to remain unchanged by either historical or cultural factors.

Judith Mayne is uncomfortable with the way Bordwell elides the real spectator and the ideal, ideologically positioned subject or textual spectator, although she tries to find some negotiated middle ground between them.[17] My concern with Bordwell's formulation of the spectator is not to do with the elision of the 'subject' and his emphasis on the real spectator. I actually agree with him that films can't corner people and explicitly position them without some active acceding on their part. The main difficulty with Bordwell's argument is his reduction of all perception to a cognitive psychology that explicitly subordinates the body to rationalistic mental functions.[18] Raising what is perhaps the crucial bone of contention between psychoanalytic approaches to the subject/spectator and Bordwell's more cognitive empirical spectator, Mayne highlights the tricky empirical problem of the validity (and non-quantifiability) of the unconscious. Bordwell rejects the unconscious as being the realm of the neurotic and the pervert, whereas his cognitive model asserts a 'normal' psychology. He writes, 'there is something quite awesome in the creative resourcefulness exhibited by ordinary people practising a well-learned skill.' Mayne counters this statement by arguing that the unconscious is not just implicated in passive deviant models of the apparatus spectator, but is also a tool in understanding the 'creative resourcefulness' of the active spectator.[19] Disappointingly, Mayne does not elaborate what this might be, and indeed within the Oedipal narratives of Freud and Lacan, especially those utilized by Apparatus theory, such a creative notion of the unconscious is hard to find.

Although Apparatus theory sought to break with mainstream realist text of the classical Hollywood film by foregrounding the ideological position of the spectator, it continued with an Oedipal narrative that splits language from the body, thereby marginalizing the bodily melodrama of film as a repressed textual relation. The embodied, psychological experience of the spectator is evacuated in accounts of classical Hollywood cinema, just as it disappears within Lacanian accounts of the textual spectator. Melodrama is, thus, reduced to *textual* bodily excess, and the phenomenological realism of film is reduced and at times flagrantly misread (in relation to Bazin), as a narrative realism that masquerades as ontology. I want to suggest that melodrama can be read as a mimetic and figural movement of the real, a phenomenological mimesis in relation to the image and object. Melodrama, then, is a bodily narrative which is not split off or repressed by linguistic representation, but mimetically moves between spectator and filmic image as a sensory and tactile 'copying' or participation with the 'other'.

The first chapter returns to the sexual-difference gaze in relation to feminist film theory, melodrama and classical film theory and rereads this gaze in terms of a phenomenological and hysterical mimesis.

Key points

- **Screen theory enabled feminist film critics to break with the realist mainstream film narrative of classical Hollywood film, by**

foregrounding the ideological construction of the spectator.
- Crucial to feminist film theory was the genre of melodrama.
- A focus on melodrama and sexual difference became a key way for feminist film critics to deconstruct the masculine structures of cinema.
- Melodrama in film has historically been associated with the nineteenth century, melodramatic imagination and a hysterical pre-Oedipal discourse.
- This hysterical discourse is seen as an 'excess' that puts 'pressure' on the dominant paradigm of the classical, narrative spectator.
- Following Peter Brooks, film theorists have associated melodrama with a Freudian narrative of the return of the repressed.
- One of the problems with this insistence of mapping melodrama in relation to a Freudian model of the return of the repressed is the textual account of melodrama that we are left with.
- Classical film theory can be broadly divided into two main trajectories that lead to very different frameworks for the spectator.
- First is the realist trajectory of classical cinema associated with 1950s French film criticism, especially André Bazin.
- Bazin has, however, been erroneously misread in terms of a tradition of realist representation, especially by semiotic film theory.
- *The Classical Hollywood Cinema: Film Style and the Mode of Production to 1960,* by David Bordwell, Janet Staiger and Kristin Thompson sums up the second trajectory of classical film theory. This second account proposes an empirically based formalism in place of ideological thematics.

1

Sexual Difference, Melodrama and Film Theory

This chapter maps but also re-reads the sexual-difference argument of film theory in relation to melodrama and classical film theory, exploring the hysterical nature of film viewing. Arguing for sexual difference and the sexual-difference spectator as hysterical reverses the historical hegemony of realist classical film over melodrama. Within film theory and history, melodrama has been read through a return of the repressed, as a bodily, pre-Oedipal excess that disturbs the dominant textual narrative. This chapter puts forward an alternative argument, exploring the hysterical and phenomenological mimesis which is at stake in relation to melodrama and film viewing.

The female spectator and the masquerade

In her exploration of the 1940s woman's film, Mary Ann Doanne historically contextualizes the male gaze of Apparatus theory and ultimately confirms it. She does this through outlining a paradox in female spectatorship, whereby the female spectator has both increased agency, but is also subjected to a dominant male gaze.[1] The answer to this paradox, for Doanne, lies in the reification of the commodity: the female spectator's over-identification with the image and object. This masochistic positioning of the female spectator as object, by a male textual apparatus, together with her narcissistic, passive desire and over-identification as a consumer, ends by reifying the female spectator herself as a commodity.

Doanne's argument for the female spectator utilizes a psychoanalytic reading of the masquerade to suggest that the position of the female spectator is untenable because of the nearness of femininity to the image. The female spectator is identified masochistically with the male gaze or cinematic apparatus, and her only relief or subversion of this masochism is the masquerade where she narcissistically takes her own image as object of desire. Doanne draws on Joan Riviere's theorization of the female masquerade, arguing that womanliness is 'a flaunting of womanliness' to cover over hidden masculine identifications that might invite reprisals. She writes, 'The masquerade in flaunting femininity holds it at a distance. Womanliness is a mask which can be worn or removed.'[2] Doanne views the female masquerade as a mask that women wear to hide their passive non-identities, to distance themselves from the passive nature of femininity. Men presumably don't need the masquerade because, according to Freud, it is only femininity that is universally rejected for its passivity. The masquerade is then the woman's resistance to patriarchal ideology: an excess of femininity that like the *femme fatale* presents a threat to masculine structures of desire and looking.

Doanne's paper is framed by Freud's definition of femininity as hieroglyphic. The connection between the hieroglyph and femininity positions the woman as indecipherable image, as other. Cinema inherits a theory of the image structured through male, voyeuristic structures of sexual difference: the male gaze. Because of this, the female gaze collapses with the very iconicity of the filmic image. Inseparable from the real of the maternal body the female gaze lacks the gap integral to the arbitrary, semiotic sign. She lacks, in other words, the necessary distance from the image (and mother) provided by castration. The female masquerade is then subversive for Doanne, because it simulates or manufactures the necessary distance between oneself and one's image. In other words, the female masquerade makes up for castration. Doanne writes,

> If Moustafa Safouan points out, '. . . to wish to include oneself as an object the cause of the desire of the Other is a formula for the structure of hysteria', then masquerade is anti-hysterical for it works to effect a separation between the cause of desire and oneself.[3]

Hysteria, as Safouan suggests, is the identification of the client or 'woman' with the analyst's 'male' desire, and it is this feminine performance that masquerades as what the other desires.[4] Luce Irigaray suggests that the female masquerade is what women are forced to do in entering Oedipal circuits of exchange: their hysterical participation.[5] Feminine mimicry, however, is a more conscious mimesis aimed at jamming that male machinery and 'recovering the place of her exploitation within discourse'.[6] Irigaray sees hysteria and the masquerade as synonymous, whereas for Doanne they are distinct.

Doanne's subversive reading of the masquerade depends on conflating the female masquerade with Irigaray's more conscious mimicry. For example, Doanne suggests that in women melodramas such as *Stella Dallas*, the woman's masquerade is taken to such extreme limits it becomes a 'double mimesis' where femininity is distanced and made strange. In *Stella Dallas*, the working-class mother Stella exhibits a tasteless, garish femininity in a sacrificial move to make her daughter leave home and join her middle-class father. Stella's exhibition and parody reveal how femininity is always excessive.[7] Although Doanne utilizes Irigaray's famous metaphor of the two lips (symbolizing women's closeness and over-identification) to shore up her Oedipal account of the masquerade, she fails to emphasize Irigaray's different reading of the so-called 'pre-Oedipal identification' between mother and daughter. As I have discussed in the Introduction, Irigaray provides an alternative 'painterly' account of the imaginary and women's relationships, with themselves and each other. This alternative, embodied imaginary, mediates and paints a relation to the real, enabling an intersubjective mediation of female narcissism. We can then suggest, following Irigaray's phenomenological stance, that the Oedipal female masquerade depicts the disembodied conflict of the hysteric whereas a playful, conscious feminine mimicry is expressed through a more embodied imaginary.[8]

Mary Ann Doanne's historical reading of 1940s women's melodrama ultimately confirms the structures of Oedipal male looking in classical Apparatus theory, and can be seen as a direct development and affirmation of Mulvey's earlier analysis of the male gaze. Perhaps it is also important to note here, that although Doanne's account is a specifically historical one, relating to 1940s and 1950s melodrama, it is taken up, like Mulvey's work, to argue for a universal. Many film critics have subsequently tried to revise this rather fixed account of the male gaze. Miriam Hansen has emphasized the historical fluidity of spectatorship between masculine and feminine positions, and David Rodowick and Teresa De Lauretis both re-read Freud to suggest the bisexual mobility of cinematic identification.[9]

Ann Kaplan finds instances of resistance by the female spectator, as well as the de-specularization that Doanne emphasizes. Linda Williams and Tania Modleski have also argued for a more positive female address within family melodrama. Williams suggests that the film *Stella Dallas* shows how women spectators identify with the contradictions of all the female figures in the films, not just the victims.[10] This account militates against a generalized theory of the male gaze, by emphasizing the positive nature of the historical contradictions for the female spectator.

Key points

- Mary Ann Doanne's study of 1940s women's melodrama confirms film theory's male gaze.
- Feminist film theory emphasizes the female spectator's passive over-identification with the image.
- Doanne sees the female masquerade as subversive because it simulates or manufactures the necessary distance between oneself and one's image, but this feminist account is dependent on conflating an Oedipal reading of the masquerade with a more conscious 'double mimesis' articulated by Luce Irigaray.

Mildred Pierce

I want to briefly discuss the classical film melodrama *Mildred Pierce*. My choice in re-reading this film is for several reasons. First, it demonstrates well the linearity of classical Hollywood plot and the subjection of the spectator within the space and time of the narrative. But this film also illustrates the division between psychoanalytic and historical criticisms within film theory. Following the distinction I have made between a hysterical female masquerade and an alternative more embodied mimesis, I want to suggest a more phenomenological reading of the female masquerade as a splitting or doubling. Here, the woman performs the body within dominant systems of the imaginary but is denied access to her own embodied subjectivity.[11] The hysterical doubling or mimesis in *Mildred Pierce* reveals femininity not as distanced, but as ambivalent and split. Moreover, this ambivalent doubling reveals the sexual-difference gaze of film, whether that gaze is male or female, as hysterical.

Mildred Pierce is a melodrama which swings, between earlier women-addressed melodramas of the 1930s and a more masculine framing of the film noir in the 1940s and 1950s. Critics of this film, especially feminist ones, have highlighted the contradictions and doubling in the text. There is a split between past tense, evenly lit episodes where Mildred relates her story of being abandoned by her husband and her struggle to raise two daughters and establish a successful restaurant business, and the film noir episodes in the present tense which seem to present Mildred as a dangerous and sinister figure implicated in murder and duplicity. Linda Williams has discussed how feminist film theory has in a sense mimicked the splits in the film by siding with, on the one hand, a more positive, sociological approach where the image is seen as a reflection of women's cultural and historical reality, and, on the other, a more textual approach where the film is analysed psychoanalytically for its linguistic repression of the feminine.[12] Andrea Walsh reads the film in relation to the complex historical changes of the time (the film was released at the end of the war, 20 October 1945, the same day as the return of American soldiers from victory in Japan). For her, the film is essentially a hangover from 1930s maternal melodramas where nobility and courage of the mother is retrospectively read in terms of emerging feminist ideology.[13] Pam Cook's 'Duplicity in *Mildred Pierce*' reads the film psychoanalytically in more negative terms, arguing for the film as a linguistic retelling of Oedipal law which represses the feminine, in the same way as historically patriarchal society has overthrown an original mother right.[14] Walsh, therefore, argues for an emergent female consciousness reflected through the historical image, while Cook emphasizes the repression of female consciousness through the text. Linda Williams suggests that we need to avoid 'simplistic realistic notions of reflection', or universal notions of textual repression.[15]

Utilizing Fredric Jameson's ideas of a 'political unconscious', Williams suggests that there are contradictions in the historical moment of *Mildred Pierce* that are both reflected and repressed by the film. Jameson's political unconscious resituates Freud's return of the repressed at a collective level, arguing that history is the absent cause of narratives and that narratives as ideology, in turn, repress history and potential revolution. The text is both the site where the strains of repression emerge and also a utopian compensation for the repression of the real. Williams uses these ideas to discuss the absent referent of the war in *Mildred Pierce*. For Williams the absence of direct referral to the war or the real in this film, foregrounds the historical contradictions of women's wartime experiences, such as conflicts between motherhood and newly found work, in relation to the absence of men and patriarchal rule. So, films such as *Mildred Pierce* repress (manage) *and* reflect women's issues about the war that other films focused more directly on wartime experience fail to capture.

I want to suggest that these contradictions in *Mildred Pierce* can be better understood, not as Oedipal/narrative repression and reflection, but as a hysterical mimesis and splitting which is intrinsic to the film's narrative position and to the wartime reference of 1945. There is a difference between understanding this film as an Oedipal narrative that linguistically represses 'hysterical' female experience, or one that is concerned with a disavowal (a splitting off) of not just history but our embodied relation to the other. *Mildred Pierce*, as Cook suggests, is indeed a duplicitous film. The masculine-framed film noir narratives, casting suspicion on Mildred as a dangerous and duplicitous woman, are distinguished from the more women-addressed stories, where she appears as the model of a sacrificial, perfect mother. But this conflict in the film is actually dealt with in melodramatic fashion, as a split, between ideal and denigrated images of the mother/woman. The spectator is carried away in sentimental and melancholic identifications with an idealized image of the perfect mother, Mildred, only to find their identifications swinging in an equally fixed way in the other direction when her melodramatic presence and image appears as one of duplicitous villainy. I would argue that in both these narratives the spectator is encouraged to take a hysterical position, a bodily performance and mimesis that weeps and feels with the ideal Mildred and denigrates her 'evil' side. The spectator is engaged here in relation to the image and narrative as ultimately disembodied and fixed, swinging in true hysterical style from one polarized binary to another. This duplicity confounds more conventional melodramas where moral polarities are established between characters, creating a simplified fixed morality, where innocence and guilt are easily resolvable.

Mildred's innocence is far more ambiguous. The body in identification with the sacrificial image of Mildred is missing, only to be projected with great violence onto her doppelgänger as a *femme fatale*. This disavowal and projection of the body in relation to the woman is, some would say, a typical Oedipal narrative. However, rather than seeing, as Jameson does, this narrative as the ideological repression of the real or political unconscious, a real which is the narrative's absent cause, we can suggest this narrative as a phenomenological mimesis. This narrative does not repress the hysterical body, but in a gestural sense mimics the relation to the other. Narrative, then, masquerades and performs the body in order to hide the split and disembodied consciousness underneath. Ideology, here, is neither pure repression nor production. Instead, it figures as our disembodied perception, a splitting off of our relation to the lived real of history. Oedipal narrative, here, is also read differently. Rather than the imaginary of narrative repressing the real, we have an imaginary that is disassociated from the real, thus freezing the image. Like the commodity or Walter Benjamin's paralysed wish images of the Arcades, the real of history and the body is severed from a more mobile and imaginative relation with the imaginary. This traumatic sealing off of the real leads to a repetitive mimesis of history as death and tradition.

In *Mildred Pierce* the disavowal of war, as a moment of history, is connected with a disavowal of the bodily relation to the other. The absence of history parallels the absence of men in the film as patriarchal figures. The male characters in the film are all portrayed as weak and irresponsible, with the exception of the paternal detective. Cook suggests that it is the present tense, male framing, of the film noir scenes, managed by the detective, which repress female consciousness through the suspicion they cast on Mildred's character. However, the film noir scenes that frame the film do not convincingly cast suspicion on Mildred. The detective is never in any real doubt of Mildred's innocence, and suspicion of her, for the spectator, is so mixed with understanding of what appears as a desperate act, that her persona as a duplicitous *femme fatale* is only really believable in the opening scenes. The real *femme fatale* in this film is of course the villainous daughter, Veda, and the duplicity of the film rests, not so much in conflict between an Oedipal repression of the feminine as film noir against a more feminist, maternal melodrama, but in a duplicity that resides between Mildred and Veda throughout. This mimetic doubling between mother and daughter dominates the film. Mildred is the sacrificial and perfect mother; Veda is her monstrous, narcissistic daughter.

Doubling between mother and daughter in this film cannot be contained within Oedipal, classical, repressive plots, or the male gaze for that matter. But neither can this doubling be explained by some kind of feminist consciousness. It is precisely the melodrama associated with the images of Mildred and Veda that casts doubt on either patriarchal or feminist readings of the film. Disavowal of the historical moment of *Mildred Pierce* goes hand in hand with a disavowal of the embodied relation to the m(other). The film is, as most critics have noted, ideologically bound up with the drive to place women back in the home after the war, an ideology which seems ultimately fulfilled by Mildred's reunion with her husband Bert at the end of the film. Mildred's mothering of Veda goes wrong because of her ambitions in the marketplace, facilitated by the absence of a paternal figure. But this ideological narrative, as Williams suggests, is more complex, speaking to the contradictory experiences of women in the war years.

However, these contradictions are not played out through notions of history and the text as a return of the repressed. Female consciousness is neither repressed nor vindicated in this film; rather it is presented as ambivalent and split. Mildred is represented at the

Fig. 1   Mother and daughter – Mildred and Veda. Joan Crawford and Ann Blyth with Jack Carson, in *Mildred Pierce* (1945), directed by Michael Curtiz. © Warner Bros / The Kobal Collection

beginning of the film as incomplete, her life a cycle of kitchens and baking cakes. A role of domestic goddess obviously desexualizes her, leaving her husband Bert scampering off into the arms of another woman. Along with Mildred's sacrificial, desexualized and hysterical role, is her desire and narcissistic involvement in her children, particularly Veda, who, Mildred repeatedly insists, must have everything. Interestingly, the younger tomboy daughter is actually rather ignored by Mildred, who makes a remarkable recovery after the girl's tragic death. No, it is the feminine, narcissistic Veda, whom Mildred adores, as a projection of all the material, sexual and selfish desires that she cannot own for herself. If Mildred occupies the transcendental realm of the sacrificial, perfect mother where the body is disavowed, then Veda is the ultimate performance of the carnal and evil woman, the *femme fatale* as a mimesis of the death drive. Both Mildred and Veda masquerade as hysterics, but as the men in the film are all feminized (and failures to boot), the hysteria is not limited to only the female players.

Mildred's consistent, compulsive desire for her daughter is because, as she quite literally says in the film, Veda is part of her. Veda must have all the feminine and middle-class commodities and accomplishments that Mildred has had to forgo. We see this in the ballet and music classes that Veda has as a child, and which Mildred pays for through working as a waitress. We also see it in the aristocratic lifestyle that Veda aspires to as an adult: a lifestyle which again Mildred pays for by losing her fortune and self-respect in marriage to the deceitful and decadent Monty, a man whom she does not love.

The spectator in relation to *Mildred Pierce* is captivated not so much by contradictory narratives that repress and reflect female experience, but through a melodramatic doubling or mimesis that moves imaginally between daughter and mother, and between the spectator and the text. We are moved emotionally to identify and weep with Mildred's melodramatic and sacrificial performance, but we are equally horrified by Veda's monstrous narcissism, a perfection and ruthlessness that feed each other. Reminiscent of Irigaray's essay 'And One Doesn't Stir without the Other', this symbiotic relation between Mildred and Veda is not repressed through Oedipal narratives. Rather, it is the hysterical result of a disavowal integral to a male imaginary, where the body (or the real) of the mother (and history) is transcended and projected onto an other. This hysterical symbiosis as disavowal can also be seen as the ultimate fetishism of the woman as image and commodity. Mary Ann Doanne notes how the relationship between Mildred and Veda is a narcissistic and hysterical excess, with Mildred's excessive mothering and Veda's role as a 'consumption Vampire' illustrated by her complaint, 'there are so many things we should have and haven't got'.[16] This excessive consumption and femininity is perceived as dangerous to a wartime economy of scarcity and lack. However, we can also see how this excessive femininity as sacrificial mothering, or consumption, brings psychoanalytic and capitalist notions of the fetish together, as an alienated splitting and disavowal of the embodied relation to the object or other.[17] Mildred's maternal sacrifice and Veda's narcissistic consumption are complementary and split halves to a disembodied, excessive femininity which circulates in terms of circuits of sexual difference and capitalism.

The melodramatic images associated with Mildred and Veda are melancholic, split between idealized and deathly identifications, an ambivalence that is not resolved by the reunion of Mildred and Bert and the narrative's ending. But these images of Mildred and Veda are also hysterical. *Mildred Pierce* can perhaps be read not just as the contradictions, for the female spectator, between feminist and paternally framed accounts, but as a mimetic splitting that disavows the real of history. This hystorical mimesis also questions classical film theory's myth of Oedipal narrative repression.

By making Veda Mildred's doppelgänger, it might be argued that the film simply re-inscribes a male imaginary that splits the woman into either absence or ground to a system of male representation. Nevertheless, *Mildred Pierce* remains a melodrama that involves the spectator in such ambivalent and emotional identifications that they cannot be contained within repressive Oedipal plots and frames. Identification in the film is not just textual or heterosexual. Mildred's desire for Veda is based on identification with an imaginary other, revealing the disembodied and hysterical symbiosis that grounds her as a 'good' mother. Mildred's symbiotic relation with her daughter cannot therefore be resolved through Oedipal plots and fantasies of the perfect mother. Such sacrifice does not narratively repress hysteria; it is the hysteria that produces such abject, pre-Oedipal accounts. Identification, for the spectator and 'subject' within psychoanalytic film theory, has historically meant being ideologically constructed through sexual and textual difference, institutionalized by the camera's male gaze. But identification in relation to films cannot be viewed simply as either ideally textual or real. If we can understand our psychological and historical identification with films as residing in our embodied and disembodied mimesis with the image, then this mimesis can also be understood as an emotional and gestural performance of the imaginary. As I have discussed, this imaginary can either melancholically disavow or reconfigure its relation to the real of the body and history. Moreover, a reading of Oedipal sexual difference as a phenomenological disavowal of the real returns us to an account of modernism and film theory that is not a textual privileging of history, as narrative, and the return of the repressed. To use Benjamin's words, history breaks down into images, not words. And, in a similar fashion, classical Hollywood films, such as *Mildred Pierce*, can also be perceived within an imaginal account of a phenomenological imaginary, where sexual difference and spectatorship become a question of bodily mimesis, not linguistic representation.

Key points

- Feminist film critics have highlighted the doubling and duplicity in *Mildred Pierce*. This criticism is divided between patriarchal accounts of repressed femininity and a more sociological account of feminine consciousness.

- Ambivalent femininity and the hysterical doubling between mother and daughter in *Mildred Pierce* refuses the binary of patriarchal or feminist readings of the text.
- *Mildred Pierce* can be read as a melodrama in terms of Freud's return of the repressed, or it can be read in terms of a more disassociated splitting. In this latter account, the masquerade of femininity simultaneously disavows an embodied relation to history and the mother.

Hysteria, melodrama and the gaze

Teresa De Lauretis suggests that one problem with film theory has been the focus on the gaze: the gaze of the woman as performance and spectacle at the expense of other forms of identification that are not with the camera. She signals the possibilities of narrative identification which might not be so restrictive to the female spectator.[18] I want to argue, nevertheless, that whether it is textual narrative or the gaze that film theory is concerned with, the Oedipal determinants remain the same: we have classical narrative repressing the melodramatic, hysterical body, or we have a controlling male gaze that objectifies the woman into passive, hysterical spectacle. A phenomenological reading of melodrama reads the relation between filmic narrative and the body differently, not as a return of the repressed but as a narrative which is structured through a bodily and hysterical mimesis.

As Tania Modleski has noted, melodrama is hysterical. Patriarchy's repression and silencing of the woman's voice is returned through melodrama. She argues if 'melodrama deals with the return of the repressed through a kind of conversion hysteria, perhaps women have been attracted to that genre because it provides an outlet for the repressed feminine voice'.[19] I have suggested that hysteria also presents as disassociation: a masquerade of the body, or seduction which performs to hide a psychic disembodiment and lack of relation to the real.

Hysteria contains all the characteristics of the melodramatic: intense moods, polarization of good versus evil, dramatic plots and an excess of emotion and spectacle, rather than in-depth character psychology. Countering Doanne's claim that the masquerade is anti-hysterical because it effects a separation between the cause of desire and oneself, I argue that the masquerade is hysteria itself whether that is manifested as Oedipal femininity or masculinity. Peter Brooks suggests that melodrama is an 'expressionist drama', in its desire to express everything that has been hitherto repressed. Against this desire to tell all, is the mute voice of melodrama, whose speech is figural of the body, rather than a semiotic language. Such non-verbal and gestural expression is linked to modernist and realist traditions but also remains distinguished from them. Brooks depicts how, like realism, melodrama focuses on the real of everyday life, but unlike realism it seeks to maximize the excitement and drama of the every-day, 'to heighten in dramatic gesture the moral crises' of life.[20] Melo-drama aims to force the representation of the un-representable within everyday reality. Its drive is to break down social prohibitions and, according to Brooks, materialize the repressed.

Whereas Brooks situates melodrama in terms of Freud's return of the repressed, as a force that breaks down narrative repression, melodrama in film can also be figured as a materialization and re-presentation of the real in relation to the image. Melodrama in this scenario is a hysterical masquerade and mimesis of the real, a mimesis of the body and history within film. This is a masquerade of sexual difference as an expression and splitting of the body in gestural form, a masquerade that unconsciously veils and unveils the history of modernism.

Linda Williams and Christine Gledhill have both argued recently for melodrama as the dominant historical imaginary or modality of film. Melodrama replaces realism, in this account, as the organizing modality of early film and classical and contemporary Hollywood film.[21] In a similar fashion I want to suggest hysteria as both the organizing force and symptom of sexual difference. But to grasp these concepts of hysteria and melodrama as being central, we have to eschew the narrative model of the return of the repressed that Freud and Brooks respectively have outlined. We have to understand them within an alternative phenomenological mode.

In the classical account of psychoanalysis and film theory, theory mediates and represses history; similarly, narrative mediates and represses the maternal body. Femininity, here, is both an unspeakable body and an unspeakable subject position within discourse. Without Oedipal or phallic strategies of the voyeuristic and fetishistic gaze, we are left to the hysterical and ultimately psychotic ravages of the body, a narcissistic over-identification with the abject maternal or feminine. This over-identification with the cinematic image provides no subject position for the 'woman' or the female spectator.

In a phenomenological account of the imaginary and film theory, an Oedipal narrative does not repress the body or the hysteric, rather it disavows and disassociates its own hysterical split nature by pro-jecting the abject body onto the other as woman, the racial, homo-

sexual other, etc. In this mapping of a disassociated and split unconscious, linguistic narrative ceases to be the privileged signifier of the
subject, culture or theory. Instead, we have the foregrounding of a
(dis)embodied, hysterical and mimetic relation to the other.

The Oedipal narrative and gaze in *Mildred Pierce* is mimetically hysterical. This gaze figures as a femininity that doubles and masquerades
as the dangerous *femme fatale* or the sacrificial, idealized mother.
Such doubling signifies the spectatorship of sexual difference, both
male and female, as hysterical. All spectatorship is over-identified
narcissistically with the cinematic image, but this is an active as well
as a passive position. Perhaps it would be more correct to state this
hysterical spectatorship and mimesis as an 'active masochism'.

Femininity and the masquerade in *Mildred Pierce* is thus an
ambivalent doubling that signifies an over-identification with the cinematic image, an identification which is narcissistically active and
desiring in relation to a disembodied other. The feminine mimesis and
masquerade in *Mildred Pierce* does not, then, signify a passive position to the female spectator in distinction to a masculine active gaze.
The fetishism and castration of the masculine look in cinematic narrative is hysterical, maintaining distance only through splitting off
and projecting the bodily relation to the mother, as femininity, onto
the figure of the woman. The doubling of the feminine in *Mildred
Pierce* thus reveals male and female spectatorship as hysterical, as
mimesis. This mimesis as I will discuss deconstructs the Oedipal
matrix of sexual difference. As Carol Clover points out in her famous
essay 'Her Body, Himself', we have to understand the processes of
viewer identification as a doubling where the final girls of Slasher
movies perform the split-off, vicarious masochism of the adolescent,
male spectator.[22] Clover's argument for cinematic viewing places
masochistic identification and desire at the heart of Oedipal looking,
a homoerotic desire which returns the castration of the male gaze,
not as a repression of the feminine, but as identification which is hysterically split off and disavowed. The desire of the spectator is, therefore, a mimetic identification with the other, which moves hysterically
between feminine and masculine positions. As Clover describes,
gender displacement in viewing can 'provide a kind of identificatory
buffer' which permits the audiences to explore emotions vicariously.

Key points

- **The cinematic gaze and narrative have been read in terms of
Oedipal sexual difference.**

- Peter Brooks reads melodrama and hysteria in terms of 'a return of the repressed', but melodrama and hysteria can also be read in terms of a phenomenological imaginary, where the relation between the body and language is one of disassociation, rather than repression.

Re-reading sexual difference

A phenomenological understanding of hysteria as bodily mimesis can enable us to re-read the sexual-difference debate within psycho-analysis and film theory. I have described elsewhere the complex, feminist debates on theories of sexual difference, and I do not have the space to rehearse them here. However, to summarize quickly, the sexual-difference debate states not just that men and women are divided (historically) according to their sex, but also that the gender debate is too superficial because it only deals with sociology or ideology, but not with bodies. Sexual-difference theorists argue there is no easy way simply to remove gender inequality through, say, political practice or the destruction of ideology, because the inequality of gender is ultimately marked through the body. In other words, gender cannot be separated from sexuality, and the cultural and symbolic markers of identity cannot be divided from the literal body.

Lacan elevated Freud's Oedipal complex to a symbolic level, arguing that sexual difference was a linguistic effect of the symbolic, and that we are all divided or split between language and the body. Femininity and masculinity are masquerades, for Lacan: they are necessary linguistic fictions which cover a splitting at the heart of identity. Luce Irigaray challenges Lacan's phallocentrism, proposing in place of the phallus, a positive, embodied feminine specificity, to combat the negative othering of femininity within Western metaphysics. Thus, Irigaray lays herself open to the charge of essentialism, through her embodiment of sexual difference. However, my project departs from both Lacan and Irigaray by arguing for sexual difference as hysterically disembodied. So, whereas I agree with Lacan that sexual difference is a masquerade, for me this fiction or masquerade is located at the level of the imaginary (not the symbolic). And although I am in accordance with Irigaray in thinking we need to find an embodied alternative to the phallus, for me a psychically embodied subjectivity can only be fostered through a more fluid understanding of sexuality. In other words, sexual difference cannot be used to delineate an embodied subject, whether that is characterized by Irigaray's 'feminine' imaginary or by Christine Battersby's more recent theorization of a 'female' embodied subject.[23]

Laura Mulvey structures the cinematic look in relation to Freud's theories of Oedipal sexual difference. In 'Some Psychological Consequences of the Anatomical Distinction Between the Sexes' and in his essay on 'Femininity' Freud explains how sexual difference positions boys and girls in different relations to the structures of looking and knowledge. The fetishization of the boy's relation to castration and looking establishes him with a distance and disavowal of the mother's body, which the girl lacks. This narcissistic lack of distance for the girl, according to Doanne, is why female spectatorship is over-identified and impossible. However, if we understand the boy's castration to be hysterical disavowal and a projection of his bodily identification onto the figure of the woman, or femininity, then we can see how the masculinity and femininity of sexual difference are both involved in a similar movement of disavowal *and* narcissistic over-identification. Projection and doubling are key processes at play in viewing films, and they reveal how the 'male' and 'female' look are both practices of hysterical mimesis. But how, exactly, does this account of hysterical mimesis re-read the sexual-difference accounts within psychoanalysis and film theory?

Film theory is indebted to a Lacanian Oedipal narrative (based on Freud) where the phallic signifier and symbolic represses the maternal body and is responsible for bringing sexual identity simultaneously into being and language. Sexual difference, for Lacan, is therefore symbolic. Alternatively, we can comprehend Oedipal, sexual difference as a defensive, imaginary structure, a rigid melancholic fixing of identification into heterosexual identities. Jessica Benjamin has argued for an early Oedipal phase characterized by rigid gender complementarity, where envious loss and repudiation of the other sex, a loss of being based on castration anxiety, lead the girl and the boy to desire what they cannot actually become, i.e., the mother for the boy, the father for the girl. Idealization of the opposite sex is bound up with aggressive melancholic loss for not being able to be that sex. For Jessica Benjamin, later Oedipal fantasies and object love compensate for this rather rigid splitting. Utilizing Freud's concept of deferred action, she suggests that this post-Oedipal phase ameliorates and retrospectively reconfigures earlier rigid identifications, introducing a more fluid bisexuality.[24] However, she also states that 'no absolute transcendence of the Oedipal is possible'; for her there is no escape from Oedipal structures.[25] I want to suggest that the Oedipal is a structure of gender instituted by society, but it is not symbolically immutable.

Judith Butler, the queer theorist and philosopher, re-reads Freud's Oedipal text in terms of her argument of gender performativity. This gender performance is understood in relation to Freud's account of mourning and melancholia. For Butler, heterosexual difference is a melancholic denial and disavowal of earlier homosexual loves. Gender is, here, an 'acting out' of unresolved grief. However, in Butler's view, performance allegorizes 'a loss it cannot grieve'.[26] In other words, performance allegorizes an incorporative fantasy of melancholia. The notion of allegory is important to Butler in this configuration because she is arguing that performance is essentially a performance reiterated within language and the symbolic. Bringing together Foucault, Derrida and psychoanalysis, Butler suggests that the symbolic law is not simply juridical and repressive, but generative too. Our identities are performances of symbolic law and language, reiterated rituals of everyday life and practices, which can produce more transgressive identities. Butler avoids the criticisms of her gender performance as simple cross-dressing or political volunteering by announcing the lack of agency in her model. Gender performance is not a willed act but in Foucauldian manner becomes a series of discursive and historical reiterations.

Butler's analysis of gender performance is intrinsically about the performance of language. Placing gender performance and identity within language is central for Butler, because in her view there is no place of desire external to the law. With this conceptualization Butler moves away from Foucault's criticism of psychoanalysis that the law is external to desire, emphasizing, through her reading of Freud, how sexual desire (and identity) are formulated in relation to prohibition. But, whereas Lacan places resistance to symbolic identity within the imaginary, Butler returns it, following Foucault this time, to the socio-symbolic. For Butler, this means situating performativity and resistance within language, the dynamics of power and the social. In a commentary on her work, Adam Phillips suggests that mourning and performativity are dialectical twins; mourning gives gravity and grounds performance, returning it to a realization of unconscious histories, our losses, whereas performance prevents mourning becoming some kind of truth act (for both analysis and the community). Phillips suggests that mourning is the way out of the magic circle of the family, meaning it is the resolution of the Oedipal complex, a Kleinian view that the analytical community agrees with.[27] But sexual difference for Phillips remains, as in Jessica Benjamin's work, not something we can transcend, for it explains how the child has to accept there is no third sex, no position beyond exclusion. Phillips seems, then, to accept some sort of sexual difference as constitutive. He argues that there is logic in the opposition Freud places between identification and desire: 'In Freud's view we become what we cannot have, and we desire (and punish) what we are compelled to disown.'[28]

Butler is not so sure, and while accepting there is no place beyond exclusion asks, 'But why is sexual difference the primary guarantor of loss in our psychic lives?'[29]

The Oedipal complex presupposes a heterosexuality which is already in place, whereas Butler sees heterosexuality as an accomplishment, achieved through a more primary repression or disavowal of homosexual desires. Heterosexuality or sexual difference is therefore melancholic, and marks a refused or ungrievable loss. As she says, loving a girl means you cannot be one.[30] Melancholia and hysteria, as Freud himself noticed, are remarkably similar. In both melancholia and hysteria we identify with the object and refuse to acknowledge its loss. Freud argued that the difference is that with melancholia we regress to narcissism, whereas with hysteria some degree of object cathexis is maintained. However, I suggest that in actuality hysteria and melancholia are both imaginary and narcissistic identifications.[31]

Sexual difference is melancholic: being masculine or feminine is a refusal to grieve homosexual loves. But sexual difference is also hysterical for both sexes. It is the way we can symbiotically remain attached to the mother and disavow loss through a certain identity. As Leo Bersani states, desire is actually predicated on the loss or dissolution of self or identity.[32] The price, then, of our hysterical identities of masculinity and femininity is melancholia: a disavowal of desire for and identification with, originally, the mother. The Oedipal boy hysterically and obsessively disavows his maternal identification, whereas the Oedipal girl hysterically gives up desire for the mother in an identification which becomes overwhelming.

In agreement with Butler, I propose that sexual difference is not the structuring loss in our lives. However, I read Butler's performativity of gender not in terms of its relation to language, but as a phenomenological mimesis of the imaginary. I suggest that sexual difference is not a symbolic loss, but can be perceived as a kind of imaginary armour against more embodied and fluid identifications. Furthermore, it is the hysterical and symbiotic nature of Oedipal sexual difference which marks our unresolved or refused loss. In this sense we are all hysterics; we all perform and masquerade to cover our refusal to leave the imaginary other.

Lacan proposes a symbolic argument for sexual difference. He argues that we are linguistically constructed and split, between the body and language, or between the imaginary and symbolic, in terms of sexual difference. This division is intrinsic to subjectivity and language. However, we can argue instead, like Foucault, for the social implementation of this division as a discourse of power. Foucault,

like Lacan, situates sexual difference as a division at the level of discourse, but for him, this is a materialistic (embodied) discourse. Foucault then suggests that sexual difference is a productive discourse of
power and the law, manipulating bodies and constructing homosexuality as an abject difference. But we can also see this discourse
of sexual difference as a hysterical split at the level of the imaginary.
Hysterical sexual difference, as a social imaginary, mimetically splits
the body from language, thus veiling a more embodied crisis of the
self. If the Oedipal complex is hysterical disassociation between mind
and body, for the woman and the man, then melancholia is the
ungrievable loss of not just homosexual loves, but a more embodied
relation to the other. Mourning becomes, in this working, not just
the way out of the 'magic circle' of the family, but the recognition of
its heterosexual dynamics as masquerade.

To return this alternative account of sexual difference to film
theory means understanding hysteria as a phenomenological and disembodied splitting that masquerades and performs in the dominant
(Oedipal) imaginary of the other. Such melancholic mimesis masks a
lack of integrated psychic embodiment. Sexual difference, masculinity and femininity, are defended modes of hysterical mimesis that are
played out in the imaginary, rather than the symbolic. The Oedipal,
cinematic and representative structures of looking described by Apparatus theory become mimetic hysterical structures of the imaginary.

Key points

- Laura Mulvey structures the cinematic look in relation to Freud's
  theories of Oedipal sexual difference.
- We can alternatively see the Oedipal, cinematic and representative structures of looking described by Apparatus theory as
  mimetic hysterical structures of the imaginary.

Film spectatorship as embodied and disembodied mimesis

Mikkel Borch-Jacobsen also proposes sexual difference as hysterical
mimesis. Returning to the Freudian project, Borch-Jacobsen interprets it as a mimesis which deconstructs any opposition between the
narcissistic ego and the object. Not only is psychoanalysis originally
rooted in the hypnotic power of suggestion (from the other), but also
the subject is constituted between self and other, and therefore

between the internal fantasy world and the outside external relationship or event. Borch-Jacobsen disagrees flatly with the idea that
desire is repressed through an external agency, whether that is the
Oedipal complex, the linguistic symbolic or indeed primal seduction.
Desires and wishes are not disguised because they are repressed by
an interdictive law or prohibitive agency. Instead, desire is from the
outset disguised or 'other' because it is mimetic.

Now in Borch-Jacobsen's work the emphasis on mimesis is negative, narcissistic and violent: 'I want what my brother, my model, my
idol wants – and I want it in his place.'[33] In her essay 'The Gesture in
Psychoanalysis', Luce Irigaray suggests a more creative identification
and mimesis between daughter and mother. Irigaray posits an alternative to Freud's 'Beyond the Pleasure Principle', re-telling his famous
Fort, Da, story of the little boy and the cotton reel in terms of the little
girl. Girls can't enter the language of culture through a death drive or
mastery that represses the mother as other, because to do this would
be to eradicate the girl's subject identity that is the same as her
mother's. The girl, therefore, plays with her doll and mimes being and
not being like her mother. This mimesis or identification is not a narcissism that repressively masters the other. Instead, the girl's identification passes backwards and forwards, miming and opening up an
imaginary and symbolic space for a desiring subjectivity.[34]

Rather than seeing this more creative mimesis as the exclusive
province of the female, we can perhaps understand it as a more social
mode of mimesis and mourning which enables the child to leave the
mother, without making her such an incorporated dead other. How,
then, can we apply this more creative mimesis to watching film?
Walter Benjamin's writing on mimesis is integral to an understanding of the experiential process of watching film. This process is both
a hysterical transportation into the dreaming collective and an
embodied, re-awakening or re-memory of historical tradition. In his
essay 'On the Mimetic Faculty', where he explores a new materialist
form of language, Walter Benjamin writes:

> Nature produces similarities. One only has to think of mimicry (of e.g.,
> insects to leaves). The highest capacity for producing similarities,
> however is man's. His gift of seeing resemblances is nothing other than
> a rudiment of the powerful compulsion in former times to become and
> behave like something else. Perhaps there is none of his higher func-
> tions in which his mimetic faculty does not play a decisive role.[35]

The human's capacity for mimesis is for Benjamin historical in both
a phylogenetic and an ontogenetic sense. In the case of the latter,

children's play is where we learn mimetic behaviour. Like Borch-Jacobsen, Benjamin does not see the desire of children as goal-directed; children's play has no aim; they mime because they identify. Benjamin remarks on how this realm of play 'is in no way limited to what one person can imitate in another. The child plays at being not only a shopkeeper or a teacher but also a windmill and train.'[36]

Mimesis, for Benjamin, was in ancient times a stronger and magical thinking of correspondences between people and their worlds. In modern times that magical mimesis of the natural world has decayed, but can be found in childhood fantasy and games. New opportunities for mimetic development are situated in new technologies such as film. He sees this mimetic power present in films as the optical unconscious. The camera surgically penetrates the unconscious space of the material world, and so film makes us aware 'of the necessities that rule our lives', opening up a sphere of action.[37] The technological reproduction (of film) 'gives back to humanity that capacity for experience that technological *production* takes away'.[38]

The mass alienation and shock associated with industrial capitalism, whether it is the urban crowd or the assembly line, is a trauma that is defended against by mimesis. With reference to Freud's essay 'Beyond the Pleasure Principle', Benjamin describes how film can be a mimetic way of defending ourselves against the everyday shock of the modern world. Freud was concerned with the defensive and hysterical mimesis and repetition that occurred in shell-shocked victims of the First World War. Unable to recollect these overwhelming experiences, the soldiers would repeat and re-enact them again and again in hallucinations and dreams. Interestingly, these war victims were the first male patients that Freud acknowledged to be openly hysterical. Benjamin, then, also recognized that this hysterical and defensive mimesis operates as a defence against the traumas and shocks of industrial life; he particularly noted the factory as deadening to the human senses. This hysterical mimesis, incapable of returning the look, like the camera, is a deadening of the senses. Susan Buck-Morss calls this mimesis an anaesthetics: a crisis of perception where experience cannot be integrated and connected to the past.[39] New mimetic technologies such as film were, in Benjamin's view, not only hysterical and defensive but were also a means of reconstructing the capacity for experience and recollection that has been shattered by the modern world.

Roger Callois' surrealist essay on mimesis (1935), was written after Walter Benjamin's essay on the mimetic faculty, but served as an originating manuscript for Lacan's thoughts on the mirror stage. In this paper, Caillois discusses the miming body in terms of the biological mimesis of insects, as magic and as human simulation; he also (like Benjamin) describes this embodied mimesis as a self-structured camera![40] Callois states that animal mimesis is paralleled by a human's mimesis with the object of art, specifically painting. Jacques Lacan famously takes Caillois' embodied notion of the human subject's mimetic faculty, manifested as painting, and extracts from it a theory of the scopic drive; a dialectic of the eye and the gaze manifesting itself as the castration complex.[41] This initial interest in mimesis and its relation to the body of the m/other, what Lacan calls 'object a', is gradually developed into his linguistic theory of the unconscious. However, in his early work *The Four Fundamental Concepts of Psychoanalysis*, Lacan cites Caillois in his description of mimesis as the organism's defence and technique of camouflage. This camouflage illustrates the defensive disguise of mimesis as a masquerade which in turn produces the sexual aim. 'Nature shows us that this sexual aim is produced by all kinds of effects that are essentially disguise, masquerade.'[42] So we have an acknowledgement from Lacan that sexuality is actually produced as a defensive mimesis. Lacan does not call this mimesis hysterical, neither does he relate it to the bodily senses, attributing it to a mental perception or imaginary which is located at the level of the gaze and the eye. However, in tracing an understanding of mimesis back to Caillois and Benjamin, we can comprehend it as *bodily* mimicry. Following Walter Benjamin, we can understand perceptual mimesis and film spectatorship as a bodily mimesis that is (1) defensively hysterical and (2) a means of cultural re-memory where experience is re-integrated and connected to the past.

Apparatus theory positions the linguistic construction of the 'subject' and the film spectator. The mimesis explored here, however, both hysterically fixes and dissolves that subject/spectator into a more fluid identification with the screen. Lacan argues that obsession and hysteria are different, oppositional and neurotic structures attached to men and women. Characteristically, men are obsessives and women are hysterics.[43] I suggest, however, that although obsession and hysteria are attached to gender, they are defensive Oedipal identifications inscribed by society that both break down into hysteria. Obsession and hysteria are thus projective mechanisms and identifications (both fixed and potentially mobile), which become involved in the defensive and melancholic disavowal of an embodied social other. There is, then, no inevitability about sexual difference as the bedrock of our identities. Rather, sexual difference and the Oedipal complex are a set of defensive identifications (masculine or feminine), endorsed by society, that hysterically defend us as an 'anaesthetics'. Sexual difference splits us off and numbs us from a more imaginative practice of an embodied imaginary; it prevents us from accessing more mobile, embodied and mournful identifications, where we can transform perception into experience, through the cultural re-memory of our histories.

Conclusion

If Oedipal sexual difference is melancholic and hysterical, then the Oedipal narrative binary of film theory that represses melodrama as a textual excess or abject underbelly to the classical realist film text has to be re-thought. This chapter has re-interpreted feminist and psychoanalytic film debates on sexual difference and the male gaze in relation to a phenomenological mimesis. Re-reading classical Hollywood films such as *Mildred Pierce* through such a phenomenological imaginary allows us to challenge the arguments that situate melodrama as the repressed bodily underbelly of more realist classical cinema.

Our hysterical and mimetic identification with the film is not repressed under the narrative. Rather, it is our disembodied, hysterical mimesis, which elaborates the narrative. Christine Gledhill and Linda Williams both propose that melodrama is the organizing modality or genre of Hollywood film. Williams in particular has stressed the nature of melodrama as a dominant imaginary in American cinema, an organizing melodramatic imaginary that moves between fictional texts and real life.[44] If the melancholic and hysterical identification with the image in *Mildred Pierce* freezes history as a melancholic mimicry of the other, a projection that is doomed to repeat itself traumatically because the real remains unmediated, then it can also be defined as part of the dominant and historical American melodramatic imaginary that Williams describes. History and film in this analysis are part of the hysterical mimesis that defines the melodramatic imaginary of Hollywood. This is perhaps a pessimistic reading of melodrama, but, as Williams notes in her exploration of the melodramatic racial imagination in America, unless we fully explore the power of this imaginary we remain in a state of denial. The melodramatic imaginary of sexual difference and race in American film are not separate, but structurally interdependent. We need to examine the force and violence intrinsic to this melancholic imaginary, and also ask how this imaginary operates to structure spectatorship within differing historical moments. The next chapter, then, examines the way in which sexual difference and film spectatorship have been historicized in relation to debates on psychoanalysis, melodrama and Weimar cinema.

2

The Sexual-Difference
Spectator in Weimar Cinema

Introduction

The last chapter explored how a conceptualization of sexual difference and melodrama as hysterical can re-read debates on the male gaze and the female spectator within film theory. Moving Apparatus theory and theories of sexual difference to an understanding of the phenomenological doubling at stake in melodrama, the idea that the double in film is our psychic and sexual unconscious, allows us to see the fundamentally split and hysterical nature of film spectatorship. Apparatus theory became increasingly criticized in the 1980s and 1990s for its inability to historicize the film spectator. On the one hand this led to a turning away from textual analysis and the rise of audience studies. On the other hand, however, there were attempts to revise the sexual, textual spectator through an attention to questions of history.

The problems of Apparatus theory stem largely from a universalizing theory of language and sexual difference, which is ultimately rooted in a structuralist theory of cinema and the unconscious. However, psychoanalysis, sexual difference and the textual, cinematic spectator are not inevitably ahistorical. Within film theory it has been the critics of 1930s melodrama and Weimar cinema who have attempted to revise the sexual-difference spectator in relation to a more historical imaginary. Critics such as Thomas Elsaesser and Patrice Petro have both sought to situate and critique Apparatus theory historically in relation to Weimar film. This chapter concentrates on film theory, melodrama and Weimar cinema in relation to a hysterical male gaze. This gaze can be understood within the

Oedipal construction of Apparatus theory. However, it can also be opened up to questions of history through a focus on a more phenomenological mimesis and imaginary. Weimar cinema is an important topic with which to examine the textual spectator, not only because it brings together psychoanalysis, melodrama and Apparatus theory, but also because it simultaneously historicizes film theory and psychoanalysis.

Psychoanalysis, especially the origins of Marxist psychoanalysis, is rooted within early Weimar culture. The intellectual scene of Weimar society was dominated by discussion of Freud and psychoanalysis. People were both suspicious of and ardently excited by this new psychology. The war had brought psychoanalysis from the margins to the centre in that it became used by psychiatrists as a treatment to cure hysterically shell-shocked soldiers so they could be fit once more for active combat.[1] Hysterical masculinity was then a key point of crisis within the Weimar period. Psychoanalysis was both a revolutionary and controlling force. It follows that the cinema of this period, as Siegfried Kracauer was so aware, is particularly situated in relation to questions of psychoanalysis, modernity and history. The critics of Weimar cinema move Apparatus theory (and the gaze of sexual difference) through an attention to cinema as an historical imaginary, but they also provide a more historical understanding of Freud by elaborating questions of the unconscious in relation to the modernist film thinkers Walter Benjamin and Siegfried Kracauer.

Key points

- The problems with Apparatus theory – a universalizing theory of language and sexual difference.
- Thomas Elsaesser and Patrice Petro have theorized 1930s melodrama and Weimar cinema, revising the sexual-difference spectator, in relation to a more historical imaginary.
- Hysterical masculinity was key to Weimar cinema and history.

Weimar cinema

Weimar cinema is characterized as the historical imaginary of German cinema because of the crisis within that society, now famously documented, for its conclusion in fascism. This crisis has also been read in terms of a breakdown in male identity, refracting the dissolution of the male subject within modernity more generally. Weimar and New German cinema is, therefore, a privileged location to examine how Oedipal Apparatus theory can be located as a historical and social imaginary. Thomas Elsaesser suggests that Fassbinder's films incorporate the very structures of Apparatus theory: voyeurism and spectacle, seeing and being seen. Elsaesser wonders if fascism can be understood less as an identification with the sadistic SS officers and more as a pleasure of being seen, 'of placing oneself in the all seeing eye of the state'.[2]

Patrice Petro criticizes Elsaesser for his reliance on a male imaginary. In concurring with the same ideas of the apparatus spectator as Baudry and Metz, Elsaesser, in Petro's view, simply provides historical credence to a spectator that is always male. Petro's own study of female spectatorship in Weimar cinema utilizes Heidegger, Benjamin and Kracauer to argue for a female gaze that is less implicated in structures of voyeurism and fetishism, and more involved with a contemplative and distracted look. Benjamin and Kracauer offer a more historicized understanding of cinema spectatorship within modernity through their attention to the impact of technology and through the differences they describe between the reception of 'art' or mass culture. The growing presence of women in Weimar culture produced an ambivalence which explains the male intellectuals' and spectators' obsession with authority: a desire to 'distance and thereby master the threat perceived as too close, too present, too overwhelming'.[3] This repression and exclusion of women in male cinematic theory and culture explains Doanne's stipulation of the non-identity of the female spectator. But, for Petro, such an over-presence of the female spectator as object and image has to be explained historically, in terms of a male imaginary which distanced a mass cultural audience perceived as both feminine and threatening.[4]

Key points

- Weimar cinema is a privileged location to examine Apparatus theory, within a historical and social imaginary.
- Thomas Elsaesser suggests that Fassbinder's films incorporate the very structures of Apparatus theory.
- Patrice Petro criticizes Elsaesser for his reliance on a male imaginary.

Petro's contemplative female gaze

In exploring an alternative female spectator Petro turns to Weimar melodrama and, following Janet Bergstrom, notes the presence of an unstable masculinity and a feminized male within these films. Petro suggests that such passive and eroticized representations of the male elicit a more contemplative 'less goal-orientated way of looking'.[5] Indeed, this contemplative gaze is implicated in Weimer melodramas generally. Such films, also known as street films or the *Kammerspiel*, are less influenced by narrative conventions and are expressive of 'composition and atmosphere'. Their 'hyperbolic gestures and exaggerated facial expression' are thus generally used to signify meaning, in excess of the narrative.[6] Intense depiction of a static *mise-en-scène* combined with breaks in narrative action, where characters are frozen, promotes a pictorial and emotive image. The spectator is drawn to this slow and gestural illustration, wondering how and why conflicts are acted out.

The contemplative gaze ushers in a different reading of the female spectator, one which is not passive but involved with the bisexual mobility and intense expressionism. This gaze is an eroticized look which historicizes a specific gendered spectator. Organized around manic and depressive gestures, this female gaze foregrounds style and expression, rather than problems with vision. Petro suggests that the popularity of these melodramas arose from the conflictual positions of these female spectators, caught between a changing 'New Woman' and more traditional modes of female identity. The female bisexuality and emotional pathos in these films was, therefore, directly related to a historical dilemma for the real female spectator, who accessed an active *and* eroticized look that cannot be attributed to either poles of classical apparatus gazing.

Petro's description is indebted to Heidegger's notion of a contemplative perception, and to Benjamin's and Kracauer's phenomenological ideas of a distracted gaze. Heidegger, along with male epistemology in general, privileges a contemplative perception in relation to art, as distinct from the degraded, distracted, non-distanced gaze of mass culture. However, Petro draws on Kracauer's analysis of 'The Little Shopgirls Go to the Movies' to argue for female viewers who are both contemplative and distracted. Kracauer's notion of the distracted spectator of mass culture is based on his ideas of the mass ornament. The mass ornament is a subject of collective experience, whose representation reflects an abstract rationalization of capitalist society linked to mythical thinking. Here, the production and unaware consumption of abstract ornamental patterns rationalizes perception and distracts attention from any desire of active social change. Aesthetic and abstract rationalization goes hand in hand with a descent into myth and irrationality, obscuring true reason. Kracauer initially characterized the mass ornament in terms of female dance troupes, like the Tiller Girls, and gymnastic formalizations anticipating the highly ornamental parades associated with Nazi Germany. Consumption of the mass ornament was also the distracted consumption of the cinema. Kracauer saw how the mass ornament allowed abstract and formalized rationalization to become infiltrated with pleasure and myth. The mass ornament is then a kind of formulaic but hysterical masquerade. In the case of the Tiller Girls it is a female masquerade that performs to obscure, not masculinity, but the alienation of capitalist systems of production.

> The legs of the Tiller Girls correspond to the hands on the machines in the factory. But beyond the manual aspect, emotional dispositions are also tested for their psycho-technical aptitude. The mass ornament is the aesthetic reflex of the rationality to which our economic system aspires.[7]

I want to note, here, the 'psychotechnicality' of emotions that Kracauer is describing – a sort of emotional disposition that is detached and manipulated. Hysterical emotion is sentimental because it is disassociated and not psychically embodied. The mass ornament is an account of the phenomenological unconscious of capitalist society, an unconscious that is located in the pure surface and externality of objects.

However, the mass ornament is also positive, because in the pure externality of mass entertainment, melodramatic films, stars and revues, the audience can actually encounter its unconscious reflection and see it for what it is. Interestingly, it is not in 'The Little Shopgirls Go to the Movies' but in his essay 'The Cult of Distraction' that Kracauer identifies this more active role of audience reception in relation to the moving-picture palaces of Berlin.[8] Arguing that audiences find a more honest reflection of their reality in popular entertainment than in bourgeois events, Kracauer describes the superficial allure of such popular spectacle and how it acts as disconnected sensory stimuli. Popular spectacle thus allows the audience self-recognition.

> Here, in pure externality, the audience encounters itself; its own reality is revealed in the fragmented sequence of sense impressions. Were this reality to remain hidden from the viewers, they could neither attack nor change it; its disclosure in distraction is therefore of moral significance.[9]

Petro tries to rescue 'The Little Shopgirls' from the hysterical distraction that Kracauer describes.[10] Although Kracauer associates low, dumb mass culture with femininity and passivity, according to Petro, he suggests another 'mode of spectatorship and form of representation that failed to keep pace with rationalised models in the realm of leisure'.[11] This alternative mode of spectatorship is found in the contemplative and emotional response of the little shopgirls at the movies. While they may be distracted from everyday life, 'they are clearly in a state of concentration at the movies'.[12] Kracauer identifies a correspondence between the female character in the melodrama and the shopgirl spectators, criticizing both for their sentimentality. Petro, in contrast, sees the sentimentality and tears exuded by the shopgirls as signs of emotional concentration, not distraction.

Nevertheless, if we are to understand melodrama and the hysterical reception it instigates as disassociated emotion, then we can see that Kracauer's attack on the sentimental response of the shopgirls is precisely the orchestrated hysteria he attributes to an abstracted and rationalized distraction. When he states that 'many people sacrifice themselves noble-mindedly because they are too lazy to rebel; many tears are shed which flow only because crying is sometimes easier than contemplation', he is depicting a hysterical feminization of the audience, a melodramatic response to the mass ornament that is not contemplative, but split off and mindless.[13] Undoubtedly, Kracauer's analysis is problematic for feminism, but his critique should also be seen in the light of a more general hystericization and feminization of capitalist mass culture.

Petro's analysis of a contemplative gaze in relation to Kracauer's sketches of the little shopgirls is not convincing. Elsewhere, however, she analyses this gaze in relation to gender experimentation and bisexuality, a look that is attributed to the film's aesthetics. Therefore, it is not so much the contemplative, *female* gaze in the reception of melodrama in Weimar Germany which is compelling in Petro's account, but a contemplative view grounded in bisexuality and the aesthetic expressionism of the image. Critical of psychoanalysis and Apparatus theory as phallocentric discourses which privilege a male epistemology of distance and differentiation, Petro offers an alternative, historical account of female spectatorship which cannot be confused with masculine structures of knowledge and gender.

Petro's contemplative gaze can perhaps be better understood through a more phenomenological imaginary. Such a phenomenological reading of the melodrama situates the spectator not with fixed textual identifications of sexual difference but within a more experiential space – a place where melancholic, distracted and hysterical identifications can potentially become mobilized within a more embodied, contemplative looking.

What is significant in Petro's analysis is the emphasis she places on an aesthetic expressionism elaborated via the image. Such an expressionism I would argue is both distracted and contemplative, but significantly moves spectatorship away from the binary poles of textual Apparatus theory and towards a more phenomenological account of cinema spectatorship. This account, then, includes real historical contradictions, rather than simply eliding them through dominant textual representations.[14]

Key points

- Petro argues for a more contemplative, distracted female gaze.
- The contemplative gaze ushers in a different female spectator, one which is not passive but involved with bisexual mobility and intense expressionism in relation to the image.
- Petro states that Kracauer's little shopgirls are not just passively distracted at the movies, but also actively contemplative.
- Kracauer's ideas of the distracted gaze are based on his idea of the 'mass ornament'.
- The mass ornament is then a kind of formulaic but hysterical masquerade.
- The little shopgirls are therefore hysterical, not contemplative.
- The distracted and contemplative gaze can be understood as part of a phenomenological imaginary, rather than attached to the binary poles of sexual difference and Apparatus theory.

The textual or real spectator?

Mary Ann Doanne criticizes Petro for confusing sexual difference with epistemology, arguing that she collapses theories of epistemology and language onto a theory of sexual difference, making knowledge a phallocentric construct.[15] Therefore, to claim an alternative position of female epistemology, one that somehow takes on the feminine attributes of femininity and closeness, is to essentialize sexual difference as attributable to men and women. For Doanne, following Lacan, sees sexual difference as a mask or construct, that ideologically and textually positions men and women within culture. But this does not mean that men and woman are contained within these

positions, although epistemology is persuasive in helping us understand the workings of 'male' power within society. This is rather a
disingenuous argument which is on some level Lacan's responsibility,
because it sets up sexual difference, language and epistemology as
socially constructed, but also symbolically immutable: there are no
alternatives. I agree with Doanne that positing a female epistemology
and a 'real' feminine spectator is dangerously essentialist, and hovers
too close to Irigaray's notion of a female 'subjectivity' or symbolic.
To claim, though, as Doanne and other Apparatus theorists have that
the structures of the sexual-difference, cinematic gaze are fictions, but
universal, seems to mirror Lacan's circular argument that the phallus
is metaphorically distinct from the penis, when actually they are
inevitably connected. Doanne and Apparatus theory privilege a
masculine, symbolic gaze, which disavows its own morphology as a
masculine imaginary. As Luce Irigaray has aptly demonstrated, the
morphology of this male Western imaginary is one that grounds
the masculine subject through a projection of the abject body onto
the image and figure of the 'woman' in our society.

However, I am also suspicious of Petro's alternative female gaze.
Surely there is no such thing as a real 'male' or 'female' spectator
who identifies either with Oedipal structures of representation within
the textual apparatus or more bisexual figurations? Although Petro's
analysis moves away from a male system of textual representation,
her argument becomes collapsed back within the binaries of this
debate, precisely because she postulates a historical 'female' gaze as
an alternative to a textual, male one. I want to suggest that the
identifications of audiences in terms of the filmic image are fairly
limitless and cannot be contained within either a theorization of
Oedipal textual representation or theories of a real 'male' or 'female'
spectator.

Whereas I agree with Lacan that masculinity and femininity are
masks and masquerades, unlike Lacan, I see Freud's Oedipal theory
as an account of neurotic defence and not an inevitable narrative of
how we gain sexed, symbolic and separate identities within culture.
So, a real alternative to the male gaze cannot be the delineation of a
female specificity, but an account that deconstructs masculine difference for men and for women. There are narrative positions in film,
and the so-called male gaze expresses a particularly dominant male
imaginary which is not universal, but always specifically historical.

Petro's argument, nevertheless, does makes sense as a historical
account of women spectators in Weimar culture, whose bisexual identifications potentially destabilize sexual-difference theory in general,
film Apparatus theory in particular. A closer analysis of Petro's thesis

reveals that she is not in fact offering up the real female spectator as an alternative to Apparatus theories of the male gaze. She argues, against Doanne's injunction of the impossible female spectator, for the contradictory experience of historical female spectators during the Weimar period. To travel beyond sexual-difference debates in film theory means moving away from the sharp distinction between the fictional apparatus spectator, and the real one. It means leaving behind Lacan's distinction between the phallus and the penis, in the realization that sexual identity does not reside purely in the imaginary (world of the phallus), any more than it is found in the real (abjection of the woman's body). Mapping a fluidly sexual spectator that moves between the real and text is perhaps the most exciting part of Petro's analysis of Weimar cinema, but her reluctance to take up the significance of this, means that while her work challenges the phallocentrism of Apparatus theory, it leaves the accompanying distance between the textual and real spectator in place. I want to suggest that while films can elicit dominant narrative positions, aligned with a 'masculine' apparatus and gaze, this hegemonic look cannot contain the fluid identifications that audiences make with films, especially in relation to the image. Although Oedipal psychoanalysis splits identification and desire along heterosexual lines, various writers and analysts have challenged the view that imaginary identification and symbolic desire are so separate.[16] If we identify with what we desire, and desire where we identify, then there can be no complete aligning of the real spectator's identifications with textual, heterosexual difference, merely a bisexual fluid identification which is augmented in various ways by the text. Petro's insistence on the expressive components of Weimar cinema points to a different emphasis on the spectator, one that negotiates the phenomenology of the image in a fluid bisexuality. However, her insistence that this contemplative gaze is located in a sexually differentiated female spectator serves to return this radical argument to the very binaries it is trying to deconstruct.

Key points

- Doanne sees sexual difference as the textual masquerade of the spectator. For her the female gaze is an impossibility.
- Petro's claim for a real female spectator is equally problematic.
- Petro's work is exciting because it maps a fluidly sexual spectator which moves between the real and text.

Siegfried Kracauer's mass ornament

I want to return to the distracted gaze outlined by Kracauer, as this gaze is one that clearly dissolves a separation between real spectator and text. Moreover, Kracauer's account of a phenomenological film reception historicizes sexual-difference theory through his notion of the mass ornament as a social unconscious of the masses. As Getrud Koch notes, there are many similarities between Kracauer's ideas of social psychology and Freud's notion of group psychology, although an important difference is that whereas Kracauer elaborates a Marxist, phenomenological unconscious, such an unconscious was latent in Freud's thinking but always disavowed in favour of his individualistic thesis of the Oedipal complex.[17] Freud followed le Bon's description of the group mind as a primitive horde bound together through libidinous identifications. His analysis of these identifications, however, seriously unravels the Oedipal complex theory, replacing it with an emphasis on bisexuality and group hysteria. Suggestive hypnosis, narcissism and the increasing split between ego and ego ideal were the key components of the group mind.[18] As this book argues, a phenomenological account of the unconscious challenges Freud's Oedipal complex and reveals it as no more than hysterical identification and rivalry that is mimetically split off and disassociated from the (social) other. Reading Freud's account of group psychology, especially the emphasis he places on the radical disassociation between ego and ego ideal, allows us to see how his understanding of a social unconscious veers perilously close to an elucidation of the unconscious as phenomenological splitting. As I shall discuss in the next chapter, this phenomenological unconscious is present in Freud's early work on hysteria and connects his thinking with that of Charcot and Jung.

Kracauer's description of the mass ornament outlines the unconscious of capitalism, where the individual is divided and desubstantialized from the process of nature and from the social, through his or her insertion into the mass ornament. This insertion destroys 'community and personality' through a fetishization of the individual as a split-off, abstract and highly rationalized function. Examples of this in Weimar culture can be seen as the mechanical orchestration of arms and thighs in the Tiller Girls revue or in mass gymnastics.[19] David Rodowick suggests that these arms and legs of the Tiller Girls are a kind of social hieroglyphics, a point I will elaborate presently.[20] The rationality of the mass ornament is an abstractness that avoids reason. This paradox is at the core of Kracauer's

thinking of the mass ornament. Capitalism's defect is that it 'ratio-
nalises not too much but rather too little', and it is the abstract reasoning of the mass ornament which collapses into mythological
thinking and chaos, thus avoiding the creative reflexivity of the
individual in relation to society as a whole.[21] It is for this reason
Kracauer talks paradoxically about the abstract rationality of the
mass ornament as also being too literal or concrete – again a fetishization where the part is made to stand in for the whole.

Such phenomenological splitting where experience and production
are disassociated and alienated is an abandonment of reason and consciousness. Although the masses produce the ornament 'they are not
involved in thinking it through'.[22] Situating his argument for the mass
ornament not just in terms of capitalism but also in relation to aesthetics, Kracauer suggests that the aesthetics of the mass ornament is
a legitimate mode of experience for people because it reflects the
reality of the economic system, and is therefore more true than
artistic productions, 'which cultivate outdated noble sentiments in
obsolete forms'.[23] Getrud Koch states that the extent to which
Kracauer puts forward a positive concept of the mass is debatable,
dependent on differing interpretations of texts.[24] What is clear is that
Kracauer's thoughts on the unconscious nature of the mass ornament
do reflect the cultural criticism of the masses aligned with thinkers
such as the Frankfurt School's Adorno. Significantly, though, this
unconscious mass is a phenomenological one, found and revealed in
surface phenomenon, not as some repressed Freudian libido, but as
disassociated and mimetic experience. For Kracauer's work is also
indebted to a tradition of social psychology and Marxist psychoanalysis, especially the ideas of Erich Fromm. Fromm was a key
member of the political Berlin School of psychoanalysis in the 1930s.
In addition, Fromm was involved with the broader cultural debates
that attempted to theorize the social and psychic effects of mass production and consumer culture, in dialogue with the Frankfurt School,
particularly Herbert Marcuse and Max Horkheimer. Rejection of a
whole tradition of Marxist psychoanalysis has occurred since Juliet
Mitchell's seminal text *Psychoanalysis and Feminism* critiqued
thinkers such as Reich and Laing for socializing the unconscious.[25]
Psychoanalysis and Feminism signalled a crucial turning away from
an empirically based, political psychoanalysis, thereby introducing a
Lacanian reworking of Freud's radical insights about sexual difference and identity, ideas which would become the central psychoanalytic paradigm through which culture and film could be studied.

Marxist psychoanalysis was failed by Lacanian feminism for
making the psyche simply an internal derivative of the social, and for

getting rid of the radical nature of the unconscious. However, this Lacanian shoring-up of an Oedipally divided unconscious eschews material and experiential accounts of the body and society. Marxist psychoanalysis has been unfairly dismissed and the radical phenomenology of some of its thinkers simply ignored. A lot of the confusion stems from a reading of experience, in relation to writers such as Fromm and (later) R.D. Laing, whereby experience is taken as an empirical sociological entity, rather than a more radical, phenomenological movement between conscious and unconscious, experience and language etc. In an early book setting out his Marxist critique of Freud, Fromm argues that daily experience and sleep are unconscious to each other: 'conscious and unconscious are only different states of mind referring to different states of experience'.[26]

The links between Fromm and Kracauer are important because they throw light on Kracauer's later book *From Caligari to Hitler*, which was essentially an exploration of the German collective consciousness or mental attitudes in the period directly before the rise of Hitler. A study in 1931 conducted by Fromm and his Frankfurt colleagues into workers, including white-collar workers, was carried out at the same time as Kracauer embarked on his own phenomenological study of white-collar workers which was printed initially in the *Frankfurter Zeitung* and then as a book. Both Kracauer and Fromm were interested in how the Nazis managed to grasp power when the political centre in Germany had been to the left. Fromm's study analysed the people's character structure in relation to authoritarian and anti-authoritarian traits, and his results showed that whereas 10 per cent of the people studied would probably be outright Nazis, and 15 per cent resistant to Nazism, the overwhelming majority would not have strong feelings either way. They would go with the flow and the crowd, and were therefore susceptible to what Fromm saw as the narcissistic, hypnotic seduction exercised by Hitler and the Nazi propaganda machine.

In his study entitled *Die Angestellten* (Office Workers), Kracauer was also very interested in what he saw as the weak democratic roots of the German people. His analysis of the surface visibility of these characters, with their mass ornamental outlook, was a reflection of the abstract rationality of capitalism. Significantly, Kracauer's and Fromm's character analysis of the subjects of Nazism and capitalism are nearly identical. This character is phenomenologically split and visibly detached or rationally abstracted from feeling. Insertion into capitalist production modes splits off people from an accessing of real emotion. Instead, they consume passively and intellectually in a hypnotic state, where sentimentality – feelings that are detached –

substitutes for a more authentic embodied sense of being in the world. Kracauer's little shopgirls are a case in point here. Getrud Koch observes how this ambivalent and fractured type of character is not only the focus of Fromm's work but is also shown by Kracauer to 'exist in the scenarios portrayed in film during the Weimar republic'.[27]

Koch counters the criticisms that are generally levelled against *From Caligari to Hitler* for its deterministic leaps from individual dispositions to a collective character. To make this criticism is to construe the Marxist psychoanalysis of the time as equally deterministic. Indeed, Fromm's understanding of the mass appeal of Hitler is a dialectical argument of how capitalist economics and Hitler's narcissism are responded to through an audience which is hysterically hypnotized because it also narcissistically consumes, through a detached and sentimental rationality, the dominant ideology. Fromm's argument of psychological types is a description of the mass ornament. What distinguishes Kracauer's *From Caligari to Hitler* from his earlier work on the mass ornament is that in the 'Cult of Distraction' essay Kracauer still seems hopeful that the mass ornament can aesthetically function as recognition of alienation. By the time he writes *From Caligari to Hitler* that hope has been abandoned, and the mass ornament is simply the aesthetic abstraction that mobilized Nazism. Elsaesser notes that, in the later work, 'Kracauer seems to have abandoned the dialectical core of his concept in favour of a more simple assertion of "the human".'[28]

However, Kracauer's argument in *From Caligari to Hitler* is not based on an ahistorical and essentialist prescription of psychological character types. On the contrary, these mental attitudes are emotional and personal: they are intertwined with the social; cause and effect leak into each other. There is no Oedipal jump or disjunction between individual and social subjects in Kracauer's work, no a priori division between the real and imaginary that we would find in classical psychology and psychoanalysis. Separation between social and psychic, for Kracauer, is not an injunction of an immutable phallic symbolic, but a mass ornamental effect of capitalism and fascism. Moreover, as Koch observes, Kracauer does not actually analyse individual or collective subjects in his analysis of Weimar films; he understands the films as artefacts and 'symbols that convey dispositions'.[29]

Films are, then, the visible or perceived hieroglyphs of a spatial unconscious. Films show this unconscious not just through their stories but also through their images, and this makes them especially inclusive, so they 'are more or less characteristic of the inner life of a nation from which films emerge'.[30]

Films are a projection of such an inner life through a collective productive process where individual dispositions come together to form a whole. This projection of psychic mentality through the mimetic work of film is an inclusive, spatial and optical unconscious. In a similar fashion to Benjamin, Kracauer sees film reflecting a phenomenological world of surface effects, spatially located in appearances, objects and images. Images of the unconscious, here, are not situated psychically, inside the individual, but appear between individuals. Mimetic identification with these images or hieroglyphs in *From Caligari to Hitler* centres on a bourgeois character disposition whose divided consciousness finds imaginary existence in an aesthetically detached doppelgänger. This split-off doppelgänger or ego 'is a traumatised interior that completely detracts from the material conditions under which it arose'.[31] This means there is no symbolic Oedipal identity, merely a hysterical and split bourgeois identity located in the imaginary, thus obscuring the social conditions of its construction. Expressionism characterizing the post First World War film *The Cabinet of Dr Caligari* emphasizes this hysterical identity; with the central character disposition in the film – the psychiatrist Dr Caligari – yielding a rather different reading of Oedipal psychoanalysis, one that challenges film Apparatus theory.

Key points

- Kracauer's theory of the mass ornament is a theory of a social unconscious of the masses.
- Both Kracauer and Fromm argue for psychological and phenomenological character types as a form of mass ornament.
- Kracauer sees films as artefacts, hieroglyphs and symbols that convey dispositions.

Masculine doubling and disavowal as a fascist imaginary

Thomas Elsaesser tracks Kracauer's interest in the hysterical masculinity that moves between Weimar cinema and culture as a mimetic doubling. Although Elsaesser does not seek to situate this hysteria within a phenomenological explanation, he foregrounds Karl Theweleit's *Male Fantasies* as a key psychoanalytic text in exploring the crisis of masculinity that arose around this time. Karl Theweleit sums up masculinity as a hysterical defence against the unbounded female body.[32] Tracing the fantasies of volunteers in German armies who went on to become fascist soldiers in Hitler's S.A., and in some cases important officers in the Third Reich, Theweleit's analysis makes gruesome reading. What is interesting for this debate is that his account rewrites Freud's Oedipal plot within the terms of a dis-associated, bodily imaginary. Theweleit describes the Freikorps soldiers in terms of an extreme masculinity. His chilling account of their murderous, hallucinatory states of perception depicts a desire for killing that quite literally wants to reduce the target to a 'bloody mass'. These fascist soldiers detest women's bodies and sexuality and are in continual dread of being swallowed up, dissolved and dis-membered by the floods of dirt, blood and black holes that women represent.[33]

Theweleit discusses how Freud's Oedipal complex is not applica-ble to these men. Their egos are disintegrated and are thus not capable of object relations, or of recognizing the other as a human being. Wilhelm Reich's ideas seem more applicable. Desire is charac-terized by Reich as a life drive or sexual force towards the world which is inhibited by social repression – hence the Oedipal complex. Reich criticized Freud for being too intellectual and too preoccupied by words and for refusing to recognize the oceanic bond of emotions and desire that vitally connects us to the world. In a famous inter-view with Eisler, Reich states that Freud's attitude to emotions showed 'not that emotions were bad, but you have to get them out of the way'.[34] Oedipal theory is, then, for Reich a neurotic defence against this embodied connection to the social. Reich's work is excit-ing for its return to an inclusion of the material real of the body, but in a sense, Reich becomes the polar opposite of Freud. Where Freud represses the bodily instincts through his concept of the Oedipal complex, Reich makes the liberation of that instinctual real the revolutionary solution to capitalist society.

Deleuze and Guattari develop Reich's ideas, especially the notion that the unconscious is not a representation or myth but an em-bodied process of the real, as 'flows' and desiring production.[35] When that desiring production gets perverted it becomes a death produc-tion. Theweleit uses this concept of death production together with Reich's arguments for a body or character armour (against free-flowing libido) to discuss the fantasies and deeds of the fascist sol-diers. The body armour of masculinity armed the fascists against their extreme fear of inner dissolution and felt bodily flows. Like the gothic, melodramatic monsters of the nineteenth century, the identity of these soldiers becomes split and doubled, between an outer and an inner disassociated self that is felt to be evil: a characterization of Dr Jekyll and the murderous Mr Hyde.

For the fascist soldiers, transgressing boundaries between inner and outer worlds meant the entry into a sort of hallucinatory state, an extreme projection of their dissolute and 'hated flows', onto women, communists and Jews. Theweleit wonders if the Oedipal edifice is just a defensive displacement of desire. If so, he asks, then what is the desire underneath, 'what is its mode of functioning in soldier males?'[36] Can the terror and persecution they carry out be explained simply in terms of projection, or scapegoating? Theweleit cites Reich's view that the masses were not duped and that under a certain set of conditions they wanted fascism. 'This perversion of the desire of the masses needs to be accounted for.'[37]

Theweleit quite correctly surmises that the acts of murder that the soldiers enter into both for pleasure, and as a defence against fear, cannot be explained by Oedipus or castration anxiety. There is indeed nothing repressed about the fascist soldiers' fantasies; they are more akin to psychotic hallucinations. But these men do not manifest as psychotics. They do not exhibit weak egos or poor adaptation to reality. They are successful and controlled, in action and words, in ways which psychotics would be powerless to achieve. Theweleit asks, 'by what type of ego, if it is not Oedipal, do these men stabilize and control themselves?'[38]

I want to suggest that just as Oedipal identity can be seen as a defence against more hysterical identifications, so can these men's extreme masculine identifications be seen as a very successful defence against psychotic collapse. The masculine control these men demonstrate is grounded through the violence and abject horror that is attributed to the 'red' soldier women that they kill. However, the mechanism operating, here, is not repression, but disavowal. Psychotic people are so unstable precisely because they lack the rigid defences that can project their madness and death onto other people's bodies. Consequently, they become hyperaware – to the point of delusion of their destructive impact upon other people.

Theweleit's male soldiers have no such awareness of their murderous fantasies or deeds. But equally, their defensive boundaries, the control that so easily tips over into psychotic violence, can be seen as the work of a defensive mental imaginary that is at war with the real. Theweleit's soldiers are hysterically split in terms of an Oedipal masculinity that has been pushed to its mad limit. Disassociated, their abstract rationality, or mass ornament, is a fetishistic disavowal of their relation to the real of the maternal body. If hysteria is the dilemma when an overly mental imaginary goes to war with the real of the body (and history), then projection of this real onto the body of the woman allows the Freikorps soldiers to stage their war in relation to an other, rather than within themselves.

The argument in this book of a phenomenological imaginary is concerned with both the splitting and the possible reconfiguration between the real and the imaginary in terms of the filmic image. Reich foregrounds the sexual body too much at the expense of a necessary social imaginary, and Fromm, in contrast, manages to evacuate the body with his emphasis on character and ego psychology. Kracauer's work, however, combines the intersubjective phenomenology of Fromm with an emphasis on the unconscious physiology that lies underneath discursive conventions. And it is of course the image, here, acting as a mimetic mirror that becomes the underlying physical layer of film and history. Kracauer suggests that the image, of the mass ornament, the film star, the photograph, confronts us with a radical negativity of how history and the body have been disassociated and excluded. Luce Irigaray and Walter Benjamin have, through different routes, utilized the image as a painterly imaginary or profane illumination which can creatively re-imagine a new embodied reconfiguration to the other and to history. However, in Kracauer's thinking the imaginary is fundamentally doubled and disassociated, split off from the bodily real. This projection of the double can be used to go to war with the real, where often in the guise of the woman, or the racial 'other', it is literally killed off, in order to ground the stability of the dominant imaginary.

Key points

- In his book *Male Fantasies*, Karl Theweleit sums up his account of male fascist fantasies and masculinity, as a hysterical defence against the unbounded female body.
- Theweleit's soldiers are hysterically split and disassociated. Their Oedipal masculinity is an abstract rationality, or mass ornament, pushed to its mad limit.

Masculine doubling in Weimar cinema

Elsaesser's most recent book on Weimar cinema highlights not so much the Oedipal controlling gaze of Apparatus theory, but an ambivalent and uncanny doubling or duplicity. Elsaesser historicizes and subverts Apparatus theory through his emphasis on the historical spectator. Elsaesser, unlike Doanne or Petro, notes that the duplicitous masquerade is not just of femininity, but of masculinity. This is a masquerade of sexual difference that is indelibly linked to the accompanying masquerade of Nazi films and culture, films which in turn mimic the Hollywood consumption and commodification of culture in the United States. I want to describe Elsaesser's argument in some detail because it links with Kracauer's study of cinema, thus providing interesting ground to explore and illustrate a phenomeno-logical, filmic imaginary.

The social and psychic imaginary of Weimar culture that Elsaesser describes is a complex mix of expressionism, theatricality, popular and high culture, pro- and anti-democracy. Such mimetic doubling of styles and genres haunts the pre-history of Weimar cinema as well as the later Nazi cinema that superseded it. Nazism was a seductive masquerade, 'a mimicry of modernity and tradition, but also a sort of dress rehearsal for some of the attitudes and values of consumer culture'.[39] German intellectuals fleeing the Nazi regime found in Hollywood's culture industries the same mimicry of ideology and style, the very simulacrum of the commodified arts that had been so seductively utilized by Nazism. Weimar cinema was also a double for the 1940s film noir cinema in Hollywood, where immigrant German film-makers found their place. So, between the historical imaginaries of Hollywood realism and German expressionism we can trace a mimetic influence and mirroring translated into genres of film noir, the musical and melodrama. This dialectic is also one of taste. The division between mainstream Hollywood film and the avant-garde pedigree of Weimar cinema was also mirrored in 1920s Weimar cinema, between art and popular culture. Popular culture wins out in this dialectic, as Petro's analysis of the immense popularity of melo-drama with female audiences reveals. Films within Weimar culture from between 1918 and 1933, are normally divided into two histori-cal imaginaries of expressionist film and Weimar cinema.[40] Expres-sionism is a style associated with the artistic historical period rooted in German romanticism. These expressionist and artistic films are demonstrated by Lotte Eisner's *The Haunted Screen* to have a direct influence on Nazism. The other historical film imaginary is of course symbolized by Weimar cinema, films mapped in Kracauer's *From Caligari to Hitler* connecting the political and social climate of the day to the rise of Nazism.

Elsaesser describes how Kracauer's and Eisner's books, written after the Second World War, recast the earlier popular view of German cinema as aesthetic and progressive. Suspicion was thrown onto a cinema that was implicated in Nazism, and studies of the film industry after 1933 and the films of the Weimar period became categorized within rigid binaries, where style and genre were divided into realist or fantasy, expressionist or kitsch. Aesthetically, films were avant-garde or commercial. Politically, they were international (progressive films) or nationalistic (hence reactionary). Elsaesser is critical of Kracauer for his storying of a culpable Weimar cinema that in its drive to make a psychologically coherent and realistic narrative of nationalist politics, reminiscent of Hollywood's classical cinema, ignored all the stylistic ambiguity and expressionistic excess that Eisner's writing is so full of. However, Kracauer, despite his negativity towards Weimar cinema captures moments of its historical truth. This truth is rooted, within his earlier analysis of film as a mass ornament. Describing the Tiller Girls' formation dancing, Kracauer shows how the girls' legs mimic industrial labour and factory machines. This public display is a mimesis that moves between entertainment and work, beckoning the spectator into a pleasurable distraction from work, but simultaneously revealing his or her disconnected, hysterical reality through capitalist exploitation.

Elsaesser suggests that the film *The Cabinet of Dr Caligari*, is a 'benchmark' for expressionism in Weimar cinema. *Caligari* stands not just for German film, but, because of Kracauer's book title *From Caligari to Hitler*, the film also figures as a historical motif of Germany and its aestheticization of politics in the twentieth century. A parody of psychoanalysis, as a metaphor of interior madness, *Caligari* was the quintessential avant-garde film of its time. In addition to the marketing of expressionist films abroad, *Caligari's* success was due also to its appeal, not just as art, but as kitsch and the latest on home design – as Rudolf Arnheim notes, 'a delightful design for wallpaper'.[41]

Retracing Kracauer's steps in mapping Weimar films as a master Oedipal narrative, Elsaesser is also critical of Kracauer's simplification of these films, *Caligari* being a case in point. Kracauer argues that the framing device in *Caligari* changes it from a radical film to an authoritarian one. While the initial story in the film sets up authority and the Oedipal psychiatrist as mad, the framing device ends up celebrating authority and pathologizing the subversive challenger to this Oedipal law as mad. Thus Kracauer reduces the formal complexities of the narrative in the film, thereby reducing multiple male and female Oedipal fantasies and scenarios into a master Oedipal plot, synonymous with more realist psychological Hollywood dramas. This reduction ignores the stylistic excesses which make *Caligari* not just a more ambivalent Oedipal narrative, but also distinguish it from classical cinema.

It is true that the framing device, which Kracauer emphasizes, does return an Oedipal master plot. Nevertheless, *Caligari* has to be seen in the context of the other Weimar films of that period. The overwhelming character disposition that emerges from the pages of *From Caligari to Hitler* is based on a phenomenological and split imaginary. This imaginary foregrounds exactly the ambivalent, Oedipal doubling of Elsaesser's account. I suggest that both Kracauer and Elsaesser deconstruct the Oedipal disposition in the film *Caligari* as split and hysterical. The abstract rationality and detached emotion of the mass ornament corresponds to the hysterical masquerade of the little shopgirls hypnotically identifying and crying with the melodramas. If the little shopgirls can be seen as the hieroglyphs with which Kracauer deciphers the feminization of mass culture, then *Caligari*, equally, is a film whose hieroglyphics decode the male hysteria of Oedipal sexuality and difference.

Elsaesser reads the expressionistic doubling in *Caligari* as completely destabilizing the Oedipal narrative, revealing its hysterical nature. *Caligari* is characterized by a performative hysteria, an uncanny doubling which unveils the disembodied splits of this 'male' historical imaginary. Now, I want to return Elsaesser's understanding of *Caligari* not to Freud's Oedipal plot but to Kracauer's phenomenological and disassociated imaginary. The importance of this is that if we rely on a stereotypical Freudian account we are left with a reductive narrative of Oedipal repression which reifies sexual difference and the textual spectator. In other words, as Petro suggests, we are simply returned to a more nuanced but equally trenchant Apparatus theory of a male imaginary.

Elsaesser's argument for the multiple Oedipal perspectives in *Caligari* warrants further attention. Kracauer describes the main protagonist, Caligari, as the tyrannical, mad doctor and military dictator mesmerizing his somnambulist population, in art as in Hitler's life. But Elsaesser notes a struggle over narrational authority which is removed from the narrative action. 'Whose story is it, who tells it, and to whom?', asks Elsaesser. In *Caligari* the position of the narrator is always being questioned and highlighted for the spectator by the stylistic excess of the text and the melodramatic, emotional pauses, which displace more goal-orientated action. For example, speeded-up drama like violent struggles or chases, reminiscent of the detective serials of the time, are made strange by filmic melodramatic images of anguished stillness.

We can highlight Elsaesser's questioning of narrative position through an analogy with the therapy session. What brings change for the hysteric in therapy, what moves her 'melancholic' mimicking and masquerade into a more embodied mimesis or reconfiguration, is not the story, but acknowledgement of what is absent and left out. Tracking the relation to the body in therapy is about following the gestural, hysterical and melodramatic movements of the clients, wondering about what they express and what they say about the structural position of both client and therapist in the story that is being narrated. The hieroglyphics of the patient's speech and action are not just to be interpreted by the analyst; they must, as R.D. Laing pointed out, be understood as the patient's phenomenological and experiential being in the world. We can also understand films as 'visible hieroglyphs', illustrated, in Kracauer's view, through silent films and the close-up:

> Slight actions, the opening or clenching of a hand, dropping a hand-kerchief, playing with some apparently irrelevant object, stumbling, falling, seeking and not finding and the like, became the visible hiero-glyphs of the unseen dynamics of human relations.[42]

Elsaesser questions whether or not the spectator in the film *Caligari* is actually asked to centre on the character of the same name. In his estimation the story equally belongs to Francis, the challenger to Caligari and the failed suitor of Jane. The story also belongs to Jane, illustrating a female Oedipal plot, where her doctor/father and Dr Caligari feature as doubles for each other. I suggest that this film ultimately defies any straightforward Oedipal reading. Interestingly, what it does reveal is a deconstruction of sexual difference through the figure of the hysteric.

Let us go back to the story. Caligari discovers papers that will yield the secret of a successful hypnosis. He then practises on the somnambulist Cesare and manages to control him. Caligari, who suffers from 'lack of status recognition', takes his revenge on a town clerk and then lures Jane to his tent where he reveals Cesare in a hypnotic trance, a sight which terrifies and repulses the young girl. For Elsaesser, this scene shows Caligari as a 'dirty old man' exposing himself through the more literal exhibition of Cesare. But this is also a black humorous attack on the founding father of psychoanalysis, the Oedipal father himself, who is revealed in all of his sex-mad hysterical neurosis. Cesare functions in this film as Jane's double. This doubling is reminiscent of Linda Williams' analysis of the classic horror film, where women's sexuality and the monster are mirrors of each other in relation to the male gaze.[43] Jane and Cesare therefore represent a monstrous female sexuality that speaks of male fear and remains an unresolved issue in the film. However, Cesare is the

Fig. 2   Dr Caligari. Conrad Veidt and Werner Krauss in *Das Cabinet des Dr Caligari* (1919), directed by Robert Wiene. © Decla-Bioscop / The Kobal Collection

hysterical double for all the characters in the film (not just Jane), and this in turn makes all the characters hysterical doubles of each other. The monstrous body that Cesare portrays as split off, both controlled and out of control, is the carnal, female sexuality, that Jane as the white 'angel in the house', hysterically transcends. But Cesare represents not just a spectacle of femininity; he also reveals the hysterical fetishism and voyeurism of the male characters. Caligari's *and* Francis's masculinity is an unstable defence against the threatening perception of a boundary-less female embodiment. It is a masculinity which defends and doubles as monstrous hysteria.

Key points

- **Hysterical masculinity moves between Weimar cinema and culture as a mimetic doubling.**

- Thomas Elsaesser highlights this hysterical and uncanny doubling as deconstructive of Apparatus theory.
- We can return Elsaesser's understanding of *Caligari*, not to Freud's Oedipal plot, but to Kracauer's phenomenological and disassociated imaginary.

Conclusion

Miriam Hansen observes that 'Kracauer in his more utopian moments understood the cinema as an alternative public sphere', and she notes that this sensory reflexivity is attributed by Kracauer, not to Weimar cinema, but to American slapstick comedy.[44] While this is true, it is important not to underestimate Kracauer's rather pessimistic analysis of Weimar cinema and history. As many critics have noted, there is some reductiveness in Kracauer's social-psychological approach to film, but this should not detract, as Getrud Koch urges, from seeing the strengths of his analysis. Kracauer's phenomenology offers us new avenues to explore a more social and Marxist psychoanalysis of film. His work further elaborates an account of a phenomenological and filmic imaginary which reads Oedipal sexual-difference theory and classical film melodrama as hysterical.

Kracauer's analysis of the mass ornament and Weimar cinema reveals the sensory mimesis of film spectatorship as fundamentally disassociated. He enables us to see that while all film spectatorship is sensory, it is only a reflexivity that acknowledges the ambivalent splitting between psyche and the social, within modernity, that can be seen as truly embodied. Through readings of Elsaesser, Petro and Kracauer in relation to Weimar cinema, this chapter has provided a critical, historical contextualization of the apparatus spectator. Moreover, it has shown how hysteria is manifest differently at specific historical moments. Despite the power of the Oedipal myth, there is no universal imaginary, with respect to psychoanalysis or film theory. Psychoanalysis has historically been harnessed to semiotic film theory, as distinct from the more historical 'modernity thesis' on cinema associated with Benjamin and Kracauer.[45] The result of this split between theory and history is that the 'psychoanalytic' implications of Benjamin's and Kracauer's work are missed, and Apparatus theory continues its celebrated, structuralist, cinematic career, immune to the vicissitudes of history.

Thomas Elsaesser comments on how Benjamin and Kracauer's cinema and film theory is a theory of the image (on the analogy with photography), as opposed to a theory of narrative (crucial in semiological accounts of the syntagmatic relations between images). Thus, its main theoretical thrust today is in the direction not of textual analysis, but in illuminating the historical conditions of spectatorship and identification, both within and outside Freudian terms in which these questions are usually posed.[46]

The next section will therefore turn to early debates on psychoanalysis, perception, film and modernity in a further exploration of the disembodied and embodied gaze.

3

Film Theory and the Visual Body

Introduction

The last two chapters have mapped accounts of the textual spectator within sexual-difference and Apparatus theory, re-reading the male gaze in relation to classical Hollywood melodrama and to the more historically located Weimar cinema. The final chapter in this section brings the debate on the male gaze up to the present day through a reading of the film *Boys Don't Cry*. This film is a retelling of the Oedipal myth; it is also a rethinking of the sexual/textual difference operating within the male gaze of Apparatus theory. In a similar fashion to *Mildred Pierce* and *The Cabinet of Dr Caligari*, *Boys Don't Cry* is also a re-reading of the male gaze as hysterical. However, this film moves beyond Oedipal determinants of sexual difference to implicate the spectator in a cultural re-memory, a phenomenological gaze of embodied sexuality. Moreover, this gaze is not purely located within a textual analysis and is mobilized to include the ethnographic audience or 'real' spectator. So, whereas the last two chapters on classical Hollywood film and Weimar cinema have deconstructed the Oedipal male gaze as hysterical, this more contemporary account offers an alternative to the male gaze through an embodied imaginary.

Psychoanalysis and phenomenology have been used more or less in terms of opposing camps of film theory, with the psychological and psychoanalytic explanations of the formally constructed or textual spectator on one hand and the realist, phenomenological accounts on the other. Such a division between the imaginary and real, metaphorically figured through the frame and the window, can be traced back to the beginning of film theory, to its original founding fathers. The Lumière brothers' early films of everyday life have been seen as an origin for realist, narrative film, and Méliès' more fantastical films are located as the origin of more formalist, avant-garde film. This history of film theory and spectatorship has been nothing if not Oedipal, and just as Oedipal theory divides the imaginary from the real, and language from the body, so has the history of film theory divided psychological explanations of the spectator from more phenomenological accounts of realist film. More recently this Oedipal split has been played out between the phallic textual spectator within Apparatus film theory, and a more cultural-studies emphasis on the real, situated audience.

A reading of *Boys Don't Cry* through a phenomenological imaginary is a counter-argument to this Oedipal split between language and the body because it explores an embodied gaze which links imaginary and real. This fluidity means that the methodologies of investigating such a cinematic spectator cannot rest solely with either textual or audience-based approaches. If Apparatus theory has sought to understand how the spectator is ideologically, linguistically and textually constructed in terms of sexual difference, then the embodied imaginary and gaze explores how the spectator apprehends the aesthetics of the image and re-members film in relation to myths of the past and the present of everyday life.

Key points

- *Boys Don't Cry* is a re-reading of the male gaze as hysterical.
- However, this film moves beyond Oedipal determinants of sexual difference to implicate the spectator in a phenomenological gaze of embodied sexuality.

Kimberley Pierce's *Boys Don't Cry*

Kimberley Pierce's *Boys Don't Cry* was heralded by some critics as one of the best films of 1999. As a film it is a starkly violent realist drama and a hauntingly tragic love story. The true story of Teena Brandon, a girl who decided to live as a man and was consequently brutally raped and murdered in 1993, is stunningly brought to life by Hilary Swank, whose performance of the transgendered youth is brilliantly captivating, drawing the audience into a drama of emotional and aesthetic expressiveness mixed with a neo-realist violence, almost unbearable to watch.

The film juxtaposes genres of crime thriller, cowboy tale and love story in ways that rewrite and remember myths of American cinema and history. But the Oedipal myth of American white masculinity that this film unravels, refuses and in a sense rewrites is one of crisis: a destruction and re-imagination of the Oedipal myths that are situated at the heart of psychoanalytic film theory. For the director and producers of *Boys Don't Cry* the film is reminiscent of a tragic and historical American heartland. Linked to classic crime novels such as Norman Mailer's *Executioner's Song* and Truman Capote's *In Cold Blood*, to such films as *Badlands, Scarface, Dog Day Afternoon, Butch Cassidy and the Sundance Kid, Bonny and Clyde* and *Goodfellas*, the film follows a tradition of literature and film that mythologizes American identity. The white trash community of Falls City mirrors the homogeneous communities of middle America, where to be an outsider, or an individual who drifts, risks violence and murder. But of course Brandon, like the outlaws in crime novels and films, is also the western cowboy who is the hero of American myth. He is an outlaw who follows his dreams and fights his way from the margins to self-realization and recognition.

Brandon, then, can be seen as an outlaw hero who represents so much of America's literary and film traditions from great literature to Hollywood, a male Oedipal hero or outlaw that has been re-imagined and passed on. The performativity of Brandon is also a deconstruction of these mythic heroes. As a girl he performs the ideal of outlaw masculinity far better than any of the other male characters in the film. He is courageous and sensitive, rebellious and deferent. He is handsome but not narcissistic, independent but vulnerable. In a sense, Brandon becomes the ideal man, from a woman's point of view, because he knows so well what it is women want from men. Brandon's charm captivates all the women he meets in the film. He wins Lana's heart because he offers her love and intimacy; even Lana's mother allows him to call her mum. The anonymous girl we see him skating with at the beginning of the film asks where he comes from and says, 'It must be some place beautiful.' Brandon, however, doesn't just win over the women; he also attracts all the men.

Boys Don't Cry is a naturalistic film: expressive, with low-key lighting and very little colour. Even though it is supposed to be summer, the starkness of the landscape and its emptiness are a surreal picture which echoes the dreariness and emptiness of the towns-people's lives. The cinematography reflects low-budget art-house film, rather than the big-screen effect of Hollywood commercial cinema.

Shot entirely on location rather than a set, the film foregrounds character development, rather than epic action narrative, plot or spectacle. Like Scorsese's *Goodfellas*, *Boys Don't Cry* is a naturalistic and intensely realistic film, but whereas Scorsese plays around with a moving camera, with editing and freeze frames to create effects, Pierce directs *Boys Don't Cry* using mostly master, medium shots. There are very few point-of-view shots, and consequently we watch the film unroll before us at a distance. No characters are captured on their own by the camera except for Brandon. His isolation adds to the sense of expectant doom throughout the film. When Brandon announces to his brother that he intends to marry the 'white trash' girl from the town that 'hangs faggots', we know Brandon's future is neither assured nor happy.

Pierce achieves a surreal and expressionistic landscape through a mixture of colourlessness and bleak, isolated buildings, like the outhouse next to Candice's home, to which Brandon retires before the final murder scene. This white shed stands out alone against the grey sky, mirroring the bleakness and loneliness of Brandon's predicament. But Pierce contrasts this stark background and solitary buildings with the sky. The low-key lighting of the ground is therefore juxtaposed with the fast-moving lights from the sky, whether these are stars or town lights. These sky lights are made to whiz faster and faster, using time-lapse photography, and depict a surrealist disjunction between the individual and the universe; for example, the confused, glue-sniffing girls on their backs on the merry-go-round, looking up at a whirling sky, or the characters in the car chase surrounded by mist with the luminous car lights following them, car headlights which also shine down on Brandon curled up in his foetal position on the ground after the rape. Extreme and violent scenes in the film contain some of the most stylized photography, moving us in oscillation, outside and then inside (nearer) the action. For example, in the rape scene we are kept at a distance, and then moved inexorably into the car. Or, when Brandon is forcibly stripped and revealed by Tom and Paul, the film cuts to everyone watching and at the back is Brandon looking down on himself as a girl.

Not a male gaze

Boys Don't Cry totally disrupts film theory's argument of a male gaze by deconstructing the Oedipal conjunction of sexual difference that has been used to interpret the viewer's identification with the camera's gaze. We are all implicated as voyeurs in this film; however, the voyeuristic camera does not replicate the fetishistic mechanisms of looking rehearsed by Laura Mulvey.[1] Freud's perverse account of the desiring look is a masculine fetishistic structure organized around castration, lack and the disavowal. Fetishism for Freud is a male perversion and look, which at one level accedes to the Oedipal symbolic of heterosexual difference, but then, on the other, disavows the castration threat, attributing a substitute phallus to the mother's body.

In *Boys Don't Cry*, the play with transexuality and gender confounds and undoes the Oedipal look. There is no *disavowal* of castration in the camera's gaze; in fact the fetish is real or indeed as real as the prosthesis that we see Brandon wear and use in actual sex. What we have is the *actual* castration of Brandon in response to the threat he poses to John and Tom. However, Brandon does not pose this threat as a woman, he poses a threat precisely because he passes (in the male community) as a man.

Where, we might ask, is the male gaze in this film? Where indeed? Is it in the scenes where the camera intimately invites us into Brandon's dressing as a man, the hiding of the tampons under the mattress, the taping of his breasts and the final insertion of his socks and false penis into his Y-fronts? For this gaze is a gaze at Brandon as a man; it is not the gaze of Brandon as an eroticized female body. Pierce's use of medium master shots, with virtually no point-of-view shots, does not privilege a male look. In fact the only character we see alone is Brandon, and the desire of the camera as well as most of the characters is directed towards him in male guise. When we see Brandon making love to Lana, the camera focuses in on her body. We see the rapture in her face, whereas Brandon's corporeality for the most part is out of the frame. This scene is remembered through Lana's own autoeroticism, in bed later with her girlfriends, providing us with a picture of female desire which is fluid, and moves between heterosexual and lesbian sex. For in making love to Brandon, Lana witnesses his breasts, and this shows why Brandon remains such an ideal man – essentially because he is also a woman.

Key points

- *Boys Don't Cry* unravels the Oedipal myth of American white masculinity.
- *Boys Don't Cry* deconstructs the Oedipal conjunction of sexual difference that has been used to interpret the viewer's identification with the camera's gaze.

Brandon's embodied imaginary

What the film offers us, then, is an imaginary of everyone's desire for Brandon (as a man who is also a woman), and of Brandon's desire for Lana (as a man who is also a woman). Within the strictly Oedipal configuration this scenario would be impossible. If Brandon was a man passing and dressing as a woman, the structure of desire could be called fetishistic, based on his disavowal of the woman/mother's castration. But the fetish for Freud is a strictly male perversion of the Oedipal drive – as a masculine structure it cannot be transferred to the woman. Being labelled as a butch lesbian, Brandon could be seen as having a masculinity complex, but Brandon does not want to be a lesbian; he wants to be a man loving a woman. Violently abused and shamed into the unwanted recognition of his female physicality by a brutal rape, Brandon tells the police officer that he has a sexual identity crisis. But, in fact the one thing made outstandingly clear in the film is that Brandon's identity crisis actually resides with the other characters. He tells the police officer falteringly that he has a sexual identity crisis because he is beaten and that is the only understanding society can have of his desire. However, in reality it is everyone else in the film, not Brandon, who questions their sexual identity in relation to him. Lana ends up not knowing or caring – *not wanting to know* – whether she is sleeping with a man or a woman. Tom and John and Lana's mother resort to the most extreme hatred and violence, not simply because Brandon is revealed to them as a woman but also because they desired him so much as a man.

Embodiment in the film is connected to representation through the image. Contrary to Christian Metz's intention to 'disengage the cinema-object from the imaginary and win it for the symbolic', the images in *Boys Don't Cry* are part of the imaginary that is connected with the real and the body. As such, they invoke imagination, feeling, creativity, transformation, hatred, abjection and violence. We participate with and project into the image, but this projection cannot be reduced to a voyeuristic textual gaze. We move in a fluid way between imaginary and real worlds, in relation to the film but also to the everyday life and myths that are imbricated with the film text. Brandon's sexuality is not just imaginary or virtual; it is also real: he embodies, passes as and enacts the masculinity he desires to be.

Fig. 3 Lana and Brandon. Chloe Sevigny and Hilary Swank in *Boys Don't Cry* (1999), directed by Kimberley Pierce. © Fox Searchlight / The Kobal Collection / Bill Matlock

Destruction of Oedipal myth . . .

Deleuze and Guattari understand the Oedipal narrative as a master discourse of modernism and celebrate its overturning through their Anti-Oedipus: *the positive flows and intensities of schizophrenic desire.*[2] So whereas Lacan posits desire as negative in terms of lack, Deleuze and Guattari articulate schizophrenic desire, or 'schizo-analysis', as a positive and anarchistic force, against capitalist hegemony and power. Liberation of this productive desire can de-territorialize repressive myths of the Oedipal family and the current social infrastructure.

Deleuze and Guattari's utopian vision does not acknowledge the importance of mediating the relationship between desire and the social in terms of the imaginary. Without such mediation, desire is not liberated into the social, but walled off from it, as an insular and psychotic space of the real. The Oedipal myth exists as a dominant imaginary. We cannot simply destroy it as Deleuze and Guattari maintain, but we can re-member it in ways that are more embodied.[3] *Boys Don't Cry* is an example of a postmodern film, that destroys and re-members Oedipal myths in ways that foreground the bodily and performative aspects of the imaginary. As a postmodern film, *Boys Don't Cry* can be contrasted with such classic postmodern films as Scott Ridley's *Blade Runner*. *Blade Runner* neatly fits with Jean Baudrillard's postmodern world of simulation where the real is lost. Here, the Oedipal myth is played out as a conflict between a Lacanian phallic symbolic and more aggressive imaginary forms. *Boys Don't Cry* foregrounds a positive embodied imaginary, situating the Oedipal myth within the hegemonic, hysterical imaginary in which it belongs.

In *Boys Don't Cry*, the loss and destruction of the Oedipal myth is manifest in the near-complete absence of any fathers. Brandon and Lana are without fathers. Candice is a single mother, as is Lana's mother. The only father we have in the film is John. His immaturity shows the aggressive imaginary underlying Oedipal symbolic law and order, signified in the film by the law courts and the police. There are no successful heterosexual relationships in the film apart from Brandon and Lana's. Brandon is loved and desired by everybody precisely because he represents the return of the ideal Oedipal hero, who, despite his youth, fills in the yawning gap for a positive and mature masculinity. The vulnerability of John and Tom is shown in their deep need for Brandon as a role model. Brandon appears to take John as his role model at the beginning of the film. John likes it and responds with pleasure, pleased at being identified with but also identifying with Brandon in turn. After a fight with other men in a bar in Lincoln, John remarks with pride at Brandon's bruised face, 'Yeah, you are going to have a shiner in the morning'; Brandon offers him a light and John stares at his hands, fascinated and perturbed: 'You got the tiniest hands.' Brandon replies, 'No they are big,' and John says, 'If you are going to get into fights over Candice, you are going to have to learn a few moves.'

. . . And hysterical identification

John is troubled by but also drawn to Brandon's masculinity. For him, Brandon represents an ideal. What John cannot handle is the growing realization that Brandon's ideal masculinity is in fact its sensitive and feminine underside. His call to Brandon, 'Come on buddy', is accompanied by urging him to prove himself as an action hero, bumper racing or in car chases. When they are in a car being chased by the police for speeding John orders Brandon to go faster. Eerie music and mist swirl together with the police lights and sirens. John cautions, 'When you hit the gravel drop to 40', and Brandon replies, 'I can't see', and John leaning over Brandon, almost caressing him, says in a voice thick with desire, 'That's O.K., neither can he – you're flying . . .' After the car stops and the police caution Brandon, pointing out the cliff drop he nearly drove over, John snarls at Brandon, 'Don't ever pull that stunt again, you almost got us killed.'

John's aggression and jealousy surface when he suspects Lana and Brandon of getting it together. Lana immediately seizes on his voyeuristic curiosity for what it is and calls him a pervert, a 'stalker'. Wounded, John insists he is only trying to protect her in a brotherly/fatherly way and comments about Brandon, 'I know he's nice and everything, but he's a bit of a wuss.' The narcissistic identification *and* desire that is directed in John's gaze towards Brandon is troubled by his feminine, 'wuss' side. But this identification is unravelled by the discovery that Oedipal sexual difference is imaginary rather than symbolic. The revelation and sight of Brandon's genitals proves not the mother's castration, but the ideal father's, and John's own imaginary erupts into aggressive violence at this loss.

Unravelling of the narcissistic violence that lies at the heart of the Oedipal imaginary, in this film, is demonstrated by the characters John and Tom. Tom reveals their emotional volatility when he tells Brandon that John has no impulse control. 'I'm the only one can control that fucker', Tom says, and then proceeds to cut himself. The violence in the film is made worse by the neediness and vulnerability that show John and Tom as psychotically mad. Their aggression is directed at Brandon, not just because they are homophobic and misogynistic, but because in representing the ideal man and then deconstructing the myth of that masculinity, Brandon's sexual fluidity rips their identity to shreds. For them, the real and the symbolic have become split off from each other and from the imaginary. Consequently there is no reality to connect their symbolic fantasies to, and the result is a spiralling madness.

Key points

- *Boys Don't Cry* is an example of a postmodern film that destroys and re-members Oedipal myths in ways that foreground the bodily and performative aspects of the imaginary.
- Brandon's identity crisis actually resides with the other characters.

Connecting the imaginary and real

For Luce Irigaray, moving away from Oedipal theories which are based on a male imaginary, involves 'an imaginary of the sexuate body whose form never detaches itself from the matter that generates it'.[4] Irigaray points out that the imaginary and symbolic value of the phallus becomes all-powerful precisely because in Lacan's account there is no sexual relation in the real. She asks 'whether the real might not be some very repressed-censored-forgotten "thing" to do with the body' and suggests 'there is no question of underestimating the real if we interpret its effects'.[5] Here, Irigaray is arguing for the transformative potential of the real relation to the maternal body through a more creative, painterly imaginary. As the Introduction mapped out, this more creative imaginary mediates between the literal and the symbolic. Whereas a linguistic Oedipal imaginary seeks to repress bodily identity, a more figurative imagination, linked to the senses, can express it.[6]

Irigaray distinguishes between a mental imaginary and a bodily imaginary which can access the creative imagination and represent the senses. In the more mental imaginary the imagination is in conflict with the affectual relation to the body, a scenario, where the imaginary is at war with the real and 'corresponds to a pathos of the senses'. In a more creative and figurative imaginary, the bodily senses become accessed through the image and painting.[7] The difference between a mental and bodily imaginary is that, with the former, the real returns as a threatening and destructive death drive, but in the latter it becomes liberated as an imaginative re-creation of the self.

Juliet Mitchell has recently discussed how Freud's very insistence on the Oedipal narrative and his role as a father has obscured male hysteria within the history of psychoanalysis. Mitchell also shows how hysteria is a form of mimetic identification and rivalry between siblings, where the oldest child feels literally eradicated by the new arrival. This rivalry then regresses or drives the child into a merged stage of identification with the parent where no separation or identity exists.[8] Such rivalry explains John's and Tom's murderous identifications and the male hysteria that lurks behind heterosexual difference.

As I have discussed, *Boys Don't Cry* is not a film in which the Oedipal gaze ever dominates. In fact, what Peirce is exploring here, is, if anything, the possibilities that arise with its crisis, or absence. Tom's and John's 'sexual identity crisis' can be contrasted to Brandon's transsexuality. Hysteria has long been associated with bisexuality, but Brandon's performative transgender suggests a fluid imaginary, that is imaginative and creative precisely because it conflates and re-members the Oedipal sexual myth differently.

The embodied imaginary and gaze

Critical of psychoanalytic film theory, Steven Shaviro notes how its emphasis on symbolic (Oedipal) theory, and the mystified, disembodied and fixed status it attributes to the image, denies the affectual and embodied pleasures of cinematic gazing: the ontological instability and the power of images to move us, materially and sensually.[9] For Shaviro, Lacanian film theory is rooted in a Platonic, metaphysical tradition which is frightened and suspicious of images: 'Metaphysics prefers the verbal to the visual, the intelligible to the sensible, the text to the picture, and the rigorous articulations of signification to the ambiguities of untutored perception.'[10] Lacanian psychoanalysis and film theory privileges the linguistic symbolic order, over and in opposition to a visual imaginary. Shaviro announces the consequences of this opposition where 'the word is the death of the thing', and where 'Percept and affect must be subordinated to textuality and the Law of the signifier'.[11] Shaviro traces how Jean-Louis Baudry, in his article 'The Apparatus: Metapsychological Approaches is the Impression of Reality in the Cinema' (1986) replicates this Platonic diction of idealistic film theory, even as he tries to critique it, because he is using a psychoanalytic paradigm that is inclusive of such metaphysical idealism. Psychoanalysis is clearly, here, insufficient as a tool to analyse images in film; as Shaviro aptly remarks, it isn't lack that makes images so powerful and disturbing.

But psychoanalysis doesn't have to be read as a self-enclosed metaphysical or linguistic system. I want to suggest that *Boys Don't Cry* is a film that offers a more embodied and mobile gaze to the viewer. In this scenario the spectator is pulled into the film as a phenomenological world.[12] In *Boys Don't Cry* this is represented though the surrealistic landscape that seems to echo and mirror the haunting emotions of the characters. Lighting also accentuates the relation between the ground and the sky, where an analogy between the individual and the universe is constantly being created. We don't have any one point of identification. Sometimes it is with Brandon as an ideal or tragic hero. More disturbingly, we identify with John or Tom (their vulnerability decides it), or with Lana in her erotic re-memory of sex, love and intimacy with Brandon, a re-memory that undoes Lana and mobilizes her sexuality to the point where physical genitals cannot eradicate the bodily sex she has experienced with Brandon. She says, 'Don't show me anything, I know you are a guy.' In all these encounters we don't just identify with the characters but with the mood which is set through the film in terms of its external setting. This setting is illustrated by the bleakness of the buildings, a sky which is constantly moving with lights or a landscape devoid of colour. The background echoes the emotional rawness of the characters and the images pull us indiscriminately into an experience and witness of what it was like.

Watching *Boys Don't Cry* does not confine the viewer to one, perverse identification with a male camera, but allows for different points of view. Images are powerful in *Boys Don't Cry* because of the relationship they establish between the body, psychic fantasy and history. In the melancholic Oedipal narrative of John and Tom, homosexuality is disavowed. This is reminiscent of Judith Butler's argument of performativity in terms of psychoanalytic notions of melancholia.[13] Reconfiguring Freud's text on *Mourning and Melancholia*, Butler refuses Freud's understanding of identification as a singular Oedipal process that delimits desire and defines the boundaries of the ego. Butler rewrites Freud's work on melancholia to argue for a *disavowed* homosexual identity. Freud describes melancholic identity as an identification that is disavowed and therefore incorporated lastingly as an unresolved other to the self. For Butler, a taboo against homosexuality precedes Freud's incest taboo. It is not Oedipal prohibition of the mother that is primary, but love of the same-sex parent that is forbidden – the homosexual cathexis. Butler suggest that the more extreme the heterosexual identification, the greater the degree of melancholia.

Heterosexuality, rather than homosexuality, is placed within the more unmediated melancholic space where loss remains unacknowledged and therefore incorporated. Within this re-reading, rigid heterosexuality is a more defensive position than homosexuality, ruled not by melancholia, but also by paranoia and hate. This melancholic and rigid heterosexuality ruled by hatred sums up much of the mentality and the masculinity of the homogeneous, white and right-wing communities of heartland America, such as that in Falls City, Nebraska. For John and Tom, there is only one imaginary, and it is fixed and rigidly heterosexual. Split off from the bodily real and masquerading (but only just) as the symbolic law, this hysterical imaginary is thrown into crisis when confronted with Brandon's more mobile and creatively embodied imaginary. When John asks Brandon, 'What the fuck are you?', he really means that Brandon's sexual fluidity and performance of masculinity is so powerful that it puts in question his own identity. Inability to root his sexuality through his own body literally sends John mad. His need, therefore, to determine Brandon's sexual identity – 'You fucking pervert, are you a girl or are you not?' – is followed by the horrifically violent rape, intended to prove John's power and sexuality: his narrative of Oedipal manhood.

I want to turn now to Brandon's embodied imaginary, which in contrast to John's melancholia is fluid and mobile. Although the hysteric might display bodily symptoms, these florid, embodied acts are witness to the real fear and absence of the body that underpins the hysteric's dilemma. Unable to ground their imaginaries within their bodies or sexuality is finally too much for John and Tom, especially when they realize what a threat Brandon poses to the symbolic representation of their identity. This hysterical dilemma for John and Tom, where they become psychically disembodied and split off, is also a situation where the imaginary goes to war with the real, sending them into a psychotic and abject rage. For Brandon, and eventually Lana, the imaginary is more connected with the body. This embodiment is transformative, actively re-reading the image in terms of the body and history.

Now it is tempting to read Brandon's gender performance in terms of Judith Butler's notion of a lesbian phallus.[14] But, actually, Brandon's performance in *Boys Don't Cry* is a practice of a situated embodied imaginary that is in some ways quite different from Butler's formulation. Butler follows Lacan's argument and turns it round by suggesting that if the phallus as symbol can be detached from the imaginary and the bodily part (the penis), then it is infinitely transferable.[15] By implication, it can symbolize other bodily parts. The lesbian phallus therefore works by displacing the privileged phallus and symbolizing other body parts: instead of the penis/phallus the lesbian phallus can represent, for example, the breast or the clitoris. Butler rescues lesbian sexuality from its abject position by transporting the lesbian body into a realm of patriarchal language and signifiers. This, then, is a question of naming. Butler doesn't change language, she changes its referent. The lesbian phallus can signify both masculine and feminine sex, and in effect removes the distinction between them. Such an imaginary calls into question heterosexual difference, based on distinct 'masculine' and 'feminine' morphologies. What is needed, according to Butler, is not so much a new body part, but alternative imaginary schemas.

Nevertheless, Brandon actually does add a new body part, and in so doing performs an alternative imaginary, blurring fixed Oedipal boundaries of sexual difference in the process. In Brandon's case his new symbolic and phallic bodily part is precisely what enables him to ground his imaginary in terms of his body, and it works as this new embodied imaginary becomes symbolically reproduced in relation to Lana. When Lana comes to get him out of jail, the dispirited Brandon whispers, 'I'm not so much a he, more of a she', but Lana responds with 'Shut up, this is your business. I don't care if you are half monkey and half ape, I'm getting you out of here.'

Key points

- John's and Tom's psychotic hysteria underlies the Oedipal myth.
- Steven Shaviro argues that Lacanian psychoanalysis and film theory privilege the linguistic symbolic order, over and in opposition to a visual imaginary.
- Judith Butler suggests that it is rigid heterosexuality, rather than homosexuality per se, that is melancholic.

A phenomenological experience of the image – and the imaginary

Following Steven Shaviro, I want to argue for the cinematic world as an activity of the imaginary, rather than the symbolic. Within this imaginary world of film we are mimetically caught up with images. These images are always connected to the real, but are nevertheless imaginary and constructed. We can perceive the cinematic world, then, as a phenomenological, parallel universe to our everyday life, but not as some fixed reproduction of reality. Vivian Sobchack emphasizes the cinematic space as a lived body.

> In its capacity for movement, the cinema's embodied agency (the camera) thus constitutes visual/visible space as always also motor and tactile space – a space that is deep and textural, that can be materially inhabited, that provides not merely a ground for the visual/visible but also its particular *situation* . . . Indeed, although it is a favoured term among film theorists, there is no such abstraction as *point of view* in the cinema. Rather, there are more concrete *situations of viewing* – specific and mobile engagements of embodied, enworlded, and situated subjects/objects whose visual/visible activity prospects and articulates a shifting field of vision from a world whose horizons always exceed it.[16]

This, then, is the cinematic world of *Boys Don't Cry*, an embodied world whose imaginary allows space a more simultaneous relation to time. Equalizing space-time enables a lived relation to the cinematic body and time. When this happens the image is no longer subordinated to traditional myths and languages and can be elaborated in a painterly way, connecting the imaginary to the body and culturally re-memorizing the past in terms of the present.

Walter Benjamin talks about the phenomenological apprehension of the image as a profane illumination.[17] For Benjamin, this profane illumination when applied to the mechanical reproduction of the cinema becomes an 'optical unconscious'. This material and optical unconscious links with the masses; it connects intersubjectively between micro and macro perception. He relates this embodied reception of the work of art to a discussion of the painterly status of the image.

In a similar fashion to Irigaray, Benjamin argues for the painterly and material elaboration of the image, but he makes a distinction between the image in an actual painting and the cinematic image. Whereas the painter establishes a natural distance from reality, the camera-man 'penetrates deeply into its web'.[18] Benjamin suggests that in film the mechanical apparatus surgically cuts into reality, fragmenting it and making it the 'height of artifice'.[19] Film reality is then a phenomenological experience, but like 'an orchid in the heart of technology' it is both material (real) and constructed. For Benjamin, reading the cinematic image can also be a dialectical re-reading of the past through the present. Cultural re-memory of the past is practised through an embodied imaginary, which in turn is opened up by the image-sphere. This active reading re-reads dead traditions and myths and connects individual memory with the community. Admittedly, this is the utopian trajectory of Benjamin's ideas on film, because he also sees it (as do Adorno and Kracauer) as an aesthetics of mass distraction and consumption, as an industry that reproduces dominant ideology within the masses.

Film viewing in relation to *Boys Don't Cry* entails both the progressive and reactionary readings that Benjamin cites, as a hysterical and more embodied mimesis. However, this hysterical and embodied mimesis is not simply dependent on a textual analysis and needs to incorporate an ethnographic emphasis on the real spectator.

Key points

- The cinematic world is an activity of the imaginary, rather than the symbolic.
- Following Merleau-Ponty, we can see the cinema as a phenomenological embodied and situated world that is both mobile and material.

Ethnography, testimony and video replay

Space-time perception is re-worked in *Boys Don't Cry* in the contrast depicted between a mythic tradition of time and place associated with the American heartland of small rural towns, and the spatial imaginary that Pierce constructs in relation to this myth. This imaginary has become, in the film and in life, a kind of nostalgic ruins of the white, male American identity. The narrative of space, time and belonging in *Boys Don't Cry* is inseparable from the struggle with identity myths which the film embodies. But these mythic stories are also a reflection of the struggles over identity which take place in everyday life.

As a temporal narrative, *Boys Don't Cry* is a film which has been made on the basis of a real-life story and documentary. Teena Brandon existed, and the film is therefore a fictionalized story of a real-life narrative. The film imbricates fact and fiction, the real of history with storytelling. The life story and murder of Teena Brandon was a significant historical event and the documentary made in the wake of his death attracted much publicity; he was talked about by journalists, feminists and crime writers. Kimberley Pierce was attracted by a story that seemed to speak straight into American myth, about identity, youth and the decline of the American heartland. Small-town rural communities, once so mythically reminiscent of the American family dream, were now dilapidated, housing narrow-minded, working-class, white communities, where violence and desperation are rife. One of the producers of the film, John Hart, remarks in the production notes (*Yahoo Movies by Fox Searchlight: Boys Don't Cry*) on how *Boys Don't Cry* is 'an examination' of American culture. He says, 'The most violent crimes are often committed in places meant to be the safest. In a multicultural environment the individual is celebrated; in homogenous ones the individual is viewed as a threat.' This, then, is the white, male myth of individual freedom and enterprise in America.

Pierce, compelled by Brandon's iconic status in the culture, spent five years researching and interviewing people connected to Brandon in Falls City. Interestingly, although she took thousands of transcripts and many personal interviews, the stories were all contradictory. She talks of the stories changing again and again: 'it was interesting to watch people's stories change the longer I stayed there. Sometimes people were lying to themselves, other times to me. But, I think people are always emotionally truthful even when they lie.' This is a significant point in thinking about ethnography: if people's testimonies are always contradictory, even over time with themselves, then how can these testimonies be any more 'factual' than the film?

Like the multiple view points that Sobchack indicates can be taken up in relation to film viewing, ethnography does not enable us to access any 'real' or 'true' experience of either Brandon's real life story or its fictionalized and filmic counterpart. Ethnography, nevertheless, can enable us to examine the cultural re-memory of myths in relation to the film and everyday life. Valerie Walkerdine's essay 'Video Replay: Families, Films and Fantasy' brings together psychic reality and ethnography. In this study, she uses her ethnographic research into the response of a working-class family, the Coles, to a video, *Rocky II*, describing how 'filmic representations are incorporated in the domestic practices of the family'.[20] Recording and observing the family dynamics, which reveal class and gender conflicts, Walkerdine writes of her own uneasy feelings about the voyeuristic position of power she occupies as academic and ethnographer. Focusing on a violent fight scene in *Rocky II*, and Mr Cole's obsessive replay of it on the video, Walkerdine links this replay to her own historical memories of being a child. In these memories the father/daughter dynamic is drawn out as only fraudulently Oedipal, revealing the hysterical and imaginary desires that inform Mr Cole's masculinity and her own historical memories of being 'Tinkerbell' as a child.

For Walkerdine, psychoanalysis can help us to understand spectators of film, not as the universal, Oedipal positioning of a textual spectator, but the fantasies of a real historical audience.

> Hence a young man can use the figure of Superman, not in relation to an Oedipal resolution, but as a carrier for his fantasies of omnipotent power. This suggests that different readers will 'read' films, not in terms of a pre-existing set of relations of signification or through a pathology of scopophilia, but by what those relations *mean to them*.[21]

Walkerdine illustrates the differing positions of spectatorship available to real spectators. The notion of 'replay' becomes the trope of the working-class father domineering the video and obsessively rewinding the fight, and the writer's own process of recall. The memory invoked is of Walkerdine at a carnival dressed as Tinkerbell. The fairy femininity of Tinkerbell is a hysterical disembodiment, whereas Mr Cole's obsessional identification with Rocky is a defensive and hysterical masculine identification, which (in true hysterical form) acts out rather than owns an embodied identity. Thus Walkerdine draws out a father/daughter dynamic which is only fraudulently Oedipal, revealing the hysterical and imaginary desires that inform Mr Cole's masculinity and her own autobiography.

The embodied imaginary described here is a movement between imaginary and real, where melancholic and hysterical identifications of violent boxer and fairy are 'replayed'. Jogged by an involuntary memory of her own past, Walkerdine's replay leads to an embodied re-memory (and mourning) of previous class identifications and longing, providing her with understanding of the hysterical, Oedipal relationship between her and her father. This cultural memory enables her to tie these defensive forms of heterosexuality (violent boxer and fairy), to a politics of class, situating Mr Cole's and her desire historically.

Nevertheless, Oedipal authority as a Foucauldian will to power and truth, one which Walkerdine so criticizes in other bourgeois intellectuals, returns in her narrative as a form of 'recognition'. Walkerdine sets out to criticize the voyeurism of the theorist and ethnographer against mass working-class pleasures of consumption, but her own position of ethnographer and academic does not sit easily with her, at times, forced identification with the Cole family.[22] This contradiction, then, can be linked to the very Hegelian language of power in which she sets out to resolve the dilemma. For Walkerdine uses and reworks Althusser's concept of 'mis-recognition' and Lacan's notion of (Hegelian) recognition as a move to resolve the antithetical oppositions between the theorist/ethnographer and 'mass' working-class pleasures. She argues, 'Often when interviewing the participants I felt I "knew what they meant", that I recognised how the practices were regulated, or that I understood what it was like to be a participant.' This 'recognition' became a tool, by which Walkerdine can take up a position of the oppressed, because she is able to re-member empathically the same imaginary, while distinguishing herself, meantime, from any forced identifications between powerful academic and oppressed worker. A major problem of course with this is that Walkerdine can't help but take up that position of power and authority as an ethnographer and academic.[23]

I think Walkerdine is trying to say that this notion of recognition can account in some way for difference and alienation: she wants to 'account for power and responsibility, rather than disavow it'.[24] Unfortunately, in this Hegelian and Lacanian master/slave dialectic the term 'recognition' determines an 'other' that is ultimately knowable and submissive. Kelly Oliver has recently taken up Drusilla Cornell's work to argue for an alternative to a Hegelian concept of recognition.[25] Using Cornell's ideas, Oliver describes a form of feminist witnessing, where the other is acknowledged even if she/he cannot be recognized or known. Oliver explores the dissolution of the Hegelian subject–object dichotomy in a reading of Agnes Varda's film *Vagabond* (1985), where she detects multiple points of witnessing in response to the film. Oliver, then, constructs a theory of phenomenological subjectivity not based on recognition, but on the more plural identifications implied by witnessing.

Juxtaposing the notions of action and testimony, Kelly Oliver suggests that there can be no authorized subject positions: all subject positions are multiple, and the idea of testimony and witness is used to argue against any one privileged position. For Oliver, we can witness and testify to what we observe, but we can also be a witness and testify to that which we cannot observe, but believe. For example, a belief in God can be testified to, but not observed. For Kelly, subjectivity always involves an oscillation between action and testimony. In her exploration of Varda's film *Vagabond*, her reading reveals the multiple positions that the viewer has to take up in relation to the film. We can, therefore, link this account of witnessing and testimony to the multiple positions which the protagonists in Brandon's real life story take up in relation to his life story. In *Boys Don't Cry*, Kimberley Pierce could not decide between the multiple, fictitious but real stories she ended up with, so she decided finally to look for where Brandon's myth intersected with her own life.

Key point

- **Ethnography as a methodology can give witness and testimony to multiple positions in retelling history.**

The bodily imaginary as a cultural re-memory of time and history

I want to end this chapter with an examination of how the phenomenological cinematic imaginary in *Boys Don't Cry* is also a cultural re-memory of history. In her analysis of cinema, Vivian Sobchack argues that cinema holds a privileged position of embodied vision over photography or more electronic media. With reference to Jameson, Sobchack aligns photography with realism (and market capitalism), cinema with modernity (and monopoly capitalism) and electronic media with postmodernism (and multinational capitalism). She argues that photography can be seen as a technological process that objectifies and literalizes the world in a self-possession. An example of this is family albums which empirically verify, 'self, other and experience'.[26]

The photograph freezes the currents of temporality into a moment, mummifying the present and delivering a nostalgic investment with death and the past. The cinema, however, involves us with an inter-subjective embodied and mobile gaze, where time is not past but experienced as a material 'coming into being'. With the cinema came pictures in motion which fragmented and re-ordered space-time, moving beyond the transcendent objectivity of realism. Cinema allows us to experience both the objective as an 'intentional stream of moving images' and the subjective as a 'mobile, embodied, and ethically invested *subject* of worldly space'. This reversible activity of viewing allows the subject to 'inscribe visual and bodily changes of situation, to dream, hallucinate, imagine and re-member its habita-tion and experience in the world'.

Embodied subjectivity is achieved only by the cinematic modernist moment, according to Sobchack. With the advent of postmodernism and electronic media we are now disengaged from our bodies and affectual situations within a world of referentiality and simulation. Blocking off the flow of conscious and temporal experience, elec-tronic media privilege the instant and construct temporality as a network of random information. Only in relation to cinema can we experience the objective 'other' as having an intentional conscious-ness and subjectivity of its own. With the advent of video tapes, for example, the ability to control, freeze and replay the film turns it into an inanimate body. Here, our experience of the objective as an intentional consciousness is lost. What Sobchack calls a 'streaming forward' of the cinematic provides a specific temporal presence which is both embodied but also mobile – connecting past and future.[27]

Obviously, through a history of technology and the development of capitalism, we can situate photography with realism, cinema with modernity and electronic media with postmodernism. But this demar-cation is far too simple; photography is not just a literal representa-tion of the real – as Siegfried Kracauer reminds us, it also confronts us negatively, in the distance it establishes from memory, with our temporal and bodily contingency.[28] Photographs are always perceived in a context, often in relation to life narratives, and, as recent cul-tural studies work on the family album has shown, photographs can be used as a way of remembering different, embodied histories.[29] I want, then, to take issue with Sobchack's contention that it is only with the modernist moment of cinema that we can access an embod-ied self.

Certainly we can agree that cinema originally suggested a more embodied, collective, phenomenological world, which was more mobile than photography and less virtual than current electronic

media. But our embodied perception is not just determined by changing representations of technology. Technology suggests a greater or
lesser embodied vision and presence. However, our embodied reception of technology as a re-memory of history and everyday life is also
a situated presence and perception which will transform technological representation. It is our subjective projection into the filmic image
which establishes either an embodied or alternatively a disembodied
relation to time. Films offer us a landscape in which we can potentially project and re-memorize our selves. Embodied or disembodied
perception is very dependent on our subjective relation to the image,
and to what we psychologically invest in it. The perception is about
how we detach the image from its object and go travelling with it in
terms of our own situated memories and histories.

Following Merleau-Ponty, we can say that film is phenomenological because it presents us with an imaginary world or landscape into
which we can subjectively project ourselves. And this is partly or
indeed centrally because, in watching film, space and time become
reconfigured in relation to each other. Embodiment of film experience is not just dependent on the act of sitting in a darkened cinema
and having no control over the projection of images. The existential
film presence is dependent on how we live temporality in relation to
images and to film. In Walkerdine's account, replaying of the video
connects the real and imaginary, enabling her to re-memorize the film
and the Cole family audience in relation to a new and embodied
perception of history. The control she exercises over the video by
replaying it does not disembody time; on the contrary, it embodies
her perception through a re-memory of history. So although we can
generalize by saying that film is a temporal experience, whereas
electronic media are a more spatial dynamic, with both there is a
relation to the reconfiguration of space-time. Our embodied relation
to either film or electronic media, therefore, depends on the phenomenological relation it puts us in touch with, in terms of everyday
life.

In *Boys Don't Cry* we have seen how the Oedipal myth and gaze
performed by Tom and John act out a hysterical and defensive, macho
identification with the male body. This myth becomes culturally re-
membered in multiple ways which historically situate the cinematic
imaginary. Pierce could not film in Falls City; that was too difficult,
so she filmed *Boys Don't Cry* in and around the outskirts of Dallas,
Texas. Visiting several towns in the area, Pierce noticed architectural
similarities to Falls City. They all contained a town square, a park,
centre shops, a police station, a big factory and a railway line not far
from the town square. Pierce describes the nostalgic, once glorious,

now dilapidated appearances of these towns, inhabited by passively drugged youths.

> Like Falls City these towns were county seats, towns of former glory, that had fallen since they were originally settled. But, best of all what we found was a whole Qwik Stop culture of narcotized kids that sleep all day and hang out all night just like in Falls City. We had all the flat farmland we needed and we found beautiful dilapidated farmhouses. It was entirely the right feel in terms of class and attitude.

Pierce constructs an aesthetics of space in relation to this representative town: big skies that reflect the beauty and starkness of the buildings and the landscape. The surreal and expressive camera work, that oscillates between sky and ground, using lighting and time compression photography creates a relation between stillness and movement, light and dark, that is somehow reflected in the relation between the individual and the community. The spatial imaginary is also embodied by Brandon, with no past or parents to speak of and no past sexual identity either – merely his innocence and embodied desire to be a male hero. As a figure, Brandon is pictured constantly in spatial isolation against the landscape, the town buildings and the community. Elsewhere, Brandon explores his embodied identity as an outlaw in breakneck bumper surfing and car chasing, or in his tragically doomed love affair with Lana. Brandon is a transformational object or profane illumination for the other characters in the community. Imaginative re-memory of Oedipal myths in this film occurs between Brandon and the other characters. Myths of masculinity in crisis, so aptly performed by John and Tom, are contrasted with their embodied re-memory between Brandon and Lana. However, with all four characters the particular white male American myth has been dissolved. In the case of John and Tom there is nothing else to replace it with, and they disintegrate into hysterical hate and violence. But for Brandon and Lana, the love and intimacy they have established provides an openness which grounds their sexual union and identities in a more fluid and embodied imaginary. At the end of the film, just before his death, Brandon burns all the images and photographs of himself in Falls City, and then Lana turns up and wants to make love to him. Unsure of his sexuality at this point and her own, Lana says, 'I don't know if I will know how to do it.' Brandon replies, 'I'm sure you will figure it out.'

This film is finally about the importance of collectively remembering new myths. Tom's and John's Oedipal story, which is also shared by the police officers and the law, is their remaining intention to destroy or castrate Brandon's embodied sexuality, and to wipe out his memory from any form of collective and public memory. Tom and John tell Brandon after they rape him that, if he tells anyone, they will silence and eradicate him for ever. The law officers, too, refuse to record or recognize Brandon as anything other than a she – Teena Brandon. Their anxieties about their masculinity are projected onto Brandon as the one with the 'sexual identity crisis'. Pierce's powerful retelling of Brandon's story is a way of putting it on public record, passing it on: a re-telling of American archetypes of masculinity that connects more marginal identities with the community. *Boys Don't Cry* is a cultural re-memory, through an embodied imaginary, of Oedipal myth and history. It is also a re-thinking of the sexual/textual difference operating within the male gaze of Apparatus theory. But how do we know that this film is not just a symptomatic, postmodern text that destabilizes the male gaze and reads it hysterically? In order to establish more firmly the hysterical nature of the Oedipal complex and film spectatorship, this book will continue by returning to an examination of the early film spectator.

Key points

- Vivian Sobchack argues that it is only in relation to cinema that we can experience the 'other' as having an intentional consciousness.
- Our embodied perception is not just determined by changing representations of technology.
- Our embodied reception of technology as a re-memory of history and everyday life also transforms technological representation.

Part II
The Early Film Spectator

Introduction to Part II

The next two chapters trace the phenomenological spectator within debates of early film and modernity. The eventual disillusionment with Screen theory in the 1980s and the consequent opposite move towards a more empirically based audience research, has left the possibilities of a more historical theory of film and psychoanalysis somewhat abandoned.

What Bordwell calls the 'modernity thesis' has stepped into this breach. As Ben Singer discusses, the critics who in the 1990s drew on Benjamin's and Kracauer's ideas of the sensual and distracted nature of modernity and cinema have been involved in rethinking cinema's imbrication with the sensory aspects of modernity and the space-time technologies of the late nineteenth century.[1] One of the implications of this body of work is a history of perception argument, that the shocks and sensual stimuli of urban modernity caused a change in human perception. Bordwell is highly critical of any structural arguments of perceptual change under modernity, putting forward a more qualitative thesis of cognitive and behavioural psychology which suggests that people merely acquired new habits and skills to adapt to the new environment. Not completely convinced by this, Singer stresses that Bordwell's skills thesis does not reach the core of what Benjamin's meant by a bodily, visceral experience of modernity. What is necessary, according to Singer, is a 'physiological formulation' of the perception and modernity argument.

Addressing this proposal, the first chapter in this section maps a debate between perception, cinema, psychoanalysis and neuroscience in the late nineteenth century. Discussing early technologies of vision, Jonathan Crary argues that perception and spectacle in the nineteenth century were based on a different model of mimesis, one that cannot be equated with the classical model of realism emerging from the classical period.[2] This new mimesis was situated in the body of the observer, but at the same time that body was denied or disassociated. In terms of the early film spectator we can see this mimesis as a hysterical split, which regulated the body, producing it in terms of the audience, projecting it as spectacle, but at the same time disavowing a more grounded bodily subjectivity. This early hysterical spectator can be linked with a phenomenological reading of the hysteric in the writings of Freud and Jung. Reading Freud's early work on hysteria through debates on neuroscience enables us to retrieve a more physiological conception of the unconscious, which in turn is used to understand the hysterical mimesis between early cinema and science. The hysterical and physiological mimesis of the spectator explored here develops a physiological formulation of the perception and modernity argument, avoiding structural determinations of society or the Oedipal complex.

The second chapter in this section brings together phenomenological film theory and psychoanalysis in a reading of early film spectatorship. D.W. Griffith's *Intolerance* and Freud's *The Interpretation of Dreams* stand out as key contemporary texts within modernism that hysterically fetishize and defend against time and history. Refusing the dichotomy in film theory which has historically defined early film as a sort of primitive pre-Oedipal cinema against later, Oedipally defined narrative cinema, this chapter explores early film in terms of a phenomenology of the image. The textual, narrative hegemony in film theory can be said to have obfuscated another more gestural or bodily imaginary. Within this gestural account it is a phenomenological apprehension of the image and filmic experience which is foregrounded. The film theories of Walter Benjamin, Siegfried Kracauer, Béla Balázs, and André Bazin all explore this mimesis of the filmic image as a mimesis which rolls between spectator and the filmic world. Balázs's aesthetic theory anticipates Benjamin's and Kracauer's optical unconscious, whereas Bazin's work is synonymous with Kracauer's later emphasis on a phenomenological realism. However, all these theorists share an understanding of film spectatorship as a mimetic defence and fetish against time. This chapter ends with a reading of the film hieroglyphs in Griffith's film *Intolerance*. Miriam Hansen reads the hieroglyphs in *Intolerance* as textuality and writing. Alternatively, they can be read within a phenomenological frame as social and archetypal filmic images. Re-reading Freud's notion of the hieroglyph as a hysterical fetish, whether we see that operating in his most famous dream text, or in his thoughts about femininity, enables us to understand the film images in *Intolerance* as a hysterical mimesis and masquerade. This mimesis is integral to the discourses of cinema, psychoanalysis and modernism, repetitively freezing time and disavowing the body.

If Freud's dream text and the film *Intolerance* signify a splitting of the body and history that is somehow constituent of modernism, then Walter Benjamin's allegorical reading of the dream images of modernity also offers us a more creative understanding of the hieroglyph. This allegory manifests as a more profane projection into the filmic image, where time and history can be embodied and reconfigured.

Key points

- The modernity thesis is Benjamin's and Kracauer's ideas of the sensual and distracted nature of modernity and cinema.
- Jonathon Crary argues that perception and spectacle in the nineteenth century were based on a different model of mimesis, one that cannot be equated with the classical model of realism emerging from the classical period.
- Reading Freud's early work on hysteria through debates on neuroscience enables us to retrieve a more physiological conception of the unconscious, which in turn is used to understand the hysterical mimesis between early cinema and science.
- Griffith's *Intolerance* and Freud's *The Interpretation of Dreams* stand out as key contemporary texts within modernism that hysterically fetishize and defend against time and history.
- The film theories of Walter Benjamin, Siegfried Kracauer, Béla Balázs, and André Bazin all explore this mimesis of the filmic image as a mimesis which rolls between spectator and the filmic world.

4

Perception and Early Film

Introduction

Michel Foucault and Jonathan Crary both address a different form of vision in the eighteenth and nineteenth centuries, one that cannot be equated with a mimetic realism emerging from the classical period. Developing this alternative account of perception in relation to a more bodily mimesis, this chapter then maps this bodily mimesis in relation to early hysterical technologies of psychoanalysis and cinema. In *The Order of Things*, Foucault traces how Kantian and post-Kantian knowledge divided the world into, on the one hand, a transcendental subjectivism where the world was understood as entirely a project or dependency on 'man's self-reflective consciousness': his 'idea'. On the other hand, however, consciousness became increasingly an objective object of study, empirically quantifiable and contradicting reflective subjectivism. Thus consciousness became created as 'a strange empirico-transcendental doublet'.[1] This contradictory split between the (individual) subject and the objective (world) meant that consciousness was on one level completely self-aware and transparent, and, on the other, obscure. Foucault describes this split as 'both in itself and outside itself, at its borders yet also in its very warp and woof, an element of darkness, an apparently inert density, in which it is embedded, an un-thought which it contains entirely, yet in which it is also caught.'[2] We can see here how Freudian psychoanalysis is a product of the split and conflict between this self-aware and rational ego and the dark unthought.

Foucault analyses how modern society was organized through the panopticon, a system of surveillance and regulation exercised by the prison, clinic, school, etc. Within this system, subjectivity is produced as both vigilantly observed and (as an internalization of this gaze) subjectively self-regulating/observing. Echoing Foucault's critique of Freud's repressive hypothesis we can say that sexuality is not necessarily repressed, it is a productive vehicle of knowledge and power. The hysteric and madman are, as the nineteenth-century psychiatrist Bleuler suggests, merely points on a continuum, where the split between subject and object, the mind and the body, have become uncontainable. However, I would also like to suggest, in line with Foucault, that the Oedipal complex (and the institution of heterosexuality) is a defensive disciplinary regulation of the body, producing the very splits between the body and self that as a narrative it attempts to master. Sexuality and psychoanalysis are, as Foucault reminds us, discourses of power, but only as long as they maintain that Oedipal narrative split between language and the body, society and the individual psyche. What is clear in Freud's work is that language remains a favoured option to mediate bodily sexuality and being, to take a distance from it. We can see this disjunction between the body and language in Freud's notion of the dream. For Freud, dreams are always linguistic tropes of metaphor, condensation and displacement. The meaning of the dream image resides in a language, which the analyst (as the one that linguistically knows) deciphers.

For Jung, on the other hand, the dream image means exactly what it says, and this phenomenological understanding of the image connects the imaginary and real.[3] The dream image is a mimetic figuration of the replay of the relation between real and imaginary. Perception of dreams and images are not based on narrative, reflexive reasoning, but on a phenomenological and embodied response that is socially contingent. All images are in a sense dream images, and in this chapter I want to re-read debates in early film eschewing what I suggest has been a pretty persistent Oedipal binary in film history. This divide has placed film as either on the side of social history or of theory, on the side of the body (ontological reality) or of artistic culture. Film has been a theory of the image or a theory of narrative; however, I want to refuse the traditions that make theory and the body, or culture and the body, line up on one side or the other.

The Lumière brothers occupy a place as the mythic origin of cinema. There is the famous example of their film of a train, which the audience perceive as coming towards them, literally out of the screen, and so they all rush out of the cinema. Now, that would not happen today, it would not have happened probably six months after the cited event, because by then the audience would have learnt that their perception of the train coming towards them was a cinematic illusion. Phenomenological psychology in the twentieth century has taught us that perception is not simply about optical seeing. Perception is an embodied affair linked to other bodily senses and it is socially learnt. Richard Gregory gives the example of a blind man who late in life has his sight restored through a cataract operation. Unable to bear crossing the road using his eyes, the man shuts them and, reverting to his old tool of perception, strides out pointing his white stick.[4] Gestalt psychology has also historically understood perception as something that conflates the real and imaginary, the figure and the ground. There is, then, nothing innate about perception; it is socially embodied in the world, and, as the Lumière brothers' film exemplifies, our perception of film is socially learnt; we bring these embodied ways of seeing to the cinema and they are culturally specific. Béla Balázs's early theory of film provides a story of a Siberian girl who goes to her first movie while on a visit to Moscow. The film, a burlesque, horrified and terrified the girl. Reporting on her experience she said, 'Oh it was horrible, horrible! . . . Human beings were torn to pieces and the heads thrown one way and the bodies the other and the hands somewhere else again.'[5]

Balázs recounts how when the film-maker Griffith first showed a big close-up in Hollywood cinema, there was panic in the cinematic audience. Cinema perception has become naturalized; as Balázs remarks, the audience in early film 'learnt to integrate single disjointed pictures into a coherent scene, without even becoming conscious of the complicated psychological process involved'. Balázs goes on to observe, 'It is amazing to what extent we have, in a couple of decades, learnt to see picture perspectives, picture metaphors and picture symbols, how greatly we have developed our visual culture and sensibility.'[6] This phenomenological understanding of the film image can be situated within differing traditions of film theory, within the formalist ideas of Arnheim and Balázs, but also in the 'realist' theories of Bazin and Kracauer. It is significant that in the history of film theory it is narrative and film language that have been privileged over the understanding of the image. This privileging of the film narrative rather than the filmic image echoes Freud's emphasis on narrative over Jung's more mysterious imaginal unconscious. A narrative understanding of film history is central to the distinction that is made between film traditions of realism and formalism developed from literary history and theory. In these traditions formalist approaches foreground the construction of film as a linguistic frame, whereas realist approaches privilege the naturalness of filmic representation as a window onto the world. Somewhat paradoxically, the dominant strand in realist approaches to cinema is understood in terms of Hollywood narrative, where realism means the dominance of the narrative integration of the spectator into the 'truth' of the fiction. Avant-garde and post-structuralist film theory rooted in traditions of formalism have been critical of realist narrative because of their anti-narrative position. But such a non-narrative stance is always based within a binary where linguistic, mental and textual play holds the reflexive centre stage, thus marginalizing the embodied experience of the viewer. Whether we trace film theory back through realism or formalism we are always, therefore, confronting some kind of Oedipal split, privileging a linguistic, rather than a bodily imaginary.

An emphasis on the phenomenological nature of the film image moves us away from the narrative distinction central to the very origins in cinema between the so-called realism of the Lumière brothers' films and the magical illusionism/formalism of Méliès. Reading the history of film theory through such a phenomenological imaginary does not polarize image against narrative. It can also reconfigure how we read the relationship between filmic categories of realism and formalism and indeed provide an alternative route to imagining the very nature and meaning of the real.

Key point

- **A phenomenological understanding of the filmic image can open up another way of understanding the history of film theory which does not polarize image against narrative.**

Perception and technologies of seeing in the nineteenth century

To explore further my argument of a phenomenological imaginary in relation to the origins of film it is necessary to go back to the technologies of perception that frame early and late nineteenth-century society in the West and elucidate the bearing these technologies of vision had on early film. Narrative and realism were inextricably linked in nineteenth-century Western culture. Brian Winston's book *Technologies of Seeing* documents how an increasing preoccupation with spectacle in late nineteenth-century popular culture and art foregrounded a mimesis of the material world in terms of exhibitionist practices of showing and telling. Winston argues for a development

of a Renaissance perspective where sight was rationalized, constructing a public audience which perceived 'space through the use
of particular codes of representation on flat surfaces'.[7] For Winston,
this realist mode of representation was a central precursor to the
popular development of the magic lantern, photography and the
cinema.

The photographic camera originated with the invention of the
camera obscura, developed hundreds of years ago. Aristotle, Euclid,
Alhazen of Basra, Leonardo da Vinci and Johannes Kepler all
realized that when light passes through a small hole in a darkened
interior, then an inverted image appears on the wall opposite the hole.
These people also made the link between this phenomenon and
human vision. By the sixteenth century a lens had been added to the
pinhole, and although Giovanni Battista della Porta in his 1558 book
Magiae Naturalis described the device, priority regarding the use of
the lens is contested. One hundred years later the darkened room
became transformed into a box, and Athanasius Kircher devised the
magic lantern by placing a candle in the box and drawing an image
on the glass between light source and lens. Descartes argued that the
camera obscura was a method by which the observer can make sense
of the world by the unique perception of the mind. The mind, which
according to Locke and Descartes was to be conceived of as an inner
empty space, was what positioned rational perception and the self,
distinct from the external world and from the troubling uncertainties
of other more embodied senses.

Winston maps how the realism of the Renaissance changes stylis-
tically over the centuries. At the end of the nineteenth century,
painting was influenced by a realist movement, a realism which
photography in a sense outstripped. Winston cites a painter hearing
about the daguerreotype as saying, 'From today painting is dead.'[8]
For Winston, the realism of the West and the Renaissance perspective that ended in photography and the cinema was also intricately
linked to illusionism. Illusionism was part of this representative
realism deeply affecting the development of Western theatre where
realistic spectacle was central to the show. This scenic theatre translated into panoramas, huge paintings circling the audience, and then
the more elaborate dioramas that introduced movement and light
changes to give an imitation of nature.[9] The tradition of the magic
lantern was also part of this realism and illusionism. Magic lantern
shows can be traced back to the seventeenth century, and at the turn
of the nineteenth century live spectacles within darkened auditoriums
and magic lantern slides created the kind of realistic spectacle and

verisimilitude that Winston suggests had 'dominated the West for pre-vious centuries'.[10]

Crucial to this spectacle of realism and illusionism, in Winston's view, was narrative. Narrative was everywhere in the nineteenth century. Dioramas and the sequenced slides of the magic lantern shows were all examples of pre-cinematic screen practice. This placing of images in a linear order displayed a narrative tendency that for Winston overturns arguments that early cinema is rooted in non-narrative forms and then takes a significant narrative turn. Winston's argument for nineteenth-century spectacle as narrative leads him to opine: 'Narrative is not the inevitable destiny of cinema – it is just that it is the inevitable destiny of any cinema created in a Western culture addicted to narrative – i.e. the only cinema there is.'[11] But what does it mean to say that the destiny for the history of cinema and the West is narrative? On one level this is obviously true as the structuralists have informed us: language universally structures experience. But to say that language structures experience through story-telling and plot does not mean that language does not also perform experience and bring it into being. There is, then, language as an embodied mimesis and gesture that is less concerned with the linguistic sign and more concerned with the figural image.

My argument returns to the phenomenological nature of the filmic image. In Jonathan Crary's *Techniques of the Observer* he argues that the camera obscura collapsed as a model for the observer and for human vision in the early nineteenth century.[12] The camera obscura provided a model for the observer based on 'a metaphysics of interiority'. Following Descartes and Locke, this observer was a solitary and privatized individual, relatively free and sovereign, but enclosed in a domestic space away from the world. Crary writes, 'The visual world could be appropriated by an autonomous subject but only as a private unitary consciousness detached from any active relation with the exterior. The monadic viewpoint of the individual is legiti-mised by the camera obscura, but his or her sensory experience is subordinated to an external and pre-given world of objective truth.'[13]

However, according to Crary, in the early nineteenth century this construction of the camera obscura disintegrated. Goethe's *Theory of Colours* in 1810, along with a series of research studies in the 1820s and 1830s, became concerned with experiences of the retinal after-image. These studies characterized vision not as separate from the senses, but as something produced by the observer in relation to the body. Vision, in these accounts, was 'an irreducible amalgam of physiological processes and external stimulation, and they dramatized

the productive role played by the body in vision'.[14] Located as imma-
nence in the physiological productive body of the observer, vision thus
was made autonomous and subjective, abstracting it away from its
previous relation between perception and external object. European
physiology in the first half of the nineteenth century no sooner
acknowledged the body as a producer of knowledge and vision, then
it started to control and quantify the body in regulatory ways, delin-
eating the senses and physiological processes (such as the brain) into
separate measurable components. We can see Crary's argument here
echoing Foucault's. Subjectivism and quantitative objectivity go hand
in hand, and the body, as Foucault himself demonstrates, becomes a
site of disciplinary power located in an empirically measured and controlled subject. Crary writes: 'By the 1840's there had been both (1)
the gradual transferral of the holistic study of subjective experience
or mental life to an empirical and quantitative plane, and (2) the division and fragmentation of the physical subject into increasingly
specific organic and mechanical systems.'[15]

This new quantification and separation of the senses went hand in
hand with the development of technical apparatuses which disci-
plined and regulated the observer's vision and subjectivity. And here
Crary brings Foucault's model of panoptical surveillance together
with the notion of spectacle. Rather than surveillance and spectacle
being distinct, as Foucault suggested, Crary reveals how integrated
they were. He cites the diorama as an example of a mechanical apparatus which simultaneously subjects and regulates the observer at the
same time as offering a mass spectacle of pleasure. The stereoscope,
an apparatus representing a stage further on from the diorama
(because it moved visual emphasis away from painting to photography) simulated the actual physical object so vividly it was tangible.
Paradoxically, though, this tangibility was the product of 'a purely
visual experience'. The reciprocity between sight and touch of early
epochs had disappeared, and vision was located optically through
an apparatus that acted on the body, but constructed the real
mechanically.

Eventually the stereoscope became outmoded, according to Crary,
because it was insufficiently 'phantasmagoric'.[16] Phantasmagoria was
a particular kind of magic lantern performance in the 1790s and
early 1800s that presented the audience with an illusion of reality and
being. It differs from the stereoscope because, whereas the latter produces reality mechanically, phantasmagoria leaves the audience with
the fantasy they have created the illusion. Photography superseded
the stereoscope because, however mechanically productive of reality
it was, it also created the illusion of the old 'free' subject of the camera

obscura. This is why photography is so often mistakenly seen as a continuation of old pictorial codes, rather than being a radical break with them. Photography, far from being a continuation of the camera obscura model (which bound observer and apparatus together), made the modern camera apparatus distinct from the spectator and 'masqueraded as a transparent and incorporeal intermediary between the observer and world'.[17] Crary concluded by remarking that however much pure vision and spectacle in the nineteenth century were rooted in the 'newly discovered territory of the embodied viewer', the success of these notions of pure perception and spectacle ultimately rested on a denial of the body and its phantasmatic rhythms as 'the ground of vision'.[18]

We can see from the above how the phantasmagoric nature of photography and film was also a technological mimesis between imaginary and real, providing an illusion of unmediated reality. In fact this mimesis was a hysterical mimesis based on a radical disassociation or split between subjective and objective epistemologies of vision – a split which regulated the body, producing it and projecting it in terms of spectacle and audience, but at the same time denying its grounded connection to subjective vision. As we shall see presently, this bodily mimesis obscuring a radical disassociation between body and self is exactly the dilemma of Freud's hysteric.

Embodied, disembodied mimesis in early modernism and film

Crary's historical interrogation of the historical conditions of the nineteenth-century observer is important, because it makes us question the status of realism and the notion that 'realism' is a form of mimetic narrative developed from the classical period depicting a dominant model of representation and vision. This narrative model of representation becomes replicated in models of mass communication in the twentieth century. Modernism is seen against this narrative model as an experimental rupture by avant-garde intellectuals, who posit a revolutionary subject with a detached viewpoint. But if Crary makes us revise our historical binaries of realism versus experimentation his understanding of the embodied observer leads us radically to reconstruct our monolithic rendering of a narrative cinematic industry.

Realism in the history and theory of cinema has been understood as a classical mimetic narrative that: 1) can be attributed to Winston's pre-cinematic screen practice or spectacle associated with storytelling;

and 2) can also serve as an explanation of the narrative integration of the spectator (within a plot of fictional/ideological verisimilitude) in terms of the classical Hollywood institution. Avant-garde, modernist films are then seen as an experimental practice of style, ideology or cultural resistance that breaks with classical mimetic models of realism through a detached, deconstructing, subjective viewpoint. But, as Crary points out, this binary obscures how the modernist rupture occurred at the beginning, not the end, of the nineteenth century, and what has been termed realism is in fact an overlapping of classical models of realist mimesis with a more modernist empirical quantification of the autonomous subject. However, as Crary suggests, in both these models the body as a ground for vision disappears.

I want to return to that suppressed bodily ground of vision through an examination of the cinematic image in terms of a bodily, rather than a classical, mimesis. A focus on realist narrative in early cinema provides us with the roots of cinema in codes of realism and modernist rupture. Realist cinema is read as a representative mimesis developed from classical models and it emphasizes a mass audience of visual spectacle. It is seen in terms of an evolving narrative cinema and a narrative integration of the audience through an external ideological cinematic apparatus (Institutional Mode of Representation, IMR), or institution. On the other hand, it is experimental modernism and the (literary/filmic) avant-garde, who break from this tradition through the use of radical form. But what is missing in both these accounts is the identification of the spectator with the cinema (and with films) in ways which are psychological, mimetic and affectual.

A mimesis of the bodily real can be documented in the early writings of Freud and Marx, but it can also be located within early film audiences. In his early writings Karl Marx describes a phenomenological intersubjectivity between subject and object which is rooted in the bodily senses. To exist humanely we must have an object and exist as an object, 'To be sensuous, i.e. to be real, is to be an object of sense, a sensuous object, thus to have sensuous objects outside oneself, to have objects of sense perception.'[19] Marx goes on to say that man is subjectively and objectively part of nature, but this embodied mimesis becomes destroyed through private property alienating the person from his senses. Thus Marx argues that private property has made us so stupid that we can only envisage our relationship to objects in terms of possessing and using them. Private property turns this having of objects into the very means of existence, namely capital, and in this process, 'all physical senses have been replaced by the simple alienation of the senses, the sense of having'.[20] Freud also talks about mimesis in a variety of ways. In his book on *Jokes and their Relation to the Unconscious* (1905; in vol. 8 of the Standard Edition), Freud describes how the comic involves an embodied copying of the other, a perception that arises in the body. His most familiar arguments on bodily mimesis, however, are his accounts of the hysteric and the death drive. Now Freud, as we all know, locates this mimetic repetition in (childhood) sexuality. But as Jung and Merleau-Ponty both remind us, hysteria is not primarily a crisis of sexuality but a crisis of embodied being. The hysterical symptom is the mad mimicking of the other that occurs when we become disassociated from the real of our bodily senses – when our relation to objects becomes alienated. This is also Karl Marx's analysis of the commodity fetish, where all objects become paralysed into social hieroglyphics in the service of capital.[21]

Debates on realism, modernism and postmodernism in both literary and film theory have been centrally focused around narrative. It is not surprising, then, that as the origins of psychoanalysis and cinema arise within similar discourses of modernity, that cinema has been theorized within Oedipally narrative terms. But just as psychoanalysis cannot be restricted to its Oedipal myths, neither can the cinema. I intend to map how the regulatory discourses of science, psychoanalysis and early film can be seen as a hysterical mimesis that disassociates the mind from the body. The Oedipal narrative of language repressing the body came into being later, after Freud's early work on the neurophysiology of hysterics and his early focus on a pathology of emotions, arising from disassociation. In my re-reading of the early debates on the unconscious between Freud and Jung, I dissolve the distinction between their respective emphases on unconscious repression and disassociation. The Oedipal complex, therefore, becomes not a healthy repression and sublimation of the body, but a defensive splitting between the mind and the body. The Oedipal, then, is a hysterical mimesis that masquerades and masks not a repression of the body under narrative but a disassociated split *between* the mind and the body.

Both Crary and Foucault enable us to understand how modernity is a competing, dialectical set of narratives where the body is regulated, divided by and from language, but at the same time mimetically performed as spectacular, hysterical sexuality. We can also re-read origins of cinema and psychoanalysis through a notion of hysterical mimesis as a disembodied imaginary.

Key points

- Jonathan Crary and Foucault enable us to understand how the body in modernity is regulated, divided by and from language, but at the same time mimetically performed as spectacular, hysterical sexuality.
- Hysterical mimesis lies at the origins of both psychoanalysis and early cinema.

Hysteria myths

Hysteria goes back a long way. The earliest Egyptian medical papyrus documenting female lassitude dates from 1900 BC. The Egyptians and Plato interpreted hysteria as a uterine disorder in women, where the disturbed womb went wandering around the body. Cure for this female deviance was pregnancy and marriage. The medieval period saw hysteria linked to witchcraft and the demonic dangers inherent within women. In the seventeenth century, however, Thomas Willis and Thomas Sydenham questioned the uterine theory of hysteria and argued that it was a mental condition. Foucault describes in *Madness and Civilisation* how this idea did not gain credence because of the conceptualization at the time of the brain as mechanical regulator of the bodily organs, which would attack the weakest bodily organ. Internal density according to Foucault became marked with moral meaning: women were constitutionally weaker, less solidly dense and therefore more prone to hysterical attacks. Sydenham writes that women are more susceptible than men because they 'have a more delicate, less firm constitution, because they lead a softer life, and because they are accustomed to the luxuries and commodities of life and not to suffering'.[22] Men in this account are seen as more embodied; having given up narcissistic fantasies and indulgences they are more connected to the world.

We can see here the beginnings of hysteria as a moral discourse, a discourse that goes on to its famous career as psychoanalysis. In the early nineteenth century Philippe Pinel, celebrated for removing the chains restraining insane patients at the asylums of Bicêtre and Salpêtrière in Paris, argued that hysteria was not organically based but a psychological and moral dilemma. Foucault reveals how Pinel's friendly but normative psychotherapy – he advocated (through discussion) a conservative cure of marriage and family for deviant female sexuality – was a disciplinary, paternalistic and bourgeois morality.

In the late nineteenth century, the clinical neurologist Jean-Martin Charcot and his famous hospital the Salpêtrière became a focal point in the study of hysteria. Indeed, Freud himself studied there in 1885 and 1886. Charcot understood hysteria as an organic, neurological disease, caused by a traumatic wound to the central nervous system. Freud subsequently revised this trauma theory, replacing it with his psychoanalytic account of unconscious Oedipal fantasy. Hippolyte Bernheim and Pierre Janet were contemporaries of Freud who influenced him and also believed in the psychological rather than the neurological aetiology of hysteria. So we can see how the conflict between whether hysteria is organically or psychologically located has been a historical one, linked, as Foucault has shown, to disciplinary powers and the morality of the social order.

Charcot's work fed into 'degenerescence theory' supporting eugenics and a scientific ideology where normality and perversity assumed positions in a hierarchy of differences premissed on organically inherited genetics. In contrast, as Foucault shows, Freud's emphasis on the repressed psychology of sex both liberated sexuality from this 'degenerescence theory' and also redeployed sexuality within a moral law. So, on one level, psychoanalysis opposed the political and institutional effects of degenerescence theory, but on another level it redeployed a legislative Oedipal sexuality that continued to distinguish between normal (hetero) sexuality and perverse (homo) sexuality.[23]

Screening the body

Charcot was a showman, according to Elaine Showalter: the hysterics he stagemanaged were performed within a 'hall of mirrors', surrounded by pictures and iconography of hysterical gestures drawn from stage and popular culture. *Trilby* (1894), a best-selling novel by George Du Maurier, which also became a hit on the *fin-de-siècle* stage, presents a young artist's model with migraine attacks who is not only cured, but becomes a famous singer through hypnosis and tutelage under the Jewish musician Svengali.[24]

Being susceptible to suggestion and hypnosis was evidence of hysteria. Charcot's methods were controversial in the extreme. He used hypnosis not only to remove hysterical symptoms, but also to produce them, inducing hysterical fits (through hypnosis) which were followed by the abreaction of the traumatic affect, again through hypnosis. Charcot staged a spectacle of hysterical and hypnotic theatre which the public flocked to witness and gaze at, Freud amongst them. Charcot showed the disassociative twilight states of

Fig. 4   Jean-Martin Charcot, French neurologist, giving a scientific demonstration on hysteria at La Salpêtrière, Paris. © Mary Evans / Freud Copyrights.

consciousness inherent to the hysteric, and Freud's spectatorship of these hysterical states resulted in his theory of the unconscious, taking the splitting of the psyche as an origin of the unconscious, a disassociated 'other' scene of desire.

Charcot also photographed his hysterics. Showalter states that two-thirds of his patients were working-class victims of the urban move to cities in modernity, where deprived of community 'they made up a third of the labour force'.[25] Some of these patients became stars of lectures and supermodels in his photography albums. The queen of hysterics was Blanche Wittman; another was Augustine, who became a 'pin-up girl' for the surrealists. Showalter notes how some of the women actually developed symptoms in relation to the photography, but what she describes is an actual mimicking of the camera work. One hysteric, Hortense, suffers from 'photophobia' as a reaction to the camera's flash, where her eye became paralysed and spasmodic, resulting in a squint which mirrors the camera man's. Augustine starts to see everything in black and white instead of colour, thereby staging a mimicking of the photograph or even early film.[26] In *Screening the Body*, Lisa Cartwright traces the relationship between Charcot's photography of hysterics and early neurological films. The head photographer for Charcot was the chemist Albert Londe, who produced photographic motion studies of the hysterics. These studies were integrally linked to the serial motion photography of physiological movement, developed by Étienne-Jules Marey in France and Eadward Muybridge in America, which were central to the technological development of cinema.[27]

A scientific and medical tradition of viewing moving bodies has been both distinct and crucially interwoven with the familiar account of narrative cinema. Categorization of Lumière's films as realist narrative overlooks how much his inventions were taken up within physiological and scientific research. Alan Williams describes how Lumière's realist images were supposed to attract audiences not because of their representation of reality, but because of their 'technical virtuosity' and ability to track the living movement of bodies.[28] Cinema prehistory stories a tradition of photography and theatre which broke with medical science in 1895. The break between science and arts supposedly occurred when Marey famously rejected the Cinématographe. Thus the beginnings of cinema became separated from physiological motion studies. Tom Gunning's illustration of his cinema of attractions through the experimental physiology of the facial-expression film shows how this break was exaggerated. Gunning illustrates how the bodily display of movement before the camera in early film centres on the close-up, an absence of narrative and the gestural performance of the actor.[29]

In Charcot's Salpêtrière, hysterics were photographed using the same techniques of neurological motion study used within Marey's and Muybridge's earlier work. A split exists, however, between the organic neurology of Charcot and the psychological aetiology emphasized by Freud which formed the origins of psychoanalysis. Jacqueline Rose and Sander Gilman both locate Charcot within a tradition of visual empiricism and neuro-biology, a tradition that formed the basis of racist science. For them, Freud's work was exemplary in breaking from this visual and empirical tradition. Cartwright contests the privileging of psychoanalysis as such a radical alternative to Charcot's empiricism, arguing that psychoanalysis's normative stance has done little to challenge the theory and practices of organic neurology.

But do we have to decide between psychoanalysis and organic neurophysiology, between Freud and Charcot? In 1895 Freud's project was to try and connect psychoanalysis with the neuroscience of the time. His trauma theories of an organic hysteria, following

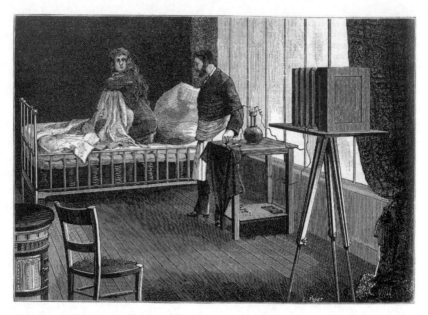

Fig. 5 Medical insanity – photographing the patient. Doctors working with Charcot at La Salpêtrière hospital, Paris, obtain photographic documentation of hysteria patients in various states. © Mary Evans Picture Library.

Charcot, were then abandoned in favour of a theory of psychological and Oedipal fantasy. But, Mark and Karen Solmes argue, there was simply a lack of scientific evidence in Freud's time. Their work completes what Freud started revealing, how neuroscience is not opposed to psychoanalysis; on the contrary, it empirically grounds it. Neuroscientific psychoanalysis is not a return to a biologically determined psyche, as older critiques of Freud have emphasized. Rather, Mark and Karen Solmes highlight the analogical relationship between mind and body and the dialectical process that exists between them.[30] Their work is strongly influenced by Antonio Damasio, a leading neuroscientist who investigates the emotional effects of brain damage.[31] Challenging Descartes' division between mind and body, reason and madness, Damasio contends that rationality is actually predicated on our experiences of embodiment and emotion. Consciousness is brought into being through the interrelationship between body and neurological images. When brain damage occurs, consciousness is impaired, but so is our ability to be reflective and understand our feelings. The developmental pathway from expressing emotion, to experiencing a feeling, to reflexive consciousness, is a neural mapping that becomes increasingly sophisticated. Emotion, feeling and consciousness are also body-related; they all 'depend for their execution on representation of the organism. Their shared essence is the body.'[32]

By the end of the nineteenth century Freud, Darwin and William James had all explored the role of emotions within scientific discourse. Freud, especially, was interested in the pathological disturbance of emotions, and his studies on hysteria were fundamentally involved with the idea that hysteria is the result of a disassociation of consciousness and emotion. Hysteria is, therefore, the performance of emotion and the body, a masquerade or *mise-en-scène* that veils a fundamental disassociation from embodied feelings and reflexive consciousness. Now, this is very different from an Oedipal account of hysteria, where hysteria becomes the failure of Oedipal mental repression and rationality, a return of the instinctual body.

Key points

- Charcot understood hysteria as an organic, neurological disease.
- Freud saw hysteria as a psychological neurosis.
- Photographic motion studies of the hysteric and the serial physiological movement studies developed by Marey and Muybridge were key to the technological development of cinema.

Hysterical regression or disassociation

Charcot's techniques of hypnotism, the production and cure of hysterical symptoms, were taken up by Breuer and Freud. For Charcot, traumatic shock was comparable to hypnosis since both were emotional moments where the will became paralysed and the trauma fixated as auto-suggestion. Whereas shock or trauma in normal circumstances is expressed or abreacted, in cases of hysteria the trauma and affect become blocked. The cathartic method in Freud's and Breuer's initial *Studies on Hysteria* (1895) was to abreact this blocked affect. Both Freud and Breuer followed Charcot in seeing hysteria as a result of a disassociation and a profound splitting of consciousness. Observing the hysterical twilight states of his patients, Freud realized that 'hysterics suffered mainly from reminiscences', an emotional and selective blocking of memory that prevented the affect from being discharged.[33] And so Freud abandoned neurophysiological explanation for disturbed psychological states in his belief that psychological repression of traumatic, sexual memories relating to childhood was the central terrain.

Freud's move away from neurophysiology and the trauma seduction theory, and towards his concepts of repressed childhood desire and fantasy, replaced initial ideas of disassociation with the more hierarchical notion of repression. Jung argued that repression was primarily disassociation (tracked through association tests), where painful complexes associated with feeling were forgotten. 'As you know, by "repression" we mean the mechanism by which a conscious content is displaced into a sphere outside consciousness. We call this sphere the unconscious, and we define it as a psychic element of which we are not conscious.'[34] Hysteria is not a suffering of reminiscences that lead back to the past, but a staged performance in the present that is in flight from present reality and takes refuge in neurotic infantile complexes. Jung says,

> The fright and the apparently traumatic effect of the childhood experience are merely staged, but staged in the peculiar way characteristic of hysteria, so that the mise en scene appears almost exactly like a reality. We know from hundreds of experiences that hysterical pains are staged in order to reap certain advantages from the environment. Nevertheless these pains are entirely real. The patients do not merely think they have pains; from the psychological point of view the pains are just as real as those due to organic causes, and yet they are stage managed.[35]

Hysteria is, then, a staging of affectual emotion – a *mise-en-scène* – rooted in a disassociation and splitting from reality. Repression is not an internal, hierarchical and intra-psychic split between the body and language, but fundamentally speaks to the phenomenological (intersubjective) relation (and splitting) between the self and the world. For Jung, it is not a return of the repressed from the past, but a regression of the libido to infantile states in the present. Jung did not privilege infantile sexuality. In his view there is no distinction between hunger and sexuality for the infant, and so-called 'sexuality' in the infant is in fact a dynamic unity of embodied and psychic energy.[36]

The Oedipal complex for the boy, and what Jung termed the Electra complex for the girl, is therefore a neurotic, heterosexual and infantile jealousy, which in optimum conditions is moved away from, as the child and young adult develops social objects outside the family. However, when things go wrong, when conflict arises (say a conflict between staying at home or going into the world), then the Oedipal complex (hitherto unconscious and inoperative) becomes reactivated, and libido is directed towards this complex – producing extreme feelings and fantasies. What is striking in Jung's account is that sexual difference is not the primary guarantor of loss; rather it becomes a hysterical retro-active defence against loss, a defence against leaving the family and entering a more social world.[37]

There are many similarities between Jung's phenomenological approach to psychoanalysis and Merleau-Ponty's theories of inter-subjective embodiment. Jung's concept of libido expands the concept of sexuality to encompass an embodied adaptation to the world where physical, psychological and spiritual aspects are connected. Disassociation of this libido from reality is also a repression. Writing about hysteria and obsessional neurosis Jung states, 'Abnormal displacements of libido, quite definitely sexual, do in fact play a great role in these illnesses. But although very characteristic repressions of sexual libido do take place in the neuroses, the loss of reality so typical of demential praecox never occurs.'[38] Following Jung, we can understand repression of the unconscious to mean disassociation. Hysteria is then a disassociation or splitting of the libido away from reality and the social, a staging of the body as theatrical presentation and sexual masquerade, which defensively masks and covers a psychic disembodiment of the self and a withdrawal from social reality. In this account hysteria stages the body to hide the lack of psychic embodiment.

I suggest that we can see this hysterical staging of the body as a masquerade of sexual difference in relation to early film. Foucault describes the way in which sexuality was deployed in the nineteenth century as a discipline of power attached to social and scientific control. Linda Williams documents how these discourses of sexuality as a 'frenzy of the visible' are also operative in early optical and pre-cinematic inventions such as the 'camera, magic lanterns, zoetropes, kinetographs and kinetoscopes'.[39] Early psychoanalysis and film apparatuses are both surveillance mechanisms and discourses that in the late nineteenth century align and produce sexuality in terms of 'Oedipal and familial norms'.[40] Muybridge's prehistoric cinema, his motion pictures of moving animals and humans, produced pleasure in the viewing audiences, as well as being part of scientific research. Williams notes how the women are fetishized in these moving pictures. Whereas the men require basic props to aid the progression of their physical movement, scientific knowledge and the narrative, the women's props are elaborate and do not even 'serve the activity illustrated'.[41] The women's bodies create a surplus meaning, an interactive, even emotional *mise-en-scène* that goes beyond the male activity sequences. Men doing and women appearing is thus a re-enactment of social mores of the time.

Muybridge's screens of animal and human locomotion suggest that the cinematic apparatus from its inception was a social apparatus that produced 'a new kind of body'; one which implanted the male Oedipal perversions of sexual difference, objectifying the woman and filming her hysterical masquerade as a *mise-en-scène*.[42] This staging of the hysteric through film brought together the neurological, surveillant gaze of science with a penetrative, pornographic desire. Both cinema and psychoanalysis are, according to Williams, 'historically determined and determining', and cinema both implanted and helped to normalize sexual perversions, making them into everyday technological and social ways of seeing.[43]

Muybridge's *Animal Locomotion* historically coincides with Charcot's neurological study and iconic photographing of hysterics at the Salpêtrière. Like *Animal Locomotion*, the *Iconographie photographique de la Salpêtrière* consists of photographs and images of the body in motion. Charcot's clinic develops Muybridge's photographic techniques to film the women convulsively writhing and moving in the grip of hysteria. In a similar manner to Charcot, Muybridge actually induced hysterical symptoms in his photographic models, making them hold a position until it induced hysterical convulsions. As Foucault notes, Charcot's clinic was a veritable 'machinery for incitement', staging and inducing hysterical attacks so they could be publicly exhibited and then cured by Charcot as a scientist cum stage magician.[44]

Lisa Cartwright's exploration of the neurological gaze in these early studies is interested in how organic symptoms and illnesses are always in excess, always in some sense subversive of the Oedipal narratives of surveillance that narrate them. She investigates two sets of films. First, some epilepsy studies produced in 1905 at a New York State public institution for epileptics, and, second, some films produced between 1919 and 1945 by neurophysiologists in New York, entitled a 'cinematographic atlas' of nervous diseases.

The epilepsy studies came about when William Spratling, in charge of an institution for epileptics, wrote to the Mutoscope and Biograph company in New York asking for help in filming his patients' seizures. Walter Chase was sent, and under Spratling's supervision filmed twenty epileptic seizures. The films were to aid prognosis and were part of the surveillant medical scientific machine at the turn of the century.[45] The filming of the epileptic seizures often meant that the seizures became induced. No difference was established then between physiological aetiology and imposed mechanical stimulus. Indeed, a researcher called Duchenne, who worked under Charcot, experimented with electro-currents applied to the faces of subjects, who were then photographed. First, he would get an actor to perform and mime facial expressions associated with emotions such as pain, happiness, etc., then he would apply electrical stimulus to the muscles of the patient's face until an identical expression was produced. As Cartwright surmises, Duchenne made his patients perform hysterically and unconsciously, mechanically inducing in them pathological expressions.[46]

Spratling and Chase were also obsessed with the difference between 'willed and involuntary, authentically pathological movement'; however, they were unable eventually to find the pathological cause simply through the camera's clinical observation of bodily expression.[47] Spratling announced that neither neurological autopsy nor cinematography could capture the aetiology behind epilepsy. He concluded that chemical analysis of blood, urine, sweat, etc. was the way forward. In a similar fashion to Charcot's photographed hysterics, the women in the epilepsy films were designated by Chase as hystero-epileptics. Cartwright shows how the biographs of these women were a mirror to both Charcot's hysterics and Muybridge's serial photographs of women's bodies, invested with the same hysterical excess of meaning, narrative causality and detailed *mise-en-scène*. The seizures of the epileptic women were more codified than the men's (the men's being more erratic), constructing a 'gestural language'. I want to suggest, then, that key to the neurological and cinematic gaze described here is the question of miming and mimesis. The hysterics of Muybridge's, Chase's and Charcot's proto-cinema, photography and film are miming, and this mimesis is induced in relation to a more powerful 'other' of knowledge that constructs them within a narrative of Oedipal sexual difference.

For Cartwright, the hysterical gestural language, particularly of the female patients, provokes the narrative *mise-en-scène*. But this hysterical and organic mimesis is not simply repressed through the surveillance of an institutional Oedipal other. Cartwright notes two instances where organic neurological illnesses are active in subverting the Oedipal narrative. One in relation to the epilepsy biographs is when a male patient recovers from his unconscious seizure and starts gesticulating to the camera; the second is in relation to a later cinematograph of encephalitis where a young woman has forcibly torn out her eyes and teeth because of her illness. Whereas the neurologists, in this latter example, make a link between Oedipal myths and sexual neurosis, Cartwright prefers the female patient's account (that the pain in her eyes was relieved by gouging them out), as an alternative reading of the text. She wonders about the horror and subsequent disavowal of the Oedipal doctors, who prize above everything else 'the knowledge and pleasure afforded by the eye'.[48]

Cartwright suggests that this female patient's self-enucleation mirrors the state of the postwar neurologist who has lost his control of the disciplinary gaze. We could equally see it as a mimesis, a copying of the desperate and ultimately frustrated attempts of the neurologists whose cinematic gaze fails to penetrate the meaning of organic illness. Early cinema as a scientific machine and gaze can be seen socially and technologically to have constructed and narrativized hysteria and organic illness, as Foucault notes, in relation to the Oedipal discourse and myth (the repressive hypothesis). However, this repressive Oedipal narrative of psychoanalysis and cinema can also be seen in terms of a mimesis of the body, a mimetic relation between the scientific camera/doctor and the hysteric, who returns the gaze through 'pathological' gestures of organic illness and embodiment.

Key points

- Jung sees hysteria as a staging of affectual emotion, a *mise-en-scène* rooted in a disassociation and splitting from reality.
- We can see this hysterical staging of the body as a masquerade of sexual difference in relation to early film.
- Muybridge's screens of animal and human locomotion suggest that the cinematic apparatus from its inception was a social apparatus that produced sexual difference.
- The early repressive discourse of cinema and psychoanalysis is also a mimesis of the body operating between scientific camera/doctor and hysteric.

Freud's cinematic analogy between body and psyche

Initially, Freud was educated as a neurologist through the German school of medicine, whose approach was one of theoretical explanation. However, influenced by Charcot, Freud became increasingly persuaded by the French school and its emphasis on detailed clinical observation. At the time, neuroscience saw organic disease related to localized lesions in the brain, diagnosed through autopsy. Charcot discovered, however, that unlike conditions such as epilepsy, hysteria revealed no sign of localized lesions in post-mortem autopsy. This led Freud's German teachers to give up on neurosis: no lesion meant no disease. This was not a problem for Charcot, who prioritized first and foremost the answers gained through the clinical picture, rather than explanations drawn from theories of anatomy and physiology. Under Charcot's tutelage, Freud turned away from theories of a localized trauma or lesion to the brain and became convinced that hysterical paralysis was due to a disturbance of the dynamic relationship between elements in the nervous system. Rather than psychology arising from a specific anatomical or physiological site, it was the result of a complex interplay within a *functional system* where the act of consciousness doubled as a bodily organ. Freud writes:

> We have several times heard from M. Charcot that it is a cortical lesion, but one that is purely dynamic or functional . . . the lesion in hysterical paralysis must be completely independent of the anatomy of the nervous system, since in its paralyses and other manifestations it behaves as though anatomy did not exist or as though it had no knowledge of it.[49]

Freud proposed instead that hysteria was the result of a psychological disturbance, a psychology that was correlated physiologically to associations between elements of the nervous system: 'The lesion in hysterical paralyses consists in nothing other than the inaccessibility of the (paralysed) organ or function concerned to the associations of the conscious ego; . . . (a) purely functional alteration.'[50]

Mark Solmes describes how Freud's abandonment of neurophysiology and his new focus solely on psychology was because he understood that localized mental functions were an inadequate explanation; the dynamic mental process at stake could not, at the time, be explained through neurophysiology. Freud's findings at this time were based on his research into the neurological condition of aphasia, not hysteria (he was then working as a neurologist). Freud's break, therefore, was not with neurophysiology *per se*, but with a localizationist tradition. Because the dynamic interplay between consciousness and physiology could not be explained at the time, Freud abandoned neurophysiology for psychology. Still believing in the correlation between psychology and physiology as a complex dynamic system, an analogical relation between the psyche and the bodily organ, Freud rejected the localizationism of classical German neurology. Interestingly, the passage in *The Interpretation of Dreams* where he announces the split between neurophysiology and psychoanalysis uses the image of the microscope and the camera. Freud ties together the psychic apparatus with the camera, but he also uses the metaphor of the microscope, an apparatus for examining the physiological body and organic tissues.

What is presented to us in these words is the idea of a psychical locality. I shall entirely disregard the fact that the mental apparatus with
which we are concerned is also known to us in the form of an anatomical preparation, and I shall entirely carefully avoid the temptation to
determine psychical locality in an anatomical fashion. I shall remain
upon psychological ground, and I propose simply to follow the suggestion that we should picture the instrument which carries out our
mental functions as resembling a compound microscope or a photographic apparatus, or something of that kind. On that basis, psychical locality will correspond to a point inside the apparatus at which
one of the preliminary stages of an image comes into being. In the
microscope and the telescope, we know, these occur in parts at ideal
points, regions in which no tangible component to the apparatus is
situated.[51]

No tangible relation between psychological perception and the
anatomy. No localized traumatic lesion, but an analogy between body
and psyche that is captured for Freud, by the camera . . . or the microscope. Baudry takes the above passage to align the psychic and cinematic apparatus as one of perspectival and pictorial representation
that can be traced back to Plato: the Oedipal gaze. Within this cinematic and psychic apparatus the subject is apprehended as a passive
subject. But, as Cartwright suggests, Freud's passage also flags up the
microscope, an apparatus which denotes a much less passive spectator, a spectator who is involved with a much 'less secure relation to
visual knowledge'.[52]

Freud's insight into the resemblance between psychic apparatus,
camera and microscope is precisely that the images they produce
cannot be fixed or located within one part of the anatomy. He real-
izes that the organic body is not a passive entity that can simply be
controlled through a locationalist, neurological gaze. Instead, a
dynamic relation exists between the physiological body and psychic
apparatus, a system that is analogical and fluid. One does not simply
act upon or determine the other; body and psyche, psyche and body
exist in an analogical relation to one another. Viewed as such, the
organic body is never completely passive or controlled by the cinematic gaze because it shares a mimetic relationship with the surveillant, scientific cinematographer. We can then argue with Foucault and
Williams that psychoanalysis and the cinema are socially constructed
discourses that produce power, knowledge and pleasure, but we can
also propose that these discourses are mimetically situated in an
embodied and dis-embodied relationship with one another.

This discussion links a scientific and cinematic gaze to a theory of
mimesis and hysteria, which in turn joins Freud's and Jung's work in

a re-reading of psychoanalysis as a phenomenological and social narrative – a narrative in which the psyche and the organic body are found in analogical motion and disassociation from each other. The cinema is historically intrinsic to this understanding of psychoanalysis in a phenomenological vein because it has historically been part of the social and scientific technology, the mimetic machine which has both produced and patrolled the hysteric. Moreover, this cinematic and mimetic machine as an Oedipal and social narrative reproduces the hysteric as other. This disembodied and disassociated other performs within the dominant imaginary as an identification which returns (like Homi Bhabha's concept of mimicry) to violently disturb and destabilize the surveillant, scientific gaze.

In Borch-Jacobsen's view hysterical mimesis lies not just at the heart of Freud's Oedipal narrative, but also exists as the central linchpin on which the relationship between Freud and Jung (and their conflictual theories) turns. Hysterical, mimetic and rivalrous identification is not prior to Oedipal desire, it *is* Oedipal desire. This hysterical, Oedipal same-sex love is at work between Freud and Jung in their rivalrous and loving relationship and correspondence, the letters that precede the famous split and parting of ways, leaving Freud as sole heir to the kingdom of psychoanalysis and Jung ousted to develop his Zurich school. As Borch-Jacobsen tells it, the correspondence between Jung and Freud involves a mimesis and exchange of ideas where each lays claim to the thoughts of the other, until no discernible difference remains.

If we return to Freud's early theories on hysteria we can see that in fact Freud agreed with Charcot, Breuer and Jung that the unconscious was a result of disassociation. Hysteria can then be summed up as a mimetic identification and disassociation that moves between ego and other: an imaginary and Oedipal identification that represses and disassociates libidinal and psychic energy. This repression or disassociation is not rooted in the past, for, as Jung states, the past is invoked as a flight from the present. Instead, it is staged as a performance and filmic *mise-en-scène* that enacts a disturbance in our phenomenological and embodied relation to the world, a disassociation in our dynamic systems, that culminates in the splitting off of mental processes from the body.

Conclusion

The hysteric and the cinema can be seen as mimetic and cultural machines, mobilizing a transference between ego and other, spectator and film text. Such a hypnotic trance cannot be reduced to language and representation, for it is not *any* language that cures the hysteric, but one in which the affect is dramatized as a *mise-en-scène*, a theatre in which hysteric and analyst, hysteric and camera apparatus are all caught up. This, then, changes the way we read the film camera; we can no longer perceive it as a textual apparatus that positions the spectator passively, any more than we can understand the Oedipal gaze of that camera apparatus to be a symbolic narrative which represses the body. For this is perhaps the ultimate myth of Freudian and Lacanian discourse, that the Oedipal is a reflexive sublimation of the hysteric's mimetic rivalry, within language and culture.

In actuality, there is no difference between the hysteric and the Oedipal; the Oedipal is hysterical rivalry par excellence, and the mimesis between them is an affectual play that is certainly communicated through language and representation, but is not cured or resolved through representation and the linguistic symbolic as Freud and Lacan seem to think. The hysteric's mimesis/transference is not resolved through representation; the hysteric does not stage herself, as Lacan thought, in order to narrate herself for the other. For the hysteric lacks access to this dream of secondary representation; she stages herself and acts not in order to enter representation and narrative but because there is no distance; she mimes and feels and exists as the other.[53] The hysteric's mime is a bodily and disembodied mimesis that exists, as Freud insists, in dynamic systemic relation between the body and psyche. This hysterical analogy also sums up the structural miming relation between psychoanalysis and cinema and between perception and modernity. This is not, after all, an argument for the structural, causal effect of modernity on the hardwiring of our perceptual systems, but an account of the psychic, social and physiological mimesis operating between spectator, cinema and society.

5

Early Film Spectatorship

Introduction

The previous chapter explored accounts of perception and early film technologies in the nineteenth century. This chapter develops an argument for the hysterical mimesis of early film spectatorship in relation to a phenomenological perception of the image. One of the key themes of this chapter is that early film cannot be seen as some kind of primitive, pre-Oedipal bodily cinema that later develops into Oedipal classical, narrative cinema. Cinema is melodramatically and hysterically Oedipal from its beginnings; the more hysterical its mimesis, the more disembodied spectatorship becomes. The origins of film and psychoanalysis occur together, and that makes their relationship interesting. Significantly, both film and psychoanalysis emerge from political and social changes associated with modernism. Charles Musser charts how film and cinema must be situated in a tradition of screen practice leading back to technological inventions such as the magic lantern, although he notes it is not in itself the technological invention of early film or the magic lantern, but the cultural practices associated with it. The emergence of capitalism and the progress in scientific reason and technology were accompanied by a demystification of the screen. In place of mystical terrors associated with ghosts and witch-burning came the 'logic of a projecting apparatus' that established a relationship between spectator and film image, between narrative and image, between theatre and the screen, that has, in Musser's view, been in existence, within screen entertainment, ever since.[1]

Freud, far from inventing the unconscious, sought to rationalize and demystify it. Philosophers such as Goethe and Schiller and the Romantic poets had all acknowledged the roots of poetic creation in the unconscious. Henry James, a contemporary of Freud, linked the unconscious with dreams and sleep.[2] It was, however, in Freud's attempt to place psychoanalysis on a scientific footing, to rationalize it, that we can see both psychoanalysis and early cinema as screen practices. As the previous chapter illustrated, the establishment of early cinema, scientific knowledge and psychoanalysis went hand in hand. Freud's move from a phenomenological tracking of the hysteric to the Oedipal moment in *The Interpretation of Dreams* where, using the image of the camera, he announces the split between neurophysiology and psychoanalysis is the beginning of his conceptualization of psychoanalysis as a meta-psychology, a depth model of reason and unreason which Oedipally divides the internal mind from the external body, the psyche from the social.[3]

The Interpretation of Dreams (1901) is not just the Oedipal beginnings of psychoanalysis; it is also an account of Freud's analysis of his own hysteria, written as Freud's melancholic difficulty in resolving the mourning and loss of his father. As Peter Gay notes, references to Rome are littered throughout *The Interpretation of Dreams*. Freud's desire to conquer Rome in the shape of the Oedipal and Semitic hero Hannibal symbolizes Freud's neurotic desire to master and triumph against (where his father had failed) a history of Jewish anti-Semitism. Phenomenologically, we can see Freud's dream book as his Oedipal attempt to master not just the unconscious, but also time and history.

A phenomenological account of hysteria and the unconscious is not pre-Oedipal, but deeply Oedipal in its mimetic and melodramatic fetishization and mastery of time and history. Quarrelling with Jung over the status of the unconscious, Freud wanted Jung to adhere to his meta-psychological theory of the unconscious, whereas Jung kept describing a phenomenological unconscious of surface effects.[4] This phenomenological account of the unconscious describes the articulation of the subject within time and history and, instead of distancing Freud and Marx as oppositional theories of mental and material existence, brings them together, perhaps most powerfully in the phenomenological film theories of the optical unconscious articulated by Walter Benjamin and Siegfried Kracauer. Early film is significant because it can help us to understand this optical and surface unconscious.

Cinema of attractions as narrative or image

Although early film has been documented in relation to nineteenth-century cultural practices of spectacle, melodrama, theatre and vaudeville, there has been a tendency to pre-Oedipalize it and to see it as primitive cinema coming before the institutionalization of realist classical film narrative.[5] This emphasis on realist narrative as the destiny of cinema not only ignores the way theatrical forms in film have persisted, but it also positions melodrama as a bodily excess of display and attractions which is repressed as an excess to the text. As Tom Gunning has documented, early cinema and the history of cinema generally have been written about and theorized under an Oedipal 'hegemony of narrative films'. For him, the early voyeurism of film was less to do with narrative and much more bound up with film as exhibition and display. Rooted in vaudeville and theatrical magic, primitive cinema can be seen as a 'cinema of attractions'. Tom Gunning's work on a 'cinema of attractions' is one area where perception and sensual psychology of the viewing spectator has been investigated. Gunning argues that instead of seeing early film-makers such as Lumière and Méliès as an opposition between narrative and non-narrative films, they should both be seen as 'presenting a series of views to an audience, fascinating because of their illusory power'.[6] Now, whether that illusion turns out to be a realist one of movement (Lumière) or a magical illusion (Méliès), this cinema of attractions is not a primitive phase of cinema that then gives way to a developed, later and more dominant form of narrative cinema. Rather, the cinema of attractions is a specific 'exibitionist cinema' linked to vaudeville shows, circuses, fairgrounds and the emergence of amusement parks at the beginning of the twentieth century.

As such, early cinema is not a primitive form of pre-Oedipal and rather vulgar experience that develops into more narrative Oedipal fictions. Instead, it is a form of cinema that privileges the perception and sensual psychology of the spectator. This cinema of attractions creates a different relation or contact with the spectator distinct from the later integration of the spectator with narrative classical forms. In the cinema of attractions there are repeated looks between actors and camera; 'from comedians smirking at the camera, to the constant bowing and gesturing of the conjurors in magic films, this is cinema that displays its visibility, willing to rupture a self-enclosed fictional world for a chance to solicit the attention of the spectator'.[7] Coining the term 'cinema of attractions' from Sergei Mikhailovich Eisenstein's film work on montage, Gunning cites Eisenstein in explaining how an attraction aggressively subjected the spectator to 'sensual and psychological impact'.[8]

For Gunning, the narrativization or indeed Oedipalization of film occurred between 1907 and 1913. Gunning's work on the famous early film director D.W. Griffith explores how Griffith's first Biograph films (from 1908 and 1909) represented a kind of transitional and transformative stage, coming after an early film or cinema of attractions, but before the classical narrative integration of the spectator.[9] The narrative argument that Gunning utilizes in his historical analysis of Griffith's films is informed by a tradition of literary structuralist theory. Gunning emphasizes how Griffith is renowned for transforming film into a medium which tells stories. Griffith was central in helping to move film away from a cinema of attractions, a display and presentation of spectacle, to a cinema of narrative integration where the film form and the spectator were subordinated to a linear development of story and character.

Gunning describes how film translates an excess of realism or the showing (in film), into a telling and narrative sense meaning: 'Film's innate tendency towards mimesis becomes a sign of narrative realism, naturalizing the process of storytelling as the inclusion of apparently useless detail does in verbal narrative.'[10] I want to stop Gunning's argument here and discuss why we have always understood film and its mimetic telling in narrative terms. Historically this has been the case, with the kind of structuralist discourse that Gunning uses making way for the post-structuralist, semiotic film theories of Heath and Metz. I aim to discuss another way of talking about narrative that does not distinguish between Gunning's understanding of an early cinema of attractions and a later classical institutionalization of the cinema where the spectator is integrated within the narrative system.

Gunning shows how Griffith's first Biograph films marked a transitional point in film-making in terms of developing a narrator system of storytelling. I shall return to Griffith's films later in this chapter, but for now I just want to make the point that my argument for a dis/embodied imaginary does not contradict arguments for a narrative turn in cinema, neither is it to be associated with notions of a pre-Oedipal primitive cinema. Rather, just as Oedipal theory in psychoanalysis represses Freud's earlier phenomenological account of the disassociated hysteric, so a narrative hegemony in film theory represses the hysterical mimesis and phenomenological apprehension of the film image. This mimesis both figures a splitting of the body within discourses of modernity, film and psychoanalysis, and reconfigures that split in a more embodied reading of film and history.

We can see the film text, then, as a mimesis of the body. Although Gunning does make a distinction between an early cinema of attractions and a later narrative mode of address, he also argues that after early film these two modes of address continue in a dialectical relationship with each other. Rather than seeing these two modes of address structured in terms of a return of the repressed, I suggest that they be seen in terms of a phenomenological splitting and reconfiguration of the body. Ben Brewster's and Lea Jacob's study on the progression of a theatrical tradition within cinema points to an alternative to the dominant history of film editing, describing a staged pictorialism in relation to dramatic situation. The pictorial 'situation' or 'tableau' is a persistent feature of film around 1910, but according to Brewster and Jacob it seems to disappear after 1917, with the advent of classical Hollywood cinema. What is striking about this argument is how it cuts across the distinction between a cinema of attractions and narrative cinema. For Brewster and Jacob, the cinema of attractions is a type of exhibition appropriate to both narrative and non-narrative films. Likewise, the pictorial tradition influences the rise of the feature film and is not identical with narrative but is seen as 'one of its modes'.[11]

Key points

- Early cinema, a 'cinema of attractions', is not a primitive form of pre-Oedipal experience that becomes developed into more narrative Oedipal fictions. It is a form of cinema that privileges the perception and sensual psychology of the spectator.
- A cinema of attractions and later narrative cinema can be seen to operate dialectically rather than developmentally.

Psychoanalysis and film as hysterical identification and bodily mimesis

An early cinema of attractions and a later more integrated narrative film can both be mapped in terms of a phenomenological imaginary, an imaginary that Walter Benjamin and Siegfried Kracauer entitle 'the optical unconscious'. The address of this optical unconscious to the spectator is not just understood in terms of a split and reconfigured body; it can also be conceptualized as the splitting and reconfiguration of time. Freud's hysterical dilemma in writing *The Interpretation of Dreams* was his melancholic disarticulation from time and history.

This dilemma was his melancholic mourning of his father, but also his need to conquer and master that history, triumphantly and Oedipally – taking his father's place. Freud's argument for a repressed unconscious in *The Interpretation of Dreams* designates the unconscious as disguised wishes and desires that we cannot know. But as Peter Gay discusses, it is Freud's own unacknowledged desire that is at stake in this book. When Abraham asks Freud directly why he failed to finish his interpretation of Irma's dream, Freud declares that his own sexual megalomania is concealed in it. The three women in the dream, Mathilde, Sophie and Anna are, according to Freud, 'the three godmothers of my daughters, and I have them all!'[12] Freud is reticent in revealing his autobiographical desires. Although he promises revisions to the text, he states, 'The Reader, does not deserve to have me undress myself in front of him even more'.[13] Freud designates femininity and dreams as hieroglyphic scripts, but it is also fair to say that Freud's hysterical, Oedipal *Interpretation of Dreams* also functions as a hieroglyphic text. This disembodied narrative aims to fetishize and master time and history. The unconscious for Freud is unknowable and timeless, but it is precisely this unknowability of his own bodily desires to triumph over his father's history and his secretive sexual ownership of the women in Irma's dream that allows them such full rein in fantasy. If the origins of psychoanalysis are so surrounded by this need to occupy such a transcendental position in relation to time, then what of film?

This hysterical imaginary as a fetishization of history, illustrated by Freud's autobiographical dream text, can also situated in relation to modernism and early film. The spectator is understood, here, to identify in terms of mimesis and a psychological apprehension of the aesthetic film image. This mimesis is associated with the film theories of Walter Benjamin, Siegfried Kracauer, Béla Balázs and André Bazin. Balázs's aesthetic theory of film anticipates, as Getrud Koch demonstrates, the phenomenological film theory of both Benjamin and Kracauer. A student of Simmel, Balázs developed an expressive theory of film, counteracting any notion of a 'naturalistic' filmic image. Balázs mapped a physiognomic film aesthetics, reflecting the mimetic play of objects in everyday life, between subjective and objective, animate and inanimate forms of nature. Balázs thought that film gives visual shape to a physiognomy in human beings, revealing the poetic mimesis of a world of objects, capturing the human face of capitalism, as the landscape of objective reality becomes mimetically replayed through the landscape of the human body and face. Although Balázs focuses most frequently on filmic characters in terms of their micro-physiognomic properties, his phenomenological argument directly links this mimicry or mimesis to a wider landscape of nature. In doing this, Balázs is indebted to a tradition of German ide-alist aesthetics and a debate on 'the beauty of nature', where the land-scape and nature return the human glance.[14] Film and the director have to find, through close-ups, the human eye in a wider landscape.

This is a romantic notion, traced directly through Simmel's writ-ings and Benjamin's, where the mediated technology of modernity, the cinematic apparatus, can provide the illusion of exploring unmediated reality: the world as an emotional poetics of animistic nature. There is, nevertheless a psychological embodiment to Balázs's ideas that situates the beauty and the horrors of nature in mimetic relation to the human body and face. For Balázs, we psychologically identify with both the world and the characters of film, 'we walk amid crowds, ride, fly or fall with the hero'.[15] Our gaze is identical with both the camera and the characters. But, and this is what dis-tinguishes Balázs's theory from more structural and linguistic accounts (although he acknowledges that films take us up through an identificatory mimesis into their world), he is not postulating a struc-turalist account of film as a verbal language. For Balázs, the phys-iognomic expression of cinema means that identification is not structured through the linguistic sign, but through a bodily mimesis. In a section entitled 'Tempo of Mimicry', Balázs argues for 'the mute soliloquies of physiognomy, the wordless lyrics of facial expression'. Gestures communicate through the medium of film what other arts cannot. Facial expression or the twitch of a facial muscle can convey emotions which language simply fails to encapsulate. He gives as an example the performance of Lillian Gish in an unnamed Griffith's film, where Gish, a naïve and innocent girl, is confronted by her sneering, corrupt seducer, and the knowledge of her ruin at his decep-tion. As Gish alternately laughs and weeps in hysterical and word-less mimicry, this 'two-minute dumb show, which one could see in close-up', becomes for Balázs 'one of the great artistic achievements of "micro-physiognomics"'.[16] Such bodily mimesis conveys the com-plexity of emotion far more than the spoken word and is evidence, in Balázs's mind, for the superiority of silent film over sound.

Balázs is talking about a mimetic identification with the facial close-up, a mimesis that Merleau-Ponty would call a gestural lan-guage. But this mimetic identification is bodily and experiential, rolling not just between self and other, but between self and the exter-nal world. Thus, it is very different from the Lacanian and Oedipal forms of linguistic identification that have been utilized in film theory, for example in relation to stars, where identification is viewed as either adherence to dominant, ideological 'reality', or in Dyer's reformulation as an alternative counter-representation.[17] In Balázs's account, identification is more embodied and more mobile (between psyche and social) and cannot be limited to debates on textual identification.[18] Balázs's ideas of a phenomenological and experiential mimesis are very similar to Walter Benjamin's and inform Benjamin's thinking in relation to the bodily image-space or 'profane illumination'.

Film spectatorship as distracted mimesis

Walter Benjamin and Siegfried Kracauer have both argued for film spectatorship as distracted mimesis. Whereas art has traditionally been allied with what Benjamin calls an aura of uniqueness, and with cultural authority, the onset of mass technological reproduction in the modernist moment destroys that sense of authentic aura. In his famous artwork essay 'The Work of Art in the Age of Mechanical Reproduction', Benjamin describes how the traditional mode of experience becomes transformed through cinema into more secularized and popular forms.

As I have discussed, Benjamin's conception of re-reading and transforming the aura is tied to the idea of the mimetic faculty of language. Although for Benjamin the mimetic aspect of language is closely tied to the semiotic, it is distinguished by its bodily and physiognomic properties. In the artwork essay, mimesis is likened to a 'sense of sameness' and the masses and placed in opposition to the aura. However, in 'Image of Proust' and 'On Some Motifs in Baudelaire', Benjamin discusses how the unconscious and negative process of mimetic similarity (not sameness) mobilizes the aura, rather than remaining antithetical to it.[19] Benjamin explores Proust's ideas on unconscious similarity and dream states, especially his story of the *mémoire involontaire*. This is where Proust's eating of a madeleine cake arouses a sensation which transports him back to the past, bringing to mind vivid images that were hitherto obscure and shadowy.[20] Benjamin discusses how this involuntary distracted memory is different to the conscious attention that remembers fixed narratives. Beyond the grasp of the intellect, this mimetic memory of unconscious experience is located, not in the mind, but in material objects that we arbitrarily encounter in our everyday life. Benjamin goes on to link this discussion with Freud's essay 'Beyond the Pleasure Principle', where Freud observes that memory elements remain more powerful when the event that triggered them did not actually enter consciousness. Benjamin remarks, 'Put in Proustian terms, this means that only what has not been experienced explicitly and consciously, what has not happened to the subject as an experience, can become a component of the *mémoire involontaire*.'[21]

Benjamin then distinguishes between a conscious, cognitive mimetic process of film technology where overstimulus to the spectator's sensory world culminates in a shock effect, psychically defending the person from further intrusion. But he also delineates a more unconscious distracted mimesis, the involuntary 'optical unconscious' where the camera creatively transforms dream images into dialectically recognizable historical images.

Siegfried Kracauer also identifies film spectatorship as distracted mimesis. The intersubjective and phenomenological film experience awarded to the spectator, in Kracauer's thinking, subverts the realist proposition that film can be passively apprehended as an objective reality that reflects the world. Kracauer's *Theory of Film* outlines a psycho-physiological perception where film images are apprehended first and foremost through bodily sensation. This sensual reaction of the spectator to the filmic image mimics the reaction of the subject to the material aspects of nature. Film therefore renders the world – and with it the spectator – in constant motion, where 'movement is the alpha and omega of the medium'. Perception of film's movement stimulates a physiological and 'kinesthetic response' in the spectator's muscle reflexes and motor impulses.[22]

Like Benjamin's 'optical unconscious' and Balázs's physiognomy of expression, Kracauer frames a spectator who moves toward the film and mimetically identifies in a limitless journey with filmic and cultural objects that are intersubjectively apprehended. Hansen describes Kracauer's optical unconscious as revealing film's much darker and more haunting dream qualities. Rather than redemption, Kracauer's distracted camera reveals the hysterical alienation of capitalism. Film becomes historical, for Kracauer, not through transforming the aura, but through its negativity. He explains this, in relation to an early essay entitled 'Photography', with reference to two photographs.[23] Comparing a photograph of a film star with that of a grandmother when she was twenty-four, Kracauer suggests that the first image of a 'demonic diva' represses history and society's fear of death, presenting us with an immediate, timeless reality. With the second image, however, there is a discrepancy between the photo of the grandmother and the memory image. The memory image for those that knew her embodies and revises the photograph, but for younger generations the old photograph of the grandmother makes them 'shudder', for it reveals not the identity of the grandmother but an arbitrary spatial configuration of a moment, which means nothing.

This negative role of the camera is 'the go-for-broke game of history' where the photograph confronts and deconstructs the memory image, revealing a void, 'nature devoid of meaning'.[24] And it is this void, the impossibility of a photograph's recapturing or representing the significance of either individuals or history that provides recognition of alienation.

This hysterical alienation of the camera is also its role in materializing and contextualizing history. For Kracauer, like Balázs, it is the mimesis and montage principle of the shot and the close-up that reveals this material contingency, and its space or distance from discourse and narrative. Miriam Hansen notes how, unlike Eisenstein, Kracauer does not locate montage with the compositional narrative effect of the shot but with its decomposition:

> The difference that erupts within the image is not one between minimal units within an oppositional system of signs (the realm of semiotics) but one between discourse and the realm of material contingency, between the implied horizons of our 'habits of seeing', structured by language, narrative identification and intentionality, and that which perpetually eludes and confounds such structuring.[25]

As Hansen explains, the 'fissure' or gap that arises in the filmic image points to an account of the 'subject' and film spectatorship which is not premissed on semiotics. For Kracauer and Benjamin, the distracted camera explores a more bodily mimesis. If Benjamin's thesis is a resolutely utopian and abstract vision, then Kracauer's is actually more grounded in the reality of a historical moment of modernism. The camera's hysterical freezing of time is, for Kracauer, a confrontation with our unknowingness, our need to master history – because we can't acknowledge time's passage – or the fantasy nature of our omnipotent desires.

Whereas Oedipal narrative film theory announces the abject real as eternally divided from language and therefore outside historical meaning, Kracauer reverses these terms. By arguing that it is precisely the abject nature of the real that makes film and history meaningful, Kracauer focuses on how the filmic camera reveals the ideological narrative memory at stake (within capitalist history, and film theory) through the alienated material surface phenomena of everyday life: the horror and the death that seem to become the necessary structural base for the onward progress of modernity. Bringing 'us face to face with the things we dread', cinema is a medusa's head. But these horrors are not integrated into meaning or narrative. As a mimetic mirror of the physical layer that underlies discursive intelligence, these filmic images of horror summon the spectator, thus incorporating into his memory 'the real face of things too dreadful to be beheld in reality'.[26]

And so, Hansen reminds us, Kracauer remains opposed to narrative film theory because, predicated as it is on drama and the novel, the narrative film evokes a development of these literary forms which is a ' "mental" – emotional, intellectual, discursive-continuum rather than a material one'. Having said this, Kracauer does not reject narrative in film; he is quite aware of the need for storytelling in the organization of space, time and the development of subjectivity and action, but for him, ultimately, the fragmentary images of the everyday such as a street or face, 'open up a dimension much wider than that of the plots which they sustain'.[27]

Balázs, Benjamin and Kracauer can all be linked in terms of an argument for a phenomenological imaginary, which moves between text and film spectator. In a traditional Oedipal account of hysteria the hysteric is repressed as a crisis of sexuality under a linguistic and phallic sign of dominant history. However, in terms of phenomenological bodily imaginary, the hysteric is understood in terms of a crisis of embodied being, and it is this disassociation and alienation from the body which also alienates the subject or spectator from participation within a wider world of social history. The imaginary world of film can, according to Kracauer, help us to confront the physical nightmares of modernity. For Kracauer, the mimetic death drive of the hysteric might be the repressed underbelly of narrative meaning and modernity, but recognition of such violence cannot be achieved through fetishistic Oedipal plots that merely repress and repeat the deathly horror at bay. Rather, as Kracauer notes, the camera can bring us 'face to face' with history as our death drives, thus incorporating the response(ibility) of this 'face to face' image within memory.

Key points

- Balázs argues for a physiognomic expression of cinema as a bodily mimesis.
- Benjamin shows how film as distracted mimesis can transform the dead aura of tradition and history.
- Kracauer's distracted mimesis provides us with recognition of our alienation.

Intolerance and hysterical mimesis

I want to ground my argument for a phenomenological imaginary and mimesis of the filmic image through a re-reading of Griffith's film *Intolerance*. Although I cannot do justice to Miriam Hansen's brilliant reading of *Intolerance*, in taking up certain points in her reading I develop them into a gestural narrative which foregrounds a phenomenological mimesis of the filmic image, rather than a textual account of filmic representation.[28]

Intolerance is a hysterical film portraying a conflict between textual and extra-textual effects. Hansen cites Phillip Rosen as remarking, 'The classical cinema has a genius father (Griffith), a first born (*Birth of a Nation*) and a magnificent freak (*Intolerance*).'[29] So, we can read *Intolerance* as an Oedipal narrative, which is rendered out of control through an invasion of affectual bodily symptoms. In my reading of the Oedipal, the body is split from language with the hysteric manifesting as an extreme symptom of this bodily alienation.[30] 'Her' bodily performance masquerades to cover a lack of embodiment: an outpouring of affect which represents the crisis of disembodiment and the accompanying split between an idealized, symbolic representation which transcends history and the body and an abject real, mimetically returned as the death drive. This film, as Rosen remarks, represents a 'transhistorical transcendence for the spectator; preserving a timeless sense of mastery and control over temporality'.[31] If in apparatus, Oedipal film theory, there is a textual split between language and the body, and the spectator remains ideologically subsumed under a dominant and linear textual trajectory, then within *Intolerance* the splitting of the Oedipal hysteric becomes active and uncontained.

As Miriam Hansen describes, *Intolerance* is split; it is a film pulled in opposing directions. On one hand is the development of a classical style, already demonstrated by Griffith, in *Birth of a Nation*. Narrative integration of the spectator within this linear and classical plot relies on the structural absence of the viewer subsumed psychologically within a diegetic effect: the continuity and presence that maintains the viewer's belief in the truth of the film's fiction. However, on the other hand it is Griffith's use of parallel montage that undermines this diegetic effect. *Intolerance* is a film made up of four different historical and geographical stories that are meant to represent how 'intolerance' passes down through the ages. The Babylon narrative tells of the fall of Babylon (in 538 BC) to Cyrus. The Judean narrative is set around the life of Christ. The French narrative portrays the destruction of a Huguenot family during the St Bartholemew's Day massacre (1572), and the modern-day narrative is a tale of a young working-class couple who struggle against the inhumanities of bourgeois capitalist labour, hypocritical liberal reformers and the law. Of these narratives it is mainly the Babylonian and modern-day narratives that are focused on and juxtaposed. These stories are edited through a combination of accelerated and parallel montage, cutting quickly between scenes within one historical narrative and then moving across to another historical narrative.

Parallel montage is accompanied by, as Hansen notes, a 'whole arsenal of meta-fictional discourse' in the form of inter-titles, prologues, title cards, archetypes and hieroglyphic symbols and characters. The title card of the 'Book of Intolerance', and 'The Woman Who Rocks the Cradle' are symbolic shots that occur repeatedly through the film, representing the archetypal Oedipal conflict of the mother versus the law.[32] Symbolic inter-texts create a metaphysical meaning to the film which is supposed to connect thematically the disparate historical narratives, but actually serves to expel the spectator from the textual diegesis. In response to reviewers' criticisms of the film's incoherence, Griffith claimed that the film aesthetics constructed the filmic images and events less as historical, linear sequence, but 'as they might flash across a mind seeking to parallel the life of the different ages'.[33] Griffith views the film, then, as a form of imaginal dreaming, rather than linear narrative and plot.

The critic Vachel Lindsay linked Griffith's explanation to Hugo Munsterberg's *Psychology of the Photoplay*, published shortly before the film's release. Hansen discusses how this analogy between *Intolerance* and the *Psychology of the Photoplay* ignores the main thrust of Munsterberg's book, based in neo-Kantian aesthetics and consistent with the classical film paradigm of unitary plot and composition. Although this is true, Munsterberg's text is, as Hansen herself acknowledges, contradictory, including a whole section on the experiences of the spectator in terms of emotion, memory and imagination. If the embodied psychological spectator returns to disturb the unity of the classical film paradigm in Munsterberg's study, similarly within *Intolerance* the hysterical body returns to disturb the Oedipal textual composition of the narrative in more ways than one. First is the way *Intolerance* moves the spectator outside the linear plot of classical narrative spectatorship through its metonymy of archetypal symbols. Second is the way that Griffith's so-called pacifist manifesto of history is continually collapsing into an abject violence of the real. This is a redemptive script, a critique of man's corrupt greed and inhumanity (the corrupt greed of the priest of Babylon, or the capitalist factory owner in the modern narrative). Transcendence through the eternal symbol of the sacrificial (virgin) mother, repeatedly falls back into its opposite, an abject, perverse female sexuality.

Hansen reads this perverse female sexuality in *Intolerance* in terms of a Freudian story and gaze of sexual difference, fetishism and scopophilia. Characters such as the 'Friendless One', 'the Uplifters' and 'Catherine de Medici' act as hysterical and out-of-control figures – a return of the repressed destabilizing the film's textual system. These perverse figures of femininity can also be read, however, as a narrative of hysteria which grounds *Intolerance* simultaneously as a disembodied, mimetic phenomenology of the filmic image, modernism and history. Although Hansen links excessive femininity to figurations of writing in *Intolerance*, I want to focus on them in terms of a phenomenology and physiognomy of the image. As Hansen shows, perverse femininity is linked to allegorical modes that form a spectatorial address, contradicting the film's narrative diegesis. Examples of this are the emblem of the 'Woman Who Rocks the Cradle' or the shocked, distorted reflection of Miss Jenkins in the mirror. Miss Jenkins' hideous grimace is a pantomime act emblematic of the metaphysical parallelism of the film but also reminiscent of Gunning's early 'cinema of attractions'.

This display and melodramatic spectacle interact in a bodily mimesis with the audience. For Hansen, these emblematic figures trouble and freeze narrative space. The close-up of the horrified reflection of Miss Jenkins' face in the mirror is, as Hansen states, an over-determined allegory of youth and love versus single, ugly, old spinsterhood. Nevertheless, this image can also be read in relation to Balázs's and Benjamin's ideas of a physiognomic and phenomenological apprehension of the object, or image, where nature mimetically returns the gaze. For Benjamin, the allegorical gaze critically re-reads symbolic, allegorical modes of timeless history, actualizing the unconscious, dissolving and reconfiguring the dreaming collective of history. Within *Intolerance* the critical allegorical gaze is not so much a redemptive reading of history (redemption is the timeless mode within this film), as a hysterical bodily address, confronting the spectator with the alienation of the senses under modernity.

Hysteria, distraction and shock

Just as Miss Jenkins' pantomimed look is associated with the attractions and distractions of early cinema's address, so we can link Miss

Jenkins' horrified grimace at her reflection to Kracauer's and Benjamin's notion of the dialectical ambiguity of film's shock and distraction. Shock, for Benjamin, was linked to the sensory technological impingement of modern life. Film was a shock that defended the spectator, like a protective shield, from the hyper-stimulus of technological modernity. Where film was not operating as a protective shield from the stimulations of modern life, it could be seen simply as a numbed reaction to sensation, mirroring the kind of deadened response of the masses to their capitalist exploitation. Miss Jenkins is the unmarried and moneyed sister of the capitalist factory owner. She is 'the catalyst' for the three witch-like Uplifters or reformers, who set about impinging upon the lives of common people, i.e., the Dear One and her family. Miss Jenkins then functions as the hysterical and domestic caricature of her more Oedipally situated capitalist brother.

Miss Jenkins is the hysterical personification of the deathly abject real, a mimesis of a capitalist world of modernity where the body is alienated and disassociated. In distinction to Freud's death drive, this mimesis is not rescued through Oedipal identifications with the social. Rather, this hysterical mimesis is a reflection of the death face of capitalism. Kracauer saw the shock of film in terms of its thrills and excitement – as nearer to the masochistic abandonment and disassociation of the subject. This is a spectator who loses him- or herself in the endless labyrinths of desire and otherness, playing with the historical contingencies of the self, mimetically reflecting and confronting the crisis of sensory alienation within modernity. Hansen discusses how Miss Jenkins' theatrical expression is an excessive allegorical meaning, displacing and abstracting narrative space. This, then, 'has important implications for the articulation of cinematic space and the organisation of the look'. We can also see how cinematic space, here, becomes opened to Balázs's analysis of the facial close-up and a phenomenological apprehension of the image. The micro-physiognomy of Miss Jenkins' hysterical expression shows the violent disassociation and death drive that underpins the ghastly social mothers or Uplifters. Miss Jenkins' hysterical face displaces Oedipal narrative authority and the textual spectator, revealing how Freud's law of sexual repression also fails to rescue us from the body of the abject mother.

If the law in this film, and indeed textual authority, is merely the other side to a deathly mimetic mother or hysteric, then we have to understand the hysterical figure in *Intolerance* not simply as repressed sexuality, but as a relation to a history, narrative and law that produces and regulates that sexuality in relation to itself. Hysteria becomes, here, a phenomenological disassociation of the body and memory, a splitting of the body that becomes projected and produced as repressed, fetishized sexuality. In a Marxist sense this hysterical image is a social fetish or hieroglyphic, masking the masses' sensory alienation under capitalism. Foucault suggests that sexuality in the nineteenth century was a product of disciplinary power that regulated women's bodies, subjecting them to a hysterization that qualified and then disqualified them. This hysterization saturated women's bodies with sexuality, integrating and pathologizing them within a medical discourse. At the same time, the hysterical female body was placed in relation to the social regulation of reproduction and as the guarantor (in the guise of the nervous mother) of the spiritual sanctity of the family. The hysteric was both the embodiment of sexuality and the personification of its lack. As the movement of sex, hysteria was both 'whole and part', one and the other, angel and whore.[34] Similarly, within *Intolerance* the perverse hysterics such as Miss Jenkins and the Friendless One are mirrored by the equally hysterical, evil and innocent mothers: the Uplifters and the Dear One. A micro-physiognomic analysis of the close-up shots of the Dear One's face in the film, together with the close-ups of her trembling fingers in the final courtroom scene, reveal a hysterical and mimetic shock, that in Benjamin's view would be the numbed response of the masses to capitalist exploitation. Indeed, the hysterical mobility of the Dear One's facial expression throughout the film is marked by the excessive emotions that move in display across her face. Although shock is a recurrent facial expression, so is excessive love and joy, marking out her innocence and childlike qualities (all hallmarks of the classic hysteric). But the Dear One is also the sacrificial nineteenth-century angel in the house, a domestic archetype of motherhood, symbolically allegorized in the film through the figure of the Woman Who Rocks the Cradle.

Hansen discusses how the allegorical symbol of the eternal cradle, rocking, belongs within a conservative and timeless meaning of history as eternally recurring. Origins of the cradle symbol can be traced in relation to Walt Whitman's nationalistic American poems. Hansen cites 'Out of the cradle endlessly rocking', the first of Whitman's Seadrift poems where the sea is analogous to an oceanic and deathly medusa or mother. It is precisely because the cradle image and shot allegorize a symbolic timeless mode of history that they deserve to be read in terms of Benjamin's slippage from a stable symbolic mode to a critical reading of the image, a reading which 'registers the historical dissolution of that very order'.[35] The cradle

Fig. 6   Lillian Gish as 'The Woman Who Rocks the Cradle' in *Intolerance* (1916), directed by D.W. Griffith. © Wark Production Company / The Kobal Collection

allegory of the ideal mother as eternally recurring history is hopelessly contaminated by a perverse femininity. This fated femininity is summed up by the three witch-like figures surrounding the cradle. It is also a linked to the three evil Uplifters and the three executioners. The mother in the cradle shot and Miss Jenkins are also indelibly linked. But this fatal femininity is also a form of writing or primitive narration that is inseparable from Griffith's authorship. Hansen thus links Freud's death drive to Griffith's (and Whitman's) fear, fascination and projection of death onto women in the film, particularly the mother. The Oedipal fantasy of the cradle shot, the eternal recurrence of history, is troubled by a 'return of repressed as perverse femininity', destabilizing the textual economy of the film.

However, I want to argue for this hysterical femininity in *Intolerance*, not as a form of textual writing, but as a mimetic repetition of the optical unconscious. Within *Intolerance* this optical unconscious takes the form of Balázs's aesthetics of the facial close-up. Such close-ups are not simply limited to the characters, for these characters are also objects and images archetypally returning and recurring to reveal an intersubjective mimesis which moves between animate and inanimate nature. As such, the embodied mimesis of the characters moves to include wider narratives of history and capitalist social relations within modernity. *Intolerance* finally invokes Kracauer's, rather than Benjamin's, filmic distraction. The optical unconscious in this film is revealed as an unmasking of the abject real. As a mimetic mirror of the medusa's death head, the filmic image confronts the viewer with the alienation of the body within modernity. Griffith might be remembered as the Oedipal father of narrative film, but *Intolerance* is his hysterical daughter, who in her exhibitionist gestures of distraction figures a mimetic phenomenology of the image at the heart of this paternal narrative unity – a mad, embodied and disembodied monster that blows up Griffith's American idyllic pastoral!

Hysterical film hieroglyphics

I want to finish this chapter with a discussion of *Intolerance* in terms of the hieroglyph. Hansen's analysis links together Vachel Lindsay's ideas of film as a new language and the universal tradition of language rooted in the Tower of Babel. The idea of silent film as a universal, phenomenological language is taken up by Balázs in his argument for an expressive, physiognomic perception of the image. Hansen is critical of what she sees as Balázs's polarization of a lost, utopian, primordial mother tongue of immediate perception versus an ' "abstract" literary culture'. I want to focus on film hieroglyphs not as a universal, direct expression of the perceptual body, nor as the form of radical 'writing' or textuality that Hansen suggests, but as archetypal physiognomic images which, as Adorno and Horkheimer state, freeze faces and images, like a 'priestly hieroglyphic script'.[36] According to Adorno and Horkheimer, the hieroglyphs of film and mass culture address images to a passive audience, so they are not experienced sensually or pleasurably as such, just ideologically read. I suggest, conversely, that such hieroglyphs are experienced pleasurably *and* ideologically, but this pleasure is a hysterical mimesis and escapist fantasy rather than being psychically and socially embodied. As commodity fetishes the hieroglyphics in *Intol-*

erance can be read as the frozen symbols of capitalist history, but, as Marx notes, they are also mimetic images that mark out the individual's alienation from the senses. Hansen argues that *Intolerance* is Griffith's (and Whitman's) narration of an enormous, transcendental and poetic ego, an ego that doubles as a cyclical and eternal reading of history. This mimesis of history ends in the teleological redemption of the modern narrative, containing the only happy ending, when the boy is saved at the last hour from execution. For Hansen, this redemptive tale signifies the 'triumph of American democracy'. We can map the hieroglyphics such as the 'Book of Intolerance' and cradle, shot as archetypes and fetishistic images, operating ideologically to naturalize the universal language of film with that of a 'progressive' history of capitalist modernity. However, the repetitive emblematic images of femininity (perverse and sacrificial), so powerfully illustrated in the 'Woman Who Rocks the Cradle' shot, are not just archetypes of an eternal history of modernity; they are also mimetic images of hysteria, paradoxically revealing the alienation of the senses under modernity.

We can therefore understand the hieroglyphs and the hysterical images of femininity in *Intolerance* in direct relation to Kracauer's thought. The film restores, as Phillip Rosen suggests, an ideal, defensive transcendence for the spectator.[37] But as social hieroglyphs these filmic images also act as a mimetic mirror bringing us face to face with Kracauer's medusa, the horrors of capitalism as a physical death drive that remains disassociated from discursive intelligence. Whereas Hansen reads the hieroglyphs in *Intolerance* as textuality and writing, they can also be read more phenomenologically as social and archetypal filmic images, images that mimetically reveal a perceptual crisis of split (embodied) subjectivity. Hansen's argument for hieroglyphic writing links Derrida's and Freud's connection of hieroglyphic writing and textuality with the 'script' of dreams, a script that cannot be immediately perceived but has to be interpreted or read.[38] Freud's textual script of films contrasts with a phenomenological approach to dreams, where the latter are read as symbolic perceptual images rather than textual phenomena. Freud likened dreams to ancient hieroglyphic scripts and argued that they are 'not made to be understood'.[39] As abstract ideas transformed into pictures, dreams hide their latent textual meaning behind manifest pictorial images, and their 'self-deception' has to be interpreted by the analyst. Jung famously disagreed with this, saying 'the "manifest" dream picture is the dream itself and contains the whole meaning of the dream. Difficulty of interpretation therefore lies with the analyst's lack of understanding, not with the dream's innate self-deception.[40] Dream images as hieroglyphics can be understood phenomenologically as symbolic pictures of our dis/embodied relation to the world. R.D. Laing argues that the schizophrenic's 'hieroglyphic speech and actions' are, as Freud said, difficult to decipher, but this is because the analyst must not simply 'interpret' or read the schizophrenic's symptoms, he must understand the bizarre hieroglyphics (both talk and action) of the psychotic as 'his experiential mode of being in the world'.[41]

We can link this reading of the dream and filmic image with Kracauer's understanding of filmic images as social and psychological hieroglyphs – the unconscious, disassociated and hysterical dynamics of human relationships. Benjamin's critical allegorical reading of the film image offers us a more creative understanding of the hieroglyph, as a profane projection enabling us to remember the new. For Benjamin, the objects of modernity are hieroglyphs that have become enigmatic, no longer generating shared meaning, as the embodied 'authentic' experience and connection between past generations is lost. Allegory becomes the active phenomenological, not textual interpretation of the hieroglyph, re-membering an embodied experience to the other and to the past.

We can see both these hysterical and creative aspects to the hieroglyph explored in the poet H.D.'s work. H.D. perceived cinema as a universal language of imaginal dreaming, consisting of phenomenological filmic hieroglyphs. H.D. was a contributor of film essays to the avant-garde film journal *Close-Up*, and she was also in analysis with Freud for several years. Although very influenced by the founding father of psychoanalysis, H.D.'s account of the unconscious language of films and dreaming is a phenomenological narrative of images and objects where life, film and dreaming coalesce. Her story of her analysis pays (mimetic) lip service to Freud and yet surprisingly refuses his more textual and Oedipal rendering.[42] Hieroglyphics are, in H.D.'s analysis and her film writing, imaginal pictures to be deciphered, not because they reveal a secret textual code or meaning, but because (as she relates in one film essay 'The Student of Prague') they say the things 'we can't say or think'. These hieroglyphs are archetypal unconscious images and film images which like Jung's unconscious are projected and are like early moving pictures, a 'writing on the wall'. In H.D.'s analysis she recounts her famous dream or visionary experience in Corfu in April 1920, where hieroglyphic images became projected onto the wall, first as magic lantern slides, then as early films. Although Freud saw these hieroglyphs as her most dangerous symptom, 'a freak thought that has got out of hand', H.D. also sees them as life-changing visionary experiences and objects that she positively identifies with. H.D. calls these hieroglyphs 'real dreams', because they include psychic experiences outside the realm of 'established psychoanalysis'.[43] Actually, H.D.'s description of a creative phenomenological unconscious comes much closer to Jung's ideas than Freud's.

As Laura Marcus suggests, H.D.'s aesthetics of cinema parallels Benjamin's optical unconscious in providing the fantasy of a reality unmediated by technology.[44] And there are other striking similarities between Benjamin's optical unconscious and H.D.'s. In fact, her hieroglyphic dreams are 'profane illuminations', which in demolishing the traditional aura between spectator and the art of film or life re-imagine them within a more intersubjective correspondence. In her essay 'The Student of Prague', H.D. describes the screen hieroglyphic as a struggle between the transcendental and the carnal, where the 'spirit becomes body, and the body becomes spirit'.[45] Here, we can see H.D. wrestling with the very splits between the mind and body which coloured the differing discourses of modernity, psychoanalysis and film in the nineteenth century. In *Tribute to Freud*, H.D. starts to question the scientific origins of psychoanalysis. Describing Dr Charcot's hospital of hysterics, the Salpêtrière, as a film or play, H.D. suggests that behind the scientific observations and quantifiable 'symptoms' is the hysteric's performative mimesis. Freud (who is also a performer) notes this hysteria as a jumbled sequence of actions, but for H.D. these actions have meaning, if seen as a two-sided dream hovering between madness and waking life. H.D. identifies the mad, hysterical patients who perform 'Caesar' and 'Hannibal' not just with her own hieroglyphic visions, but with Freud's own identity behind his role as doctor.[46] Correctly linking 'Caesar' and 'Hannibal' to Freud's own (Oedipal) struggles to master time and history, H.D. shows how the 'picture' hieroglyphs of dreams and film are a universal language of the unconscious and of man who seeks to 'forgo barriers of time and space'.

At the end of her film essay 'The Student of Prague', H.D. argues for her vision of a universal language of film as a hieroglyphic art which is 'open alike to the pleb and the initiate'.[47] We can compare this with Hansen's understanding of the hieroglyphic connection between high art and popular culture in *Intolerance*.[48] Hansen notes that the tradition of American hieroglyphics that Griffith's *Intolerance* speaks into is convoluted, mixing a popular tradition of hieroglyphics with a much older tradition of mystical mimesis 'prefigured by the divine script of nature'.[49] Hansen traces the hieroglyphic language in *Intolerance* to a genealogy of literary history. She writes: 'If *Intolerance* is proposing to recover a unity of popular and high art, it does so not by replacing writing with a superior language of visual presence, but by retrieving the common roots of both film and literature in the hieroglyphic tradition.'[50] However, we can also read the hysterical film hieroglyphics in *Intolerance* in terms of an ambivalent phenomenological presence, a distracted, hysterical perception and gaze. This mimesis of the real via the image subverts the dominant narrative form of Griffith's film and any easy recuperation of an Oedipal, repressive and textual history of modernism.

Conclusion

Of course Griffith's *Intolerance* is extremely Oedipal in its hysterical transcendence of time and history. *Intolerance* and *The Interpretation of Dreams* stand out as key texts within modernism that hysterically fetishize time and history – suggesting, perhaps, that there is something significant about the relation of film and psychoanalysis to this historical moment? Here, the splitting of modernism and film are located in a defence against time, a timeless preservation of the unconscious and the individual's (Freud's) need to defend 'himself' against the passage of time and desire: to disavow, or unknow its imaginary nature. There is a danger in reading film images (and hieroglyphs) through an idealized account of embodied redemption of both the spectator and history. Benjamin is perhaps guilty of this at times, and H.D.'s writing also colludes with a certain idealistic enthusiasm in unifying the carriers of culture with the working classes whom she so charmingly calls the 'plebs'! Hansen is understandably wary in aligning her analysis with a phenomenology of visual presence that seems to recuperate an ideal unity of superior art. Although both H.D. and Griffith's *Intolerance* depict a hieroglyphic mimesis between imaginary and real, these gestural discourses have to be distinguished in terms of taste. Reading film cultures within modernism in terms of a dialectics of taste, Janet Harbord describes how shifting distinctions and divisions, between art and life, culture and economics become reinstated with the publication of the film journal *Close-Up*.[51] This film journal was the one in which H.D. regularly published. Emerging out of an avant-garde, literary tradition, *Close-Up* emphasized experimental film aesthetics and was produced in response to the growth of mass culture, a culture characterized by the standardization and institutionalization of mainstream narrative films such as Griffith's. Harbord notes how an early cinema of attractions, which was rooted in popular traditions of the fairground and everyday life, paradoxically crosses over into avant-garde art, transforming Méliès' magical mimesis into a Kantian category of formal play. Meanwhile, mainstream film remains economically tied to the narrative realism and audience identification implicit to mass culture and profits.

A distracted mimesis of film, within Harbord's analysis, will therefore signify different things, depending on whether it is situated within an avant-garde or a mainstream narrative film. The mimesis of H.D's filmic hieroglyphs reconfigures art and life, but this embodied reconfiguration is firmly tied to a reflexive, literary space of formal language and 'high' art. In contrast, the hieroglyphics in *Intolerance* do not reconfigure art and life. The popular and the redemptive, the carnal and the transcendental, are not united in this film, but horribly split. Mimesis of the real in this film and the apprehension of the hieroglyph and film image remain a hysterical abjection that grounds the timeless and redemptive narrative of modernist, Oedipal history. On another level, the gestural and imaginal address of this hysterical film can also be seen in relation to Kracauer's negative mirror, as a deconstruction of the material ground of that history; revealing its alienated, physical base. The mimesis and splitting of the hysterical body in *Intolerance* reflects how pure perception and spectacle in the nineteenth century were rooted in 'the embodied viewer', but their continued performance rested ultimately in a denial of the body as the ground of that vision and knowledge. Such disavowal fuels the secret hieroglyphs of 'Caesar' and 'Hannibal', secret images that also haunt the Salpêtrière in H.D's film vision and in Freud's dream book. If Freud arrived at the Oedipal complex as both a defence and disavowal of his 'own' hysteria, then this myth also castrates and disavows a more phenomenological account of the unconscious. This imaginary as both hysterical mimesis and embodied reconfiguration situates the origins of psychoanalysis and cinema in relation to epistemologies of early modernism. Knowledges which have divided and regulated the body construct a colonial and narrative subject in relation to a projected, hysterical bodily other. However, it is only through the image of the embodied and disembodied hysteric, not the regulating discourse of the Oedipal subject, that we can begin to understand the dialectical nature of psychoanalysis and film history. How, in other words, we can comprehend the twin narratives of psychoanalysis and film as figural mediums of mimesis and memory, as forces that repetitively freeze but also actively reconfigure time and history.

Key points

- *Intolerance* is a hysterical film split between its classical style and an extra-textual parallel montage.
- The perverse figures of femininity in *Intolerance* can be read not simply as a return of the repressed, but as a hysterical, mimetic phenomenology of the filmic image, modernism and history.
- Miriam Hansen reads the hieroglyphs in *Intolerance* as textuality and writing; they can also be read more phenomenologically as social and archetypal filmic images.

Part III

Audiences, Stars and Aesthetics

Introduction to Part III

This book has argued for an account of film spectatorship and psychoanalysis as a phenomenological mimesis of the body which moves between hysteria and more culturally embodied forms of identification. This last section of the book examines more contemporary debates on film spectatorship in relation to themes of experience, memory and time. The first chapter in this section returns to cultural studies' approaches to the 'real' film spectator, utilizing a central psychoanalytic theme of the relationship of memory to the real. Cultural studies associated with the Birmingham school approach in Britain has been historically interested in locating the 'real' social audience and spectator. Within film studies, however, it is Miriam Hansen's early work on audiences and the alternative public sphere that explicitly thinks through the real audience or spectator in terms of concepts of phenomenological experience and time. Miriam Hansen develops her ideas of a more public dimension to film viewing through her concept of an alternative public sphere which is rooted in the same account of mimetic experience utilized by Siegfried Kracauer and Walter Benjamin. Unlike Habermas's bourgeois and rationalist public sphere, Hansen follows Negt and Kluge's study, *The Public Sphere and Experience* (1972), arguing for a social horizon of alienated experience which has been abjected from the dominant. Cinema then acts as an alternative public sphere, not for some bourgeois and rationalist, liberal collective, but for more embodied 'social groups at particular historical junctures'.[1] Now this notion of 'experience', as Hansen makes clear, is not empiricist, but follows the Frankfurt thinkers, Adorno, Kracauer and especially Benjamin. This concept of experience is then a phenomenological concept, described by

Hansen as that which 'mediates individual perception with social meaning, conscious with unconscious processes, loss of self with self-reflexivity; experience as the capacity to see connections and relations (Zusammenhang), experience as the matrix of conflicting temporalities, of memory and hope, including the historical loss of these dimensions'.[2]

Exploring the historical space between the textually inscribed spectator and the empirical viewer, she attempts to overcome the divisions between textual and theoretical film approaches and more historical and empirical studies. She cites David Bordwell's inclusion of cognitive psychology within his project of historical poetics. Bordwell's view of psychoanalytical film theory is that it makes the viewer a passive consumer of the dominant ideological text. For him the spectator is also active, 'a hypothetical entity' who is cued from the text but also constructs a story in relation to the filmic text that involves 'inter-subjective protocols'. Hansen develops this rather vague gloss on intersubjectivity, illustrating how the different forms of cinema, Hollywood, art films and modernist cinema all construct different paradigms of narration. But this intersubjectivity also involves the empirical viewer. For Hansen, formalist film theory erases the individual and historically contingent empirical viewer, but more importantly it also eliminates 'the hermeneutic constellation in which a historical spectator makes sense of what he or she perceives, how he or she interprets the filmic narration'.[3] This hermeneutic constellation signifies a 'specific social horizon of understanding' that moulds the spectator's reading of the film: a social horizon or public sphere that subverts conventional narrative systems by its emphasis on the autonomous nature of reception. When we watch films, we are not simply subject to the ideological script, but we also read and actively distinguish in relation to a variety of tastes, influenced by class, race, sexuality and gender. This public dimension to film viewing is independent from the narrative and cultural determinants of the script in that it is not necessarily controlled through the context of production. So although film reception is always being appropriated by dominant industrial and ideological apparatuses, it also 'harbours a potentially autonomous dynamic'.[4]

Hansen is concerned with Bordwell's cognitive psychology because of its universal and ahistorical framework which disposes with the necessary tension between textual spectator and empirical viewer. Also, the cognitive approach implies a perception that is positivist and conscious, leaving little room for either the unconscious ambivalence of the sexual subject, or indeed the more marginal and hence 'unconscious' stories that are abjected outside of dominant frameworks. Hansen, therefore, rejects cognitive psychology and classical psychoanalysis for their ahistorical notions of human universals. However, her work fits with the argument in this book, which reclaims psychoanalysis for film studies in a more experiential and phenomenological mode.

Hansen's concept of an alternative public sphere in early film audiences is also a cinema of attractions that mobilizes not the middle classes, but differing immigrant communities in terms of Benjamin's optical unconscious. Migrating from pre-industrial 'nature' to the capitalist, industrial and urban centres of the New World, these immigrant audiences experienced competing temporalities between old, more communal and extended familial lifestyles and a new privatized work force. In their alienation from their old communal lives and their exclusion from more dominant public spheres, the cinema became for them a form of memory where through a filmic reception of the optical unconscious these audiences could re-member and re-imagine their past. This optical unconscious is not the intentional linguistic representation of established and conscious memory. Rather, it is the profane illumination of surrealist experience where the past as some kind of 'primary nature' becomes imaginatively transformed through an embodied imaginary. Citing Foucault, Hansen notes that such a horizon of differing temporalities, where 'men' break with traditional time, only occurs at specific historical junctures. The immigrant communities' utilization of the cinema as an alternative public sphere was their experience of it, not as a narrative, textual aesthetic, but as a cinema of attractions. This cinema of attractions became a refuge from the factory or from the drudgery of the domestic sphere, where it not only helped people to 'come to terms with competing temporalities, it also lent itself to the unceremonious actualization of memories'.[5]

Although Hansen's alternative public sphere is situated at a particular historical conjunction where the cinema of attractions became a prevailing distraction from the competing temporalities of daily life, Hansen does not make any simple dichotomy between this more socially transformative leisure activity and the ongoing implementation of classical cinema and consumer culture. Acknowledging Siegfried Kracauer's broader work on filmic reception, Hansen notes how Kracauer's own particular theorization of the projection and reconfiguration of the film spectator points out the ideological escape of the viewer into the world of objects and things on the screen.[6]

This ideological escape into the world of consumption and film is also the development of a classical narrative of textual spectatorship that gradually takes precedence over the cinema of distractions and attractions. But what is interesting in Hansen's work is how she uses Kracauer's and Benjamin's work in relation to a historical analysis of the space-time dynamics of cinema spectatorship. If the cinema of attractions and an early filmic alternative public sphere give way to classical paradigms of narration, this does not mean, in Hansen's view, that a more embodied spectatorship is simply abandoned.

I have argued so far for melodrama and hysteria as dominant structures in understanding film spectatorship. In this reading, then, the distinction between the classical Oedipal textual spectator and the real audience collapse. Consequently, we are left with a dialectic of disembodied hysteria in relation to a more culturally reconfigured re-memory of the filmic text. Rather than locating an embodied spectatorship and cinema of attractions with early film, and attributing a more mental, Oedipal narrative of film to later classical cinema, we can see a disembodied *and* embodied dialectic of spectatorship operating within distinct historical periods. This is, then, a filmic or optical unconscious moving between melancholia and mourning. In Hansen's work on a specific historical moment of early film audiences we can see how a cinema of attractions, embodiment and cultural re-memory is tied to the temporality and mourning of what she calls an alternative public sphere. Implicit in Hansen's work is the notion that film is a medium and methodology of time and memory.

Film as a mediation of time and memory is therefore the theme of these last three chapters. Hansen's emphasis on the space between filmic text and empirical viewer can be traced forward in time to the cultural studies' emphasis on the 'real' ethnographic film spectator or audience. In focusing on the real spectator in terms of ethnography, the first chapter in this last section foregrounds the work of memory in understanding how the real is culturally re-membered by the spectator. Reading film ethnography in relation to hitherto antithetical discourses of psychoanalysis and cultural studies defines film spectatorship as a phenomenological and retrospective screen memory.

The second chapter develops this argument for a phenomenological imaginary in terms of contemporary debates on film in relation to stars, fandom and melodrama. Identification with stars involves a phenomenological mimesis of the body. This star image is not a text, in the sense used by Richard Dyer in his 1979 book *Stars*, but occupies a transitional space between the real and language which finds representation within films and inter-textual forms such as magazines, advertisements, etc. Performative spectatorship of film fans in relation to stars moves between hysterical melancholia and a more active, social memory and spectatorship. This bodily performance can be used, in turn, to read debates on melodrama and Hollywood film. The last part of the second chapter therefore develops an argument for the hysteria of Hollywood film. If melodrama is interpreted not simply as a discreet genre but as the organizing hysterical force of a dominant Hollywood imaginary, then this imaginary also reveals film spectatorship in terms of hysterical identifications. The 'hysteria' of Hollywood structures spectatorship in terms of Oedipal relations of race and gender. Such ambivalent Oedipal desire is the film spectator's hysterical performance of the body which repeats, but cannot re-member, a more embodied aesthetics of the film text.

The final chapter, therefore, moves to an examination of a phenomenological aesthetics of film which can mobilize melodrama in terms of a more cultural and social re-memory. Time and memory are intrinsic to more social forms of identification and film spectatorship, and this last chapter brings together debates on film aesthetics and postmodernism. Opening the film image up to time means connecting the imaginary world of melodrama with the real of the body and history. It is only this connection between the body and the dream world of film, a meeting point between the time image and narrative, where the hysteria of melodrama can evolve into more social and political forms of film spectatorship.

Key points

- In film studies it is Miriam Hansen's early work on audiences and an alternative public sphere that explicitly thinks through the real audience or spectator in terms of concepts of phenomenological experience and time.
- Rather than locating an embodied spectatorship and cinema of attractions with early film, and attributing a more mental, Oedipal narrative of film to later classical cinema, we can see a disembodied *and* embodied dialectic of spectatorship operating within distinct historical periods.

6

Cultural Studies, Ethnography and the 'Real' Film Spectator

Introduction: psychoanalytic film studies versus the real spectator

Phenomenological film experience, as a psychic and social optical unconscious, was first imagined by Kracauer and Benjamin and has since been developed through the innovative work on early film by Miriam Hansen. Film studies in general, however, has historically divided the psychic fantasy operating within the textual viewer from the social experience of the real audience. Screen theory and the cultural studies' audience approach are located at opposite ends of the spectrum. Stuart Hall's famous article 'Cultural Studies: Two Paradigms' was an attempt to integrate the antithetical approaches of structuralism's textual subject and the more culturalist emphasis on lived experience. But as Hall himself admitted, it didn't work. Screen theory's focus on the textual spectator has been on the inner world, fantasy and the imaginary at the expense of concepts of history, memory and social reality. Susannah Radstone's excellent essay on the film *Forrest Gump* addresses this issue, highlighting an opposition between psychoanalytic film studies and a more cultural studies emphasis on historical memory. This division between fantasy and history is not just observed in the different focus on a textual or a real spectator. It is also mirrored in the split between psychoanalysis and trauma theory.

Freud originally theorized neurosis and hysteria as symptoms resulting from repression of a traumatic event: child sexual abuse. Freud's subsequent abandonment of the seduction theory developed from his increasing realization that he could not distinguish between the truth and fiction of his patient's memories. Through his famous case history of the Wolfman Freud argued that the traumatic, historical event was a delayed experience or deferred action (*Nachträglichkeit*). Freud hypothesizes that the Wolfman's trauma was located primarily at the age of eighteen months, witnessing a primal scene of parental sex. This scene only became traumatic later through his sister's seduction and is only experienced by the patient in terms of his dream of wolves. In other words, the primary traumatic event is not remembered at the time, and it is only through its recall in a later therapy session that the wound is felt. Memory is not simply factual recall but also a fantasy or fiction, a story that is recreated or constructed to incorporate lost, traumatic events.

Trauma theory, which is becoming increasingly popular within psychiatry and cultural movements, emphasizes the real event rather than fantasy. Its core belief is that a traumatic event, too painful to be assimilated, is walled off. False memory syndrome or 'recovered memory syndrome' is where patients remember previously forgotten sexual abuse (often through therapy). The central idea, here, is of a damaging traumatic event which leads to an experience becoming incorporated but not internalized. For Susannah Radstone, trauma theory parallels a 'victim culture' so eloquently documented in Elaine Showalter's *Hystories: Hysterical Epidemics in Modern Culture*.[1] Showalter's thesis is that modern culture is in the grip of a cultural hysteria, in which false memory syndrome, chronic fatigue syndrome, multiple personality and Gulf War syndrome are the psychological symptoms that result when people are unable to articulate their stress, anxiety or oppression.[2]

Radstone privileges Freud's account of deferred action over trauma theory because trauma theory, for her, simply posits a linear registration of the event or history, which becomes disassociated. Freudian psychoanalysis pays a more sophisticated attention to how the real of history is mediated by the inner world and by fantasy. The film *Forrest Gump* can be read in terms of trauma theory and victim culture: a melodramatic world of villains imposing suffering on innocent victims. Reviews suggesting that audiences became the passive recipients of the film's ideological brain-washing and deceit would foreground this reading. Radstone, however, proposes a less judgemental account of the film's popular appeal by showing how the spectator in *Forrest Gump* is caught up in a more complex process of deferred action, or '*Nachträglichkeit*'. Here, the spectator struggles over the historical event, remembering and revising the past through active fantasy. Radstone recuperates a Freudian reading of the textual form, narrative and address of *Forrest Gump*.

This reading suggests that the film's temporality foregrounds a kind of innocence, reminiscent of victim culture, but then revises this victim position, through a psychoanalytic understanding of revision, a revision which 'speaks to that audience's ongoing struggle with the past'.[3]

Radstone's reading is a compelling one that moves between historical and filmic cultures. As Janet Harbord has recently noted, we cannot simply locate texts or readers, but have to understand the circulation of films within the space of culture.[4] For Nick Couldry, this means understanding the flow and production, but also how meaning is negotiated by real audiences.[5] Textual readings of films also have to take into account inter-textual relations of genre and stars that move the spectator outside the film text to the social. And, indeed, Radstone does address issues of inter-textuality with her emphasis on contemporary debates on victim culture and her comparison of the film with other critical reviews. Nevertheless, we can't necessarily privilege her textual account over, say, Robert Burgoyne's trauma reading of the film, which argues that *Forrest Gump* splits off and evacuates history and agency. In Burgoyne's narrative, the film splits off from history, the traumas of the 1960s and 1970s, through a hysterical division of memory (an argument I find equally compelling). This is not in any way meant to negate Radstone's analysis, just to emphasize that it is a partial account, a textual and inter-textual reading of the reconfiguration of the real within *Forrest Gump*, which actually leads me to wonder about the 'deferred action' and memory work at stake within Radstone's own reading. In other words, I wonder about the autobiography that informs her reading of the 'real' filmic event. For textual analysis, by its very nature, is not just what we objectively find in a film, but also what we imagine and in a sense re-member in relation to our own situated histories. If retrospective memory work can be identified both within the film text and the critic, then how can it be identified with respect to the real spectator or audience?

If there is no objective position ethnographically which we can take up as a researcher in relation to cinematic knowledge, what does that mean for empirical and audience research? Alternatively, if we say all ethnography is autobiography doesn't that just evacuate real spectators and audience work completely and return us to wall-to-wall textual analysis? I propose that, although ethnography is filtered through fantasy in the sense that it is always mediated by the subjective autobiography and memory work of the researcher, it does not mean that the 'real' cannot exist and that it does not contribute valuable knowledge. In fact, within this argument the real is continuously reconfigured through the imaginary and memory of not just the researcher but through the practice of the audience themselves.

What methodologies can then be utilized in carrying out this research into intersubjective film spectatorship? Neither textual nor empirical methodologies can address the intersubjective nature of a phenomenological perception that moves between them. It is not enough simply to focus on the textual address of the film, but in order to understand the real ethnographic spectator and audience we cannot rely on empirical concepts of experience. To break this opposition between text and empirical audience, or between psychoanalytic film studies' emphasis on an inner fantasy world and cultural studies' focus on memory and the event, entails a rethinking of the real spectator: a re-evaluation of the real spectator in terms of phenomenological experience. As Miriam Hansen has shown, such a conceptualization of experience does not distinguish between conscious and unconscious, or between individual psychic perception and social meaning.

If we understand the unconscious to be based on a model of phenomenological experience and disassociation, rather than narrative repression, then trauma theory and psychoanalysis, or fantasy and reality, cease to be polarized in such opposing planes. Trauma theories are based on disassociation of the traumatic real, a splitting off of the event, because it is too painful to assimilate.[6] But if, as I suggest, psychoanalysis can be understood through hysteria as a mimetic disassociation from the body and the 'real', then we don't have to choose between psychoanalytic accounts of fantasy or trauma theories of the disassociated event. Moreover, we can't synthesize these two positions through Freud's original account of deferred action as this takes us back to memory as a virtual past, a memory based purely on mental representation and fantasy.

R.D. Laing did not believe that Freud's meta-psychology, his account of an internal world, held the key to, or route out of, the petrified hysterical or schizoid state. For Laing, it was the person's ability to exist within phenomenological and lived time, which released him or her into more intersubjective relating. Hysterics and schizophrenics are chronically disarticulated from time. Disembodied, as inauthentic 'false selves' they remain split between imaginary and real, and this lack of two-way connection between imaginary and real leads the hysteric and schizophrenic to lead an increasingly fixed imaginary existence. For the schizophrenic the traumatic petrification is complete, 'the world is in ruins and the self (apparently) dead)'. In this dead world, 'Real toads invade the imaginary gardens and ghosts walk in the real streets.'[7]

Key points

- Film studies has historically divided the psychic fantasy operating within the textual viewer from the social experience of the real audience.
- Opposition between psychoanalytic film studies and a more cultural studies emphasis on history and memory is also mirrored in the split between psychoanalysis and trauma theory.

Screen images and memory

What would it mean to re-read Freud's account of deferred action through a phenomenological lens? Such an account would argue for a retrospective memory of 'real' phenomenological experience, rather than mental, textual representation. R.D. Laing challenged Freud's conceptualization of a mental imaginary through his more phenomenological reading of D.W. Winnicott. In a similar move we can also read the work of the Winnicottian analyst Christopher Bollas in a more phenomenological mode. Bollas describes how trauma in childhood leads to forgetting and psychic disavowal, producing an arena of deadened, unthought experience. Such dead experience can be brought back to life through the rememory (or *Nachträglichkeit*) operating in the analytic session. Re-memory of the bodily real and the movement from hysterical trauma to a creative and embodied place within time occurs, according to Bollas, through the liberation of what Freud called 'screen memories'. These screen memories are not actual memories of real events, but as images they form what Juliet Mitchell calls an iconic memory that 'stands in for the overall experience'.[8] Creating and rebuilding a two-way circuit between fantasy and reality, these creative screen memories and images become the reconstructive work of historian and analyst. The Lacanian real is not walled off, here, from representation, but allowed significance within imaginary and symbolic registers.[9] Bollas provides an explanation of the psychic re-memory of history which is not based on the return of the repressed or linguistic repression by the phallus, but which is nevertheless identical to Freud's coding of the term '*Nachträglichkeit*'.[10]

This theorization of psychic history based on a return and re-creation of a lost, internal (maternal) object understands the past as trauma which has been self-destructively obliterated through amnesia. Re-memory of this lost maternal object is synonymous with the creation of an embodied sense of place within the self. Martin Heidegger calls this embodied sense of place *Dasein*, or dwelling.[11] For Heidegger, embodied dwelling and *Dasein* is a being 'towards death' whereby the person can inhabit time; 'she' can belong in her embodied self because she is conscious of her mortality and of time's passing.[12]

Screen memories are a mixture of (childhood) experience and fantasy, and they constitute an iconic memory, elaborating the hysteric and the schizophrenic within time and space. Whereas Freud's deferred action privileges a mentally reflexive working through of the past, a phenomenological account of retrospective memory reveals the hysteric's (and schizophrenic's) split in embodied being, their crisis and disarticulation in terms of temporality. This uncanny disarticulation from interpersonal belonging means the hysterical or psychotic person is ontologically homeless within time and the community.

Walter Benjamin describes such a phenomenological screen memory and image, revealing how the past is recognized in the present as an uncanny moment or haunting. Here, loss of the historical object is apprehended through a more material sense. Benjamin explains this through Proust's famous story of involuntary memory, where Proust tells of a visit to his mother and the eating of a madeleine cake. For Proust, it is the sensual experience of eating a madeleine cake that opens up an image sphere where he free-associates about his childhood in Combray, elaborating on an important bit of his past. Proust thus reveals how the past is located beyond the realm of the intellect and discovered accidentally in external material objects. He says, 'it depends on chance whether we come upon this object before we die.'[13]

These images and objects, like dreams, do not just return when we want to recall them – they are not lodged in a conscious and mental representation. In fact, 'they have never been seen before we remember them'.[14] According to Benjamin, these images, like dreams, therapy or 'a prehistoric past', are 'developed in the dark room of the lived moment', confronting us with a mimetic image of ourselves as a relation to the real of the body and history. They are like photographs, the ones on cigarette boxes, or the ones when we see our whole life run before us in a filmic way in moments of life-threatening danger. Like images of our childhood that are 'precursors of cinema', they are images of the objects and people we want mimetically to be.

Instead of understanding the screen image and film spectator in terms of Freud's mental imaginary of deferred action, we can instead see it as a more experiential, retrospective fantasy. Walter Benjamin's ethnography of history (as always a lost object) returns the real spectator, not to the empirical knowability of the subject, but to an idea of material re-memory underlining a particular phenomenological concept of experience.

If we understand the unconscious, not as the contents of an internal world, but as a phenomenological experience which is disassociated (Laing re-read Klein and Winnicott in this way[15]), then we have to reconsider exactly what we mean by the term 'experience'. Ann Gray argues cogently for the importance of ethnography and the category of experience within cultural studies work in critiquing the idealism of theory. For her, experience is a non-unified category which can be mobilized in a number of ways, for different purposes and for different epistemological outcomes.[16]

Key points

- Retrospective working of memory in relation to the film image can, in a phenomenological sense, transform a traumatic space of fantasy and experience into a lived historicity and future.
- Benjamin's screen memory is not an Oedipal narrative of mental representation and fantasy; rather, it is based on the embodied, material apprehension of the image.

Cultural studies and the 'real spectator'

Audience research into film has arisen out of the field of cultural studies, particularly the British Birmingham school, formerly known as the Centre for Contemporary Cultural Studies (C.C.C.S.). Here, the methodological shift has been away from textual analysis to ethnography, concentrating on the real, experiential spectator or consumer. This spectator is not monolithically interpellated through ideology, and can therefore resist through more located, resistant readings of the text. Emphasis on the social, rather than the psychic identity of the spectator in cultural studies has arisen due to frustrations with the universal textual theories of sexual difference within feminist film theory that tend to position the cinematic spectator in relation to fixed, heterosexual, Oedipal identifications. One of the difficulties with some audience research within a cultural studies tradition has been the rather unproblematic way such work has presented the political subject. Constructed as a positive, social identity prior to the interpellation by media texts, this subject remains untroubled by unconscious processes and identifications.

There are, however, some notable exceptions within cultural studies work, especially in relation to feminist theories of film spectatorship. Jacqui Stacey's *Star Gazing* and Annette Kuhn's *Family Secrets* introduce, albeit in ambivalent form, a psychoanalytic discourse with which to connect to wider social narratives of identity.[17] Admittedly, Annette Kuhn's work is so ambivalent about psychoanalysis that she renounces the terminology altogether, writing her own account of psychic and social memory through a discourse of autobiography. Such uneasiness with respect to psychoanalysis in these texts interests me, not only because I agree on the whole with these writers' criticisms of Oedipal, textual film theory, but also because their attempts to forge links between psychic and social identities, in relation to film spectatorship, articulate a narrative of a more phenomenological imaginary.

My re-reading of their work demonstrates how psychoanalysis can be utilized within a phenomenological account of the real audience and spectator. Here, the real spectator is located historically and experientially, and oscillates between self and other, and between real and imaginary registers. As this feminist work will demonstrate, ethnographies of film audiences, or the real spectator, cannot obtain objective empirical evidence; instead it produces a material, situated and imaginary reading of that real spectator. This is not to say that the real spectator does not exist, or that audience work in film studies is obsolete, for then we are left with just more textual analysis. Rather, the emphasis is on the existence of the real spectator whereby that 'real' is immediately bracketed. Thus acknowledging our access is always refracted through the imaginary, leading us to an ethnography that must, by necessity, endlessly problematize itself through autobiography, memory and fantasy.

In a sense it is these ethnographies – perhaps they could be called Weberian, non-ideal ethnographies – that can be articulated through a phenomenological bodily imaginary, thereby replacing the more positivist emphasis in empirical audience studies. Non-accidentally, perhaps, these ethnographies have been articulated by feminist scholars whose awareness of being disenfranchised through class, sexuality, race and gender have led them to question research methodologies in terms of relations of power and knowledge. Jacqui Stacey has argued that where psychoanalysis has been utilized in relation to ethnography, the problems of Oedipal hierarchies have, if anything, been exacerbated, with the interview session being likened to an analytic session where the research subject is psychoanalysed by the interviewer.

Ethnography and audience studies within a cultural studies approach have historically sought to understand the 'lived experience of media consumers' and have accordingly challenged the passivity of the purely textual spectator.[18] In an early piece on encoding and decoding (1980) Stuart Hall argues that textual meaning is always negotiated between the reader and the text, producing dominant oppositional or negotiated meaning.[19] The meaning of a text is always, therefore, mediated and informed by the cultural context and identity of the reader. David Morley and Charlotte Brunsdon analyse television audiences in terms of the programme *Nationwide*; they study the active responses of audiences in terms of relations of class and in terms of their everyday, familial context. In a similar vein, Ann Gray examines the gendered and social relations of video consumption by female spectators in their domestic environment.[20] The role of fantasy in relation to audience consumption has been explored by feminist and cultural critics in relation to romance novels and soap operas. Tania Modleski's study of romance and gothic novels and daytime soap operas examines the pleasures these popular texts provide for women, using the psychoanalytic tropes of the hysteric (for the female reader of romance novels) and the ideal mother (for the female spectator of soaps). Whereas Modleski seems to replicate a textual and universal Oedipal trajectory, which is then uniformly applied to the actual reader, Janice Radway's analysis of women's consumption of popular romantic fiction focuses on the mobility of reading as an oppositional practice which subverts their sacrificial domestic role.[21] Ian Ang's study *Watching Dallas: Soap Opera and the Melodramatic Imagination* explores the pleasure and fantasy of female spectators of *Dallas*, using Pierre Bourdieu's account of popular and sensual taste and consumption. Women sensually identify with the soap in terms of their everyday life, and so fantasy becomes for Ang an embodied identification, a psychic and social play between everyday life and the text. Instead of splitting language from the body and experience from the text, reality and fantasy are put into play. The imaginative pleasure for the female spectator in watching *Dallas* does not transcend the embodied real, as Oedipal textual theory would suggest, rather the spectator becomes involved in 'a game that enables one to place the limits of the fictional and the real under discussion and make them fluid'.[22]

How then do we conceptualize this fluid relation between imaginary and real in terms of the spectator or reader within studies of media consumption and film? Before I turn to examine the feminist ethnographic work of Stacey and Kuhn, I want to consider the phenomenological framework that Paddy Scannell develops in conceptualizing television and radio in modern life.

The 'real' spectator and time

Scannell uses Heidegger's *Being and Time* to explore how television and radio structure our everyday lives in a temporal manner: 'Broadcasting, whose medium is time, articulates our sense of time.'[23] Heidegger distinguishes between lived phenomenological time and chronological clock time which is institutionalized and regulated. Lived time, the ordinary, might be abiding with planned mental timing and procedure, but it might just as well be dreaming or doing nothing. This experiential life-time, or 'my-time', exists for me or anyone. It is the socially projected me, the possible me that is accounted for in the structure of the media programme.[24] Broadcasting is *directed* at audiences' my-time, although it remains outside life-time, inhabiting conventional, institutionalized time. According to Scannell, because broadcasting tunes its services to audience 'my-time', it can be said to also partake of this life-time.[25] Broadcasting, then, mediates between abstract clock time (oneself) and lived time (myself). Radio and television both mediate between the 'for anyone' time of public tradition and mass production, and the 'for someone', or my-time, structure of personal belonging, evidenced by family photos, letters and videos.[26]

Scannell identifies a third structure of lived time, or *Dasein*, called 'ownself', but he neglects it, because unlike the socially projected myself, the 'ownself' represents cherished but ultimately inexpressible parts of experience and memory. As such, the ownself is a by-product of broadcasting, only approached tangentially by public media such as radio and television.[27] Heidegger, however, might not agree. He describes how blindness to the 'ownmost' self can pervert the aim of *Dasein*, which is to clarify the meaning of Being.[28] Such blindness promotes anxiety and an uncanny homelessness within, time which Heidegger terms as a falling of *Dasein*. This fall causes us to flee. But rather than fleeing from the world, we run into it and become lost in an anaesthetized public realm, where we forget our embodied dwelling. The fall of *Dasein* 'does not flee in the face of entities within the world; these are precisely what it flees towards – as entities alongside which our concern, lost in the "they", can dwell in tranquillized familiarity'.[29] This uncanny, tranquil living in the imaginary of the other captures, precisely, the dilemma of the hysteric. If we come back now to Scannell's account, we can see how *Dasein* falls and becomes lost in the 'they' of public broadcasting and temporality.

Scannell idealizes the participation of television and radio audiences. He suggests that the outside world that broadcasting brings – with all its everyday concerns – becomes transformed in relation to a lived my-time, where the 'they' becomes a 'we'. Audiences are touched by the world of television, radio and newspapers. Their encounter is through a lived temporality of the everyday, endlessly being caught up, 'remarking, observing, commenting, blaming, ridiculing, laughing, worrying'.[30] Scannell's description misses the harsh truth that for many people watching television and listening to the radio is exactly a falling of *Dasein* and a fleeing into a public world of tranquil familiarization.[31] Watching television is as much a tranquil and hysterical forgetting of dwelling as it can also be at times the kind of lived everyday experience that Scannell so eloquently depicts.

The key, then, to whether *Dasein* becomes lost within the world, or whether it can find its situated place of dialectical and interpersonal belonging, depends on the 'ownmost' self. This 'ownmost' self is a personal belonging evidenced by family photos, videos and letters. For Heidegger, it is the experience of the uncanny as anxiety, an awareness of the uncanny that can bring *Dasein* back from its falling into the world to properly authenticate being. If we think about this in terms of family photos and videos we can see that they also signify a tranquil falling into the 'they' of the 'family romance', as much as they signify a more authentic recognition of uncanny anxiety and belonging. It is perhaps important to note here that individualization of *Dasein* does not mean 'privatization'; rather it points to a symbolic and existential recognition of 'being in the world'.

Heidegger's 'ownmost' self is depicted in Roland Barthes' essay on photography *Camera Lucida*.[32] Barthes suggests that the photograph reveals history as hysterical and divided. Unlike the filmic image or the Proustian evocation of the past, the photograph cannot remember, dream or mourn; it cannot work through the monstrous melancholy of 'engorged and immobilised time' that it presents. Therefore, the photograph in Barthes' view is undialectical; there is nothing about it that can 'transform grief into mourning'.[33] Unlike the cinema whose referent always moves, the photograph makes a claim on the real, and we are confronted with the actuality of the referent once being there. Barthes divides photographs into the *studium*, which are public, cultural codes 'for anyone', and the *punctum*, which is the personal detail in the photograph, that flash of recognition where we are caught up into structures of interpersonal belonging with the other.

Barthes describes how it is the one photograph of his mother that summons up this *punctum*, and her being, for him. The *punctum* confronts us with the meaning of time, the irreversibility of death; as such, it is a 'mad' confrontation with our existential being, which paradoxically dims down our uncanny mode of being 'not at home'.[34] Barthes distinguishes between photography and cinema, with the former hysterically immobilizing time and the latter allowing its passage as dream and memory. Quoting Bazin, he discusses how film is like a 'hideout': the filmic images and characters move and live on; they are not like photographic images which are immobilized and pinned down, as butterflies by the frame.

However, Barthes' analysis of the *punctum* collapses this distinction, because, where the *punctum* occurs within photography, movement within time is allowed, setting up a 'blind field'. The *punctum* as a detail in the photograph points to a historical beyond of the frame; it re-articulates the dead, objectified fetish in relation to the larger whole of history and the body. This embodiment of the *punctum* reverses the hysteria of photography and history. Like the photograph of Barthes' mother, the *punctum* releases the spectator into a shared structure of belonging, and, despite Barthes' protestations, it moves *him* into the realms of memory and lived time.

Photography is designated as the private, whereas television, radio and film are seen as more public and socially mediated transmissions. But they are all involved in the temporal movement of *Dasein*. Therefore, the photograph as an 'ownmost' self, or *punctum*, can also release us into shared belonging with the world – just as the consumption of film and television can hysterically lose us to the imaginary events of that public world, a familiar falling where we forget the 'real' of our dwelling. I now want to apply this phenomenological argument for a psychic and social re-memory of the real to the ethnographic accounts of film in cultural studies by Jacqui Stacey and Annette Kuhn.

Key point

- Paddy Scannell's conceptualization of television and radio in modern life also enables us to understand a phenomenological account of the real spectator.

Star gazing

The textual dominance of feminist film theories of spectatorship, exemplified by Laura Mulvey's theory of the male gaze, maps how the cinematic apparatus Oedipally constructs the spectator to identify with dominant textual representations of sexual difference. Mulvey herself revises this argument in a subsequent article entitled 'Afterthoughts', where she turns to Freud's notion of the difficulty for women in negotiating a passive route out of the Oedipal complex, highlighting how they remain stuck between active male and passive feminine positions.[35] This might make sexual difference more mobile, but as Jacqui Stacey observes it still leaves the spectator oscillating within a binary of heterosexual difference, where the only access to active looking is through a phallic metaphor or gaze.[36] Indeed, with subsequent feminist film theory this problem of not being able to escape the Oedipal binary is still apparent, leading to an inevitable collapse of women's desire into notions of privatized narcissistic identification. This ignores the fact that identification and desire are not mutually exclusive in either heterosexual or lesbian women.[37] Jacqui Stacey's *Star Gazing* is an exemplary work in feminist film spectatorship in that it refuses to accept the reduction of psychic and social fantasy to Oedipal binaries. Indeed, Stacey's attempts to think female homoeroticism in terms of desire and identification becomes critiqued, as she states, in terms of the very binary she is trying to escape: 'My appeal to move outside this framework to address feminine desires more broadly, or to rethink narcissism in relation to the feminine other, is ignored and instead Freud is called upon to refix the binarism I attempted to disrupt.'[38]

In her attempts to make the female spectator move more flexibly outside sexual difference binaries and between psychic and social identities, Stacey considers the work of Elizabeth Cowie and Constance Penley. Cowie and Penley utilize the ideas of Laplanche and Pontalis in order to theorize a cinematic structural fantasy, one that is rooted within the *mise-en-scène*. In this scenario, the scene of film and cinema representation mirrors the early pre-Oedipal and structural staging of desire, where fantasy and pleasure are not gender-orientated and can be identified in multiple ways in relation to the screen. As Stacey notes, the problem with this approach is an over-riding analogy between film fantasy and the unconscious, an analogy that negates more conscious and social forms of fantasy and identity. Ultimately, for her, Cowie's approach refuses, rather than explores 'the relationship between psychic and social'.[39]

Undeterred by not finding a social explanation of fantasy and spectatorship within Oedipal psychoanalysis, Stacey follows a cultural studies tradition and turns to the analysis of real female spectators, rather than textual ones. Her study is located in 1940s and 1950s Britain in relation to Hollywood female stars. The embodied imaginary that Ian Ang describes in terms of the female spectator is taken up by Stacey in relation to her study of female spectatorship of Hollywood stars. Active audiences do not necessarily signify ideologically resistant or free spectators. Ang's methodology of concentrating on the audience's letters as texts, which do not inevitably reveal the 'truth' of the spectator, is also implemented by Stacey. Analysing letters to cinema magazines in the 1940s and 1950s Stacey realized she had not got enough material, so she advertised in contemporary leading women's magazines for women in their fifties (and over) to write in about their experiences of watching film, forty and fifty years previously. Stacey subsequently compiled a questionnaire based on those responses, which was explicitly structured to elicit memories.

As Stacey points out, 'the relationship between memory and history is a slippery one.' This is because popular memory highlights not an objective recuperation of historical fact, but the personal investment and selection that occurs in choosing certain events over others.[40] Stacey uses cultural studies work on popular memory to analyse her female spectators' letters and questionnaires. The female spectators in Stacey's study remember with great pleasure and nostalgia their cinema-going days in the 1940s and 1950s, linking their experiences to their daily lives. For these women, cinema-going and identification with glamorous Hollywood stars was a pleasurable escape from the relatively deprived existence in wartime and postwar Britain. Adolescence and young adulthood are remembered in terms of the ideal identifications these women experienced in relation to Hollywood film stars. Retrospective nostalgia of feminine ideals, never fully realized, become treasured moments of memory and fantasy recorded by these female spectators. Stacey defines two sorts of memory operating in their texts. First, an iconic memory where the frozen image is remembered, and second, a narrative form of memory where the spectators reconstruct self-narratives through temporal recollections between present and past.[41]

Examining the identification of female spectators with their Hollywood stars, Stacey divides their identification between fantasy and cultural practice. This distinction, Stacey admits, does not really hold, but is made nonetheless because she wishes to highlight the exclusion of social practices of identification within psychoanalytic accounts. Cinema studies, generally, has used identification in terms of literary or narrative models, aligning the spectator's identification with a visual and narrative point of view, i.e., with the screen characters. Elaboration of the term 'identification' in film studies through psychoanalysis has used Freudian and Lacanian theory to examine how the cinema's identification with sexual difference is textually replicated within the spectator. Identification in these Oedipal theories of (hetero)sexual difference is about separating desire from identification. You desire what you don't want to be, and want to be what you don't desire. Identification is, then, heterosexually fixed, unless of course you are pre-Oedipally immature. Freud believed this was more likely in women, who (in his account) are therefore more prone to shifting identifications between both sexes and homoerotic desire.

Stacey rightly takes issue with this narrow account of identification within film studies and psychoanalysis, arguing through reference to her case studies that homoerotic desire between women involves identification as desire. Many of the heterosexual female spectators in Stacey's account wrote to her, stating their identification, but also their adoration and love of the film stars they admired. One of Stacey's respondents, a Patricia Robinson, admits her adoration of Deanna Durbin: 'I think perhaps that it would be considered to be a bit of a giggle today, if a large number of women confessed to feeling love for a girl. Nobody seemed to question it then. Just in case; I have been married since 1948! Have two sons and a daughter, one grandchild.'[42]

Recent feminist research into psychoanalysis has shown that desire and identification are not distinct but hopelessly entwined.[43] However, Stacey's intention to conceptualize cinematic identification beyond Oedipal formulations, as a cultural process with social meanings, leads her to distinguish between psychic fantasy and social practice.[44] For Stacey, cinematic identification also takes place beyond the cinema in a social world where the female spectators will often transform aspects of their appearance and behaviour in relation to their adored stars. Hairstyles, clothes, a particular way of walking, talking or rolling the eyes, become the mimetic play. Stacey describes how the spectators imitate and copy the appearances of the female stars. Moreover, copying is a practice which transforms the spectator's physical appearance. She concludes that whereas identificatory *fantasies* relate to cinematic viewing and connote difference, the focus is on the stars, not the spectators. Identificatory *practices*, on the other hand, relate to the spectator's use of the stars in a different cultural time and place. These practices take place in everyday life, outside the cinematic space, and are more connotative of sameness, as the spectators are more involved in 'closing the gap produced

by the differences'. Here, self-transformation of the spectators themselves is accentuated. Stacey observes that whereas Lacanian and
Freudian psychoanalytic models fix identity in terms of cinematic
spectatorship, her research shows how identification involves the
production of new identities, rather than simply the conformation of
existing ones.[45]

I disagree with the distinction Stacey makes between fantasy and
practice, for this limits the work of the imaginary to a mental psychic
mechanism, whereas in a phenomenological account of the imaginary, fantasy, imagination and embodied practice are all imbricated
with each other. Such a bodily imaginary can sum up the fantasy and
the practice of these female spectators. Rather then just imitating or
copying their favourite stars, the female spectators are also involved
in a practice and language of mimesis which oscillates between similarity and difference. This mimesis does not just confirm existing
identifications, it also produces new ones.

Movement from a private to a more embodied imaginary is
dependent on a phenomenological, retrospective memory of the real
which can re-articulate hysterical and frozen identifications within
shared structures of belonging. This screen memory, whether we con-
ceive of it in relation to film spectatorship, media audiences or the
more personal consumption of photographs, mediates between public
institutional time and experiential lived time. Another way of putting
this is to say that screen memory, in film spectatorship, mediates and
fluidly connects between embodied psychic fantasy and everyday
life. In relation to Stacey's film viewers, it is not just the self-
transformation of the spectator that is achieved but also a mediation
of the idealized star or image.

We can distinguish between two forms of perception and memory
that operate in film spectatorship. The first is hysterical, incorporative or melancholic. Second, a more embodied re-memory occurs, a
mourning where the past is reworked and re-imagined in terms of the
present. Stacey's spectators don't travel *from* psychic (cinematic) *to*
social (extra-cinematic) identification. They move from a melancholic, hysterical and idealized identification with the stars, to a screen
memory and practice that is socially embodied within time.

Both hysterical memory and a more psychically embodied memory
operate within film spectatorship. An example of these idealized or
hysterical images is characterized by the 'treasured' and frozen
moments or memories of the female spectators in Stacey's study.
Fantasy and identification, here, are with the star's difference and
unattainability. Such moments are characterized by 'Bette Davis's
flashing eyes' or 'Rita Hayworth's flowing hair'. These 'treasured'

moments that have been frozen in time become reworked in the spectator's embodied play and practice within everyday life. They are also
involved in the act of retrospective memory, a process which is also
a central methodological tool of the study. However, I don't want to
suggest, as Stacey seems to, that this embodied re-memory only operates in an extra-cinematic space. Radstone's reading of *Forrest Gump*
and my own analysis of *Boys Don't Cry* (see chapter 3) are both
examples of how hysterical, Oedipal memory can be reworked, in
relation to lived time, within the textual address of the film itself.

The frozen, 'treasured' moments of time, remembered by the
female spectators in Stacey's study, are similar to photographs which
hysterically immobilize and repress the passage of time and our fear
of death. However, the treasured images of time in Stacey's study are
also like the Winter Garden photograph of Barthes' mother, expressive of the *punctum*. They figure as a more embodied dwelling. So,
on one level Stacey's female audiences are uncannily lost to the
'public' world of their stars. But, on another level they are pierced,
like Barthes, into a '*heimlich*' recognition of their being. Patricia
Robinson recalls how she remembers first becoming aware of Deanna
Durbin through details of her mouth and her perfect teeth, in magazines and newspapers. She then connects the facial images with a
lovely singing voice she has heard on the radio. It is only later when
she sees the star on screen that these fetishistic images become fully
embodied with a realization of the star's name. The effect on Patricia is 'electrifying' and signifies the beginning of a lifelong love affair
with her adored idol.

Iconic images remembered by Stacey's spectators are screen memories that summon up both experience and fantasy. Elaboration of
these images moves them beyond a fetishistic and hysterical identification with the image/text to a practice of embodied memory and
lived experience within everyday life. As in Stacey's study, this re-
memory can be temporal and retrospective, replaying films from
within another cultural time and space. Or it can occupy the present
viewing situation itself – films that haunt you, precisely because that
re-memory occurs within the film experience that is taking place.

If Barthes' photograph of his mother is his 'ownmost' self, a self
that informs the wider cultural text of *Camera Lucida*, then in
Stacey's study perhaps what is missing is the problematization of
Stacey's own role as ethnographer, her personal narrative of place and
belonging. Like the treasured moments of the Hollywood spectators,
we are offered a performative, idealized image of femininity at the
beginning of Stacey's book, a photograph of her in her mother's
1950s attire, at a memorabilia ball in the 1970s. Interestingly, this

photograph is not explored further, as the focus moves onto 'other' female spectators, although it implicitly sets the scene and subject for debate.

Key points

- Jacqui Stacey's project is a rethinking of the female spectator in terms of homoerotic desire, identification and narcissism, as a more intersubjective relationship which moves between social and psychic identities.
- Stacey divides cinematic spectatorship into fantasy and practice. Identificatory *fantasies* relate to cinematic viewing; identificatory *practices* relates to the spectator's use of the stars in everyday life.
- Dissolving the distinction Stacey makes between fantasy and practice allows us to see film spectatorship as a phenomenological mimesis.

Family Secrets

Family Secrets by Annette Kuhn also begins with a personal family photograph; it then moves on to an ethnographic reading of film. Annette Kuhn offers an account of psychoanalytic and social 'memory work'. The fact that she refuses explicitly to align her 'memory work' with psychoanalysis is perhaps telling of the historical difficulty in being able to both use psychoanalysis and prevent the narrative being recuperated into Oedipal frameworks that exclude embodied histories and social meanings. Annette Kuhn starts with a 'toolkit' of what memory work is and how to do it. Using family photographs, Kuhn refers to Rosy Martin's and Jo Spence's work on phototherapy and the family album, and discusses how the photograph can operate as a starting image. She provides the reader with some simple rules on how to read such photographs. First, describe the photograph, imagine yourself as the subject and connect with the feelings associated with this image. Examine the context of production, what circumstances gave rise to it, and concentrate on the technology that produced the image and on the aesthetics of the image. Lastly, consider the circulation of the photographic image then and now: what were the conditions of reception when it was taken and what are they now?

Kuhn uses private family photos, but also public images of films, news and a painting, to trace and elaborate on memories. For her, whether these are categorized as private or public, all forms of individual memory are also always collective. She writes:

> I observe too, the unfolding in memory texts of connections between memory and the past, memory and time, memory and place, memory and experience, memory and images, memory and the Unconscious. And I note, finally, that in all memory texts, personal and collective remembering emerge again and again as continuous with one another.[46]

For Kuhn, the photographs of her family album are a re-memory of the past in terms of a living history of the present. Traces of the past are endlessly re-membered in terms of remakings of identity and meaning in the present. Kuhn recounts painful Oedipal conflicts through her excursion down memory lane. These memories make her aware of anger and aggression at her mother's narcissistic identifications and the loss of her father. As ambivalent memories they contradict and subvert the 'happy' linear progression of stories advertised by the family photography business in the 1950s. Providing an ironic twist to the Kodak slogan on 1955 advertisements, which ran 'She'll always be your little girl because you took the picture', Kuhn takes this title to recount the family story behind a picture of her as a six-year-old child, taken by her father, a story that reveals the possibility but also the loss of that father/daughter relationship, barred through the mother's possessiveness. The mother's story of the photograph competes with the daughter's. For Kuhn, this is yet another example of her mother's blurred boundaries in identifying and appropriating her daughter's desire/identity, although, as Kuhn acknowledges, the two stories challenge each other for the 'truth'. So, although Kuhn is recounting and remembering a private story of her loss and desire for her father, this largely psychoanalytic account of Oedipal dramas is also connected to a wider family romance: the narrative of consumption espoused, and put into play by the family photography industry. However, the private melancholy of Kuhn's past, where Oedipal competition means choosing between father and mother (or between identification and desire), reveals a painful irony encapsulated within the public slogan promoting the happy family, 'She'll always be your little girl'. In this way, Kuhn moves a psychoanalytic exploration of her childhood to wider social registers of meaning and structure.

Kuhn's family narrative is a story of paternal claim and identification which is eradicated in favour of the mother. Thus Kuhn examines, in a similar vein to Carolyn Steedman, the painful politics of class that contribute to this narrative of maternal envy and narcissism, versus the daughter's angry melancholy. Kuhn's family photo is painful, an Oedipal hysteria that, in Barthes' words, cannot 'transform grief into mourning'.[47] It is only when Kuhn moves this autobiography of her everyday life away from photography and towards an analysis of film that the narrative seems to integrate space and time through a process of mourning and re-memory.

Mandy (1952) is a film first seen by Kuhn as a child and then remembered from the perspective of an adult, postgraduate seminar twenty-eight years later. In this second story it is Kuhn's identification with the deaf girl in the film, the little girl's struggle for naming, language and social identity that has an unforgettable emotional impact on Kuhn. Reminding her of her childhood, this identification intrudes into her more academic conversations about the film when teaching as an adult. Kuhn describes the textual, post-structuralist analysis of *Mandy* in the postgraduate class as lacking an account of the spectator's emotional, embodied response to the film. For Kuhn, that response returns through the images of the film, particularly with an analysis of the images of 'waste ground' outside the family home. These 'waste ground' images in the film prove a 'transitional space' for the protagonist Mandy in a journey towards identity and naming. But this 'waste ground' is also an image that figures for Kuhn as a social memory of postwar reconstruction in Britain: an image that paints a mythical archetype of war and conflict, and also circulates as a more personal image of Mandy's struggle. Like Walter Benjamin's profane illumination, this image of the 'waste land' operates for the spectator as an embodied re-memory of the present in terms of the past. As a work of mourning and re-memory this film is a social and psychic practice of the embodied imaginary.

Interestingly, Kuhn's last chapter in *Family Secrets* brings together Freud and Barthes in a discussion of mourning. Entitled 'A Phantasmagoria of Memory', this conclusion links photography, painting, documentary and film in terms of British heritage. Social memory of the texts is interwoven again with Kuhn's autobiographical memories. Her sense of London as a place and as a kind of dreaming state is elaborated on with reference to Michel de Certeau's essay 'Walking in The City'. Just as de Certeau and Kuhn connect dreaming memories of city, space and place to the experience of childhood, so too can their social and psychic memory work be linked to Walter Benjamin's collective phantasmagoria or dream world. Kuhn's memory work explicitly uses Barthes' sense of the *punctum* to analyse a photograph of St Paul's Cathedral during the Blitz. Two films are also analysed: the first a documentary entitled *Listen To Britain*, made after the Blitz; the second a more recent film made by Derek Jarman in 1987, entitled *The Last of England*.

Iconography of the photo and the films, in this account, are the practice of memory and the imaginary: both personal and social. Images, here, are also perceived as screen memories which are interwoven, for Kuhn, through the particular image of fire. These screen images figure, like the 'waste ground' in *Mandy*, as a reworking of familial psychic fantasy and experience, but they also operate simultaneously as a social memory of postwar Britain. The films operate, therefore, as a cinematic imagination analogous to the 'inner' workings of the mind. As such, they are ascribed very different stories of place and belonging by Kuhn: two different phenomenological memories – of hysteria and mourning. The first screen memory and experience of *Listen to Britain* summons up pleasurable feelings of belonging and unity, which for Kuhn is a nostalgic disavowal and longing for an imaginary united family and community. The second screen memory, *The Last of England*, unsettles, fragments and 'pierces' Kuhn with anxiety in an uncanny sense, marking for her the retrospective work of mourning. If *Listen To Britain* figures as a falling and forgetting of *Dasein* into a public 'they' of nostalgic familiarization, then *The Last of England* becomes a turning away from that falling, an awareness of the 'ownmost' structures of time and belonging. Kuhn's reading does not distinguish between the iconography of the photograph of St Paul's and the films. In fact, the distinction she makes of memory is *between* the films. As such, Kuhn rewrites Barthes' phenomenological division between photography and film.

For Barthes, the photograph arrests the viewer with the thing-ness of the referent, the thing that has 'posed in front of the tiny hole and remained there forever'.[48] In contrast, cinema negates that pose; time passes with the series of continuous images. This phenomenological division of the melancholia of photography or the mourning of film is reflected in Kuhn's narrative of her family photograph versus her reading of the film *Mandy*. However, in 'A Phantasmagoria of Memory' this distinction collapses, with the hysterical memory of one film versus the mourning of another. Technological difference, here, is not determining, rather it is the dialectical play of time and being, the structures of interpersonal belonging that the spectator enters into, in relation to the technology and text.

Key points

- Kuhn's family photo is a painful melancholy, an Oedipal hysteria, that in Barthes' words cannot 'transform grief into mourning'.
- It is only when Kuhn moves this autobiography of her everyday life away from photography and towards an analysis of the film *Mandy* that the narrative seems to integrate space and time through a process of mourning and re-memory.
- However, Kuhn's last chapter in *Family Secrets* rewrites and dissolves Barthes' distinction between the hysteria of photography and the mourning of film.

Conclusion

Stacey's and Kuhn's elaboration of cultural re-memory cannot be reduced to classical psychoanalytical conceptions of *Nachträglichkeit*. As I have indicated, the Oedipal fantasy operating within their texts is a melancholic, hysterical and idealized identification that is then opened up, through a social and embodied reconfiguration of the psyche, as a mourning and creative image play. The film text cannot be divorced from the experiences of the real film spectator or audience; they are both always caught within a flow of phenomenological experience oscillating between real and imaginary. If this is so, then the Oedipal/semiotic understanding of the split between text and spectator is no longer viable and we have to look beyond Althusserian and Lacanian understandings of ideology and identification.

Cultural studies work on ethnography has always problematized structuralist and post-structuralist textual approaches through its focus on social experience. But I suggest that a more phenomenological understanding of notions of experience and psychoanalysis refuses a dichotomy not just between text and spectator, but also a division between linguistic meaning and embodied experience that has underwritten so many founding cultural studies texts. Stuart Hall's 'Cultural Studies: Two Paradigms' article and his piece on 'Encoding/decoding' to some extent rely on this division, although I suggest that we don't have to perceive spectator's responses to texts as either wholly meaningful or unconscious or as ideologically placed.[49] Forms of identification that move between real and imaginary worlds articulate the relation between the spectator/ethnographer and the image/text within structures of time, place and belonging.

Psychoanalysis is not forever Oedipally wedded – or I should say divorced – in Oedipal disharmony, from social accounts of experience and identification. Indeed, the practice of a phenomenological imaginary is premissed on the very refusal of this disjunction or split between linguistic text and the experiential, real spectator. If we understand the Oedipal split between language and the body to inform a particular, hysterical form of film memory and spectatorship, then we also have to acknowledge a more social, embodied, screen memory. The retrospective, phenomenological memory I have described can thus be used to problematize the different methodologies of ethnography, rather than resolve them. We need to persist in thinking through and breaking down the melancholic and Oedipal boundaries between the imaginary and real, so allowing a fluid play of being between the real spectator and the film text.

7

Stars and Melodrama

Introduction

So far I have argued for the mimetic 'gaze' of a phenomenological or bodily imaginary. In re-reading debates on the textual and film spectator it has been suggested that neither a post-structuralist focus on the apparatus nor an imaginary free emphasis on the real spectator can help us to understand the bodily and psychological encounter between the spectator and the film text. The spectator is, therefore, neither completely ideal nor fixed through ideology, but neither can 'he' or 'she' be understood in terms of an objective, empirically quantifiable audience. Chapter 5 discussed the historicization of the textual spectator, while the last chapter has focused on the cultural re-memory implicit within ethnographic models of film spectatorship. However, we cannot really historicize the textual spectator without reference to inter-textuality and contemporary debates on stars and genre mixing.

Identifying with stars as texts and as ideology

The attention to stars in contemporary film theory has arisen largely due to the widespread dissatisfaction with Apparatus theory.[1] In Apparatus theory and textual analysis the star is simply a function of the narrative, part of the textual system, albeit, influenced by the persona of the star external to the film. Current emphasis is focused on the inter-textuality of stars that circulates and flows between a wide range of differing texts, such as the film, television entertainment, magazines, fan internet sites, advertising and the music business where increasingly film stars and musical stars cross over. Bjork, Nicole Kidman, Ewan McGregor and of course Madonna are examples. Richard Dyer's two monographs, *Stars* and *Heavenly Bodies: Film Stars and Society*, have been central to this study. Drawing on a tradition of semiotics and structuralism, particularly Lévi-Strauss and Althusser, Dyer understands the appeal of stars in relation to cultural myth. Following Lévi-Strauss's idea that myths are intrinsic to how a culture thinks and resolves myth, Dyer argues that stars speak to social contradictions. Sometimes stars resolve these contradictions and sometimes they heighten them. Marilyn Monroe fascinated audiences because she was both sexy and innocent. She seduced men but did not threaten them, at a time when social upheaval was also destabilizing conventional gender roles. For Dyer, there is a 'structured polysemy' to the images of stars, multiple elements that are in tension with each other, thus raising contradictions to any linear flow of meaning. It is important to note Dyer's use of the word 'image'. He is not referring to the star as a person, but to the star as a conglomeration of texts. The star's image is therefore complex, and this image can either conform or clash with the narrative character a star plays in a film. For example, Tom Cruise's character in Kubrick's *Eyes Wide Shut*, where he played a psychologist, sharply contradicts his macho image of a sexual action hero both on screen and in life; his subsequent great performance in the film *Magnolia* goes one further in satirically deconstructing that macho performance.

Dyer also draws on the same sources as Apparatus theory to define the ideological functioning of stars. Utilizing Althusser's ideas of how ideology interpellates us as individuals and social subjects, Dyer argues that stars present us with the contradictions of this ideology of individualism: they 'articulate both the promise and the difficulty that the notion of individuality presents to all of us who live by it'.[2] Judith Mayne suggests that although Dyer does not reduce his notions of contradiction to resistant ideology, within the terms of 1970s Apparatus theory, all arguments based on finding the contradictory gaps and fissures within the dominant ideology become read as a contestation. She warns about the danger of positing a dominant/resistant binary where everything becomes collapsed into hegemonic ideology or its subversion.

Christopher Williams echoes these views, and asks how useful is ideology as a concept for understanding the circulation of cultural forms.[3] Using the example of Bette Davis, Mayne describes the relationship of the spectator to the film star as too complex to be contained within a dynamic where the spectator is passively inside

dominant ideology and complicit, or outside it and therefore resistant. Pointing to how Davis's star image circulated within a number
of inter-textual forms such as fan magazines, advertisements,
women's magazines and consumer products, Mayne documents how
her star image has been one of stark contradiction, moving between
binaries of domestic wife versus career woman, female rivalry versus
feminist power, self-determination versus consumer goddess. This
complex relation invites

> the opposing terms of love, hate, devotion and obsession, life and the
> movies, butch and femme to inflect each other constantly. I am sug-
> gesting that the appeal of stardom is that of constant reinvention, the
> dissolution of contraries, the embrace of wildly opposing terms.[4]

Stars and gender as bodily performance

There is a complexity to the spectator's embrace of binary opposites
in relation to the inter-textual circulation of star images. But I don't
think we can understand this complexity within the structured terms
of Lacanian and Althusserian film theory. The model of identification
advocated here is based on the necessity of an Oedipal model, utilized (within 1970s film theory) as a cinematic apparatus that textually inscribes ideal or ideological positions of sexual difference which
the spectator then takes up. Lacan might well have announced the
masquerade of sexual difference, but for him it was also immutable,
an inescapable fact of language and the symbolic, which we can only
foreclose at the peril of psychosis.

I would like to suggest a different model of identification in relation to stars in terms of a bodily imaginary, an identification with
star images that does not reduce them to purely textual, Oedipal, or
ideological determinants. In his book *Stars*, Dyer discusses how our
understanding of stardom is always structured between seeing them
as special or different and seeing them as the same as, or like, us in
a more ordinary way. This interplay of desire and identification is at
odds with an Oedipal heterosexuality where desire and identification
are seen as mutually exclusive. We can think, therefore, of the bisexual forms of identification and desire that operate in relation to stars,
where Judy Garland has for a long time been an icon for male gay
culture, or how Tom Cruise is on one level an all heterosexual male
star, and precisely because of that 'macho' performance becomes a
representation of homoeroticism for gay men.

Indeed, the rumours about Cruise's alleged gay identity, which he
has strongly rebutted, only add to this complexity. Steven Cohan

discusses the masquerade of the bachelor playboy in 1950s and early 1960s Hollywood films where stars such as Cary Grant and Rock Hudson played the stereotyped straight, hunky and masculine leads.[5] However, the romantic sex comedy films in which these stars played also parodied male identity, with the male leads adopting feminine identities to either seduce or trick the woman. And of course in real life, Grant was, as Cohan points out, bisexual and a cross-dresser, whereas Hudson was gay. We can argue that the spectator's identifications don't just swing from one Oedipal binary to another. Part of the complexity of star images is that they incorporate a much more fluid and bisexual movement between desire and identification. Cohan's notion of the bachelor masquerade operating with these male stars is based on Butler's ideas of gender performance, rather than Oedipal psychoanalysis. In other words, the gender operating here is a performance constituting identity. Cohan states that the kind of masquerade he is describing is not hiding a dark (phallic) secret, rather it is marking out an identity in terms of 'opposing planes' a movement of gender mobility between sameness and difference.

However, there is a problem with Butler's idea of gender performance if we see it simply as willed or voluntary cross-dressing. She would argue anyway that there is no willed agency as such behind gender performance. It is only through the recitation of its discursive practice that gender can be performed differently. We can certainly apply Butler's notion of gender recitation to Dyer's and Cohan's notions of the textual and inter-textual performance of star images. As image texts and inter-texts, star images become performed and repeated in oppositional ways that confound or contradict any singular/stable notion of ideology, gender or identity. Butler places her notion of gender performance within a post-structuralist register of discourse. For her, the imaginary is flawed because in Lacanian accounts it is pre-Oedipal and therefore inaccessible to language and culture. We can, though, understand the imaginary not within Oedipal dualisms, but as phenomenological experience: a mimetic performance which moves between hysterical sexual difference and a more social re-memory of the real.

Key points

- In Apparatus theory and textual analysis the star is simply a function of the narrative, part of the textual system.
- Current emphasis is focused on the inter-textuality of stars.

- According to Dyer, stars present us with the contradictions of an ideology of individualism.
- We can understand a different model of identification in relation to stars in terms of a bodily imaginary and gender performance.

Star identification as fans

Now, this argument can be seen to operate with spectators as fans. Dyer's emphasis on stars as sites of contradiction and resistance paved the way to connect film studies with cultural studies, opening up questions of film spectatorship and linking them to issues of fandom and subculture. Dyer's ideas that stars embody meanings which are contradictory, complicit and resistant to dominant ideological meanings have been developed into discussions of how the duality of stars and the contrast between their ordinary and spectacular lives circulate through a range of texts and are taken up in active ways by the audience. John Fiske proposes that audiences and fans choose films and stars that make sense of, and transform, their own social experiences and identities.[6] Yvonne Tasker accentuates the 'complex personas' of stars that are constructed from 'far more than the texts in which they appear'.[7] In her analysis of Hollywood action films Tasker highlights the active and resistant roles that male stars offer their fans. Bearing in mind Mayne's reservation about dissolving contradiction into resistance, about avoiding the complexity of star images by reducing their reception to either dominant or subversive ideological meaning, I want to explore further the performance of stars in relation to questions of fandom, reception and embodiment.

Constance Penley and Henry Jenkins have both mapped the differing ways that fans appropriate meanings from the dominant television series *Star Trek*, exchanging and remaking them in terms of their own social interactions and communities. Jenkins highlights Michel de Certeau's ideas, arguing that fans are 'rogue readers' poaching and raiding media texts as a basis for their own cultural productions.[8] Moreover, Jenkins warns against seeing this fan cultural production in terms of pure 'ideological struggle'; he argues that fans do not see themselves in political terms and that they 'rework media material as the basis for their own social interactions and cultural exchanges'.[9]

Constance Penley also investigates the fan reception and production of *Star Trek*, exploring the slash stories and fanzines of a group of heterosexual women. Slash stories are a genre where women reread and produce the fictional male heterosexual relations in science fiction and action adventure stories in terms of homoerotic desire. Slash fanzines of *Star Trek* focus especially on the figures of Spock and Captain Kirk. Penley reveals that these texts are full of homo-erotic fantasies between the two male stars which are rendered as both romantic and explicitly pornographic. These bisexual fantasies of Kirk and Spock allow the female spectators the pleasures of both identifying with and desiring the male stars.

In her exploration of the slash fan's homoerotic texts, Penley utilizes the psychoanalytic writings of Laplanche and Pontalis to argue for positions of fantasy and sexual identification that are mobile, rather than fixed for the spectator.[10] Laplanche and Pontalis re-read Freud's origin of the sexual drive. Where Freud posits an experience of satisfaction between the infant and breast, Laplanche and Pontalis argue for an autoerotic hallucination of the absent breast as fantasy. In other words, sexuality begins, not with bodily drives, but with fantasy, and this is an autoerotic staged setting of fantasy and desire, where the subject does not pursue an object of desire, but is caught up 'in the sequence of images'.[11] Elizabeth Cowie has famously matched this theory with film studies, arguing for the staged setting of desire within the film as the *mise-en-scène*, where multiple points of identification and desire can be taken up by the spectator.[12] Whereas Cowie's argument is a textual analysis of film spectatorship, Constance Penley develops similar ideas within a discussion of an active participation of the audience through fandom.

Penley's study is fascinating, but there remains a problem, for me, with her use of Laplanche and Pontalis. For while their argument frees us from the Oedipal binaries of Apparatus theory it roots all fantasy in representation, thus evacuating the other's body as a site of desire. Let us consider the desire and identification of Penley's slash fans in terms of a sensual imaginary and mimesis. The fantasies of these women are not just a representation of homoerotic desire between men, they are a graphic and pornographic embodiment. Within this account Spock and Kirk are identified with and desired mimetically because that is the basis of desire and identification with the other. These heterosexual women's fantasies and their exchange of fanzines is a copying and mimesis that reconfigures Oedipal oppo-sitions between activity and passivity. Through identifying with Kirk and Spock as a homosexual couple, these women also confound Foucault's institutionalized opposition between gay and straight sexuality within our culture. This might not be a conscious political act and therefore ideological in Jenkins' eyes, but it does resist dominant ideologies of sexual difference, however unwittingly.

I contend that identification with stars is a phenomenological mimesis of the body which is both conscious and unconscious and moves between the real and representation in terms of an imaginary that is presented through the image. This star image is not a text, as in Dyer's sense, but a liminal space between the real and language which finds representation within films and inter-textual forms such as magazines, advertisements, etc. But this image is at the same time rooted in a 'real' relation to our bodies and histories. Mimesis of the star image is both textual representation and a figuration of the real.

Penley's study, like Jacqui Stacey's *Star Gazing*, illustrates a mimesis of the spectator between textual identification and a more active and located community and audience. But as Dyer, Mayne and more recently Tasker portray, the spectator's identification with the film star image is always moving between the text and everyday life. This doubling is often apparent through the differing inter-textual appearances of the star image; in the contradiction, say, between the stars' ideal performance on the screen and their more ordinary behaviour in everyday life. Sometimes, the star image, as Tasker and Christine Geraghty have recently pointed out, can remain more stable. Here, as in Tasker's discussion of Stallone in films such as *Rocky* (1976) and *First Blood* (1982), the image of the actor in real life and on screen merge. In Stallone's star image it is the story of poverty to riches, the immigrant's successful struggle with the establishment, against all odds.

Perhaps the doubling of star images as both contradictory and consistent is significant in that it returns us to a consideration of the psychological, split and embodied perceptions of the spectator. In our identification with stars, we are, as Dyer suggests, always in search of the star's real 'life' and self because it is also a projection of an important part of ourselves.[13] This similarity is always augmented by the star's difference or specialness. We only want in stars, mind you, the differences that we want. In other words, as Geraghty points out, Stallone's everyday star image as a happily married dad with glasses, 'clutching babies', is distinctly unwelcome and 'dysfunctional' to his fans because it contradicts his action hero performance.[14] The specialness of the star is a hysterical mimesis where we are caught up in the other's imaginary, an idealistic identification in relation to the other's body and desire. Apprehending these stars in their everyday lives, on chat shows and in magazines is fascinating for the audience, because these godlike star images appear ordinary and like us.

Princess Diana is a key example of this; the manipulation of her image, especially through the famous *Panorama* interview where she revealed her bulimia, her husband's adultery and the problems with her mother-in-law, made her ordinary, but it was an ordinariness and difference that still fitted her star image. Diana, as a princess like us, is ideally special and similar, but her appeal rests essentially on being the same. Our fascination with Diana is being hysterically caught up in the other's imaginary, a hysteria which indeed her death made highly visible. If this is so, then how are star images ever really different? How, in other words, do we find an outside to the other's desire, and what does this mean in relation to questions of ideology and language? In a post-structuralist sense, placing oneself outside the other's imaginary is also putting oneself in relation to language and the law. In Lacan's view, difference is achieved within the symbolic alterity of language. There is then no outside of ideology, just the difference of actively wielding power or being a subject. And this is the kernel of Butler's thinking too, that performative difference is only achieved through the recitation and differences in language. There is no outside to power, then, just its reiteration and performance, a miming of the dominant through language and speech that eventually makes a difference.

François Roustang disagrees with Lacan; for him the desire of the other is not the law, and neither is the analyst simply an impersonal function of that law or ideology. In order for the hysteric to resolve her transference onto the other, or the 'one that knows', she has to perceive the analyst as a real 'somebody'. Not too real, for that would paralyse any projected fantasies, but not completely imaginary either. Roustang calls Lacan's phallic law Nobody, and in order for analysis to work and for the transference to be resolved the hysteric or the analysand has to move away from the idealism of both the other's imaginary and the law.[15] This is achieved by the therapist realizing that a) what the hysteric really wants is out of the infernal circle of desire that 'she' is bound to, a desire that is merely encouraged by the analyst's impersonation of Nobody; and that b) this entails the therapist not acting on his desire, but implicating it by introducing aspects of the real. In therapy this is often achieved through finding traces of the 'real' life of your therapist in or outside the session. But real, here, does not mean authentic, just that someone has a different imaginary. There is no such thing as 'Nobody', un-embodied ideology, or the law, in an abstract sense. Nobody is always somebody, and this means acknowledging the dialogic status of different imaginaries. When we stop hysterically splitting our desire off onto the one that is supposed to know and embody what we want, then we can move to a more social (or shared) recollection and practice.

Fandom entails a hysterical, disembodied mimesis in relation to the star image, as 'the other's imaginary', but this mimesis also moves to a miming and practice in everyday life where the 'real' of difference can be negotiated.

Key points

- Constance Penley and Henry Jenkins have both mapped the differing ways that fans appropriate meanings from the dominant television series *Star Trek*.
- Identification with stars is a phenomenological mimesis of the body.
- The spectator's mimetic performance moves between the text and everyday life, and between disembodied and embodied apprehensions of the star image.

Stars, genre, melodrama

I have specifically focused on the movement between textual and extra-textual understanding of star images in relation to film spectators, as fans and subcultures, but what of the spectator's embodied apprehension of the star image in relation to texts and genre? Christine Geraghty distinguishes between three sorts of stars. Celebrity stars function between everyday life and the text. These stars circulate within extra-textual formats, and their 'real' life is pieced together by the audience through tabloids, gossip columns and celebrity interviews. Stars as professionals and performers are products of a relationship based more firmly on the filmic text. Geraghty focuses on stars as performers and takes up Christine Gledhill's analysis of method acting as a way of understanding how certain male actors have acquired cultural value distinct from garnering celebrity status in extra-textual formats. I want to explore Gledhill's analysis of method acting and its implications, not just for the star as performer, but for our performative identifications with stars.

Gledhill argues for melodrama as a self-transforming genre which has moved from nineteenth-century Victorian theatre to twentieth-century Hollywood. Marginalized as a women's form, playing second fiddle to a dominant realistic aesthetic in Hollywood, melodrama also occupies the same realm as realism – the world of bourgeois capitalism.[16] As Peter Brooks has noted, realism is compensated for by the melodramatic imagination. Moreover, as I discussed in the Introduction, Brooks' sense that melodrama externalizes psychic conflict is a phenomenological typology of the hysteric. Gledhill argues that the double movement of melodrama that Elsaesser traces, between a tradition emphasizing a dramatic, public persona, and one derived from an internal world of romantic drama, can help us understand the construction of film stars.[17] Stars reach audiences through their bodies, and just as melodrama has an intrinsic relation to realism, so the star's image manages melodrama's tensions as a mimesis between an emblematic persona and a more private and ethical force.

By the nineteenth century melodrama became less focused on public types and more revealing of an inner private life. Actors at the end of the nineteenth century took over the functions of the Church as representatives and 'exemplars of morality and lifestyle'. Gledhill discusses how the production of melodrama in America was central in transferring the melodramatic imaginary from stage to screen. Constantin Stanislavski's ideas were central to the American acting ideology of the 1920s, emphasizing the psychology of actors through 'affective memory', where the performers were skilled in using their own emotional experience to portray characters. With Lee Strasberg's development of these techniques 'the Method' of acting came into being, a practice which Gledhill suggests 'virtually dissolved the boundaries between acting and psychotherapy'.[18]

Method acting grew out of the relationship between psychoanalysis and acting, a partnership centrally due to the growing popularization of Freud in 1940s and 1950s America. Method actors were encouraged to utilize unconscious emotion and gestural expression in place of more rehearsed dialogue. Dyer describes both melodrama and the method approach as a rhetorical search for authenticity. Within this ideology the surface is controlled and public, a masquerade veiling the private or spontaneous self. Brando, Montgomery Clift, Julie Harris and Rod Steiger are all 1950s method performers who are divided into an 'unresolved tension between an outer social mask and an inner reality of frustration'.[19] Modern melodramatic and method acting is a mimesis of our moral world, dramatizing social and psychic conflict. Male method acting can provide a theatre for the contradictions in masculinity and provide cultural status for the star.[20] Female method actresses are less successful, and Colin Counsell contends that the emphasis on the divided self in method acting works less well for women because they are more likely to be demonized for being neurotic.[21] Geraghty notes how the success of Jodie Foster in *The Accused* and *Silence of the Lambs* was partly due to their masculine genre natures as either gangster or thriller genres, whereas Foster's performances in *Sommersby* and *Nell* were far less popular.

I want to consider why male method acting is so much more successful than female performances. We can categorize male method

Fig. 7   Nicole Kidman as Satine in *Moulin Rouge* (2001), directed by Baz Luhrmann. © 20th Century Fox / The Kobal Collection / Sue Adler

acting not just as a melodrama of the moral occult but as a theatrical performance of the male hysteric. But why is male hysteria or neurosis so much more appealing than hysteria in women? Certainly it is worked into many more hero roles, whereas as Counsell notes women become villainized. But the nature of the hysteria is also different. Hysteria in female star performances is more often routed through spectacular body images, whereas, as Geraghty points out, in method acting attention is drawn to 'the body as a site of performance, worked over by the actor'.[22] Perhaps this is also because the male method actor manages a space between social and psychic imaginaries. The hysteria is there lurking, as passion, division, frustration, but because it is worked over and controlled in an active way it becomes a melodramatic performance that also promises in some way to resolve the private hysteria. Because the male method actor does not allow his hysteria to sabotage action, then he avoids the hysterical division associated more with women, a hysterical victim position which cannot embody agency.

I want to consider briefly the method acting of the female star Nicole Kidman. Kidman's most emphasized method-acting role is in Campion's adaptation of *Portrait of a Lady*, where she literally embodies and personifies the gasping, mute, inwardly claustrophobic of Isabel Archer's hysteria. Geraghty notes how Campion's use of facial close-ups is a dramatization of the body to express inner turmoil. In her more recent film *Moulin Rouge*, we can see this method performance invoked by Kidman, a performance that covers over a more private turmoil of the consumptive hysteric. Significantly, in this film the control and management of inner division is through a more spectacular, feminine masquerade. *Moulin Rouge* is then hysterical melodrama taken to comic levels. Kidman hysterically embodies all the splits of the hysterical and melodramatic modern occult. She is both angel and whore, consumptive interiority and publicly displayed and consumable sexuality. But rather than sentimentalizing ethics as melodramas are inclined to do, *Moulin Rouge* parodies them and sends them up. Even the sentimental heterosexual romance between Kidman and McEwan is idealized to such an extent it is made ridiculous, frozen into perfect unattainability by her death.

Key points

- Christine Gledhill links her analysis of stars' method acting to issues of melodrama, psychoanalysis and genre.
- Male method acting is more successful than female performances; why is this?

From melodramatic genre to melodramatic modality

In her essay 'Rethinking Genre', Christine Gledhill argues for the cyclical nature of film genres.[23] Gledhill maps how the traditional notions of genre within film studies as a question of texts and aesthetics has moved to incorporate a more recent focus of the social circulation and context of film, its intersection with industry, institution, culture and audiences. For Gledhill, melodrama as a genre is a cultural hybrid which is found not just within textual reflections or at the site of production, but as a mimetic copying and shifting that refuses any singular or original definition.

Melodrama can then be conceived in terms of early cinematic production as an apparatus that puts into play popular genres for mass, mainstream audiences. But it is also, according to Gledhill, an organizing modality, and by that she means an aesthetic register or form that is fluid across a range of genres, across historical moments and across spatial geographies such as national cultures. The modality of melodrama is of course double, articulating distinctive genres at particular moments, but also providing a practice of oscillation and transformation between genres. Melodrama, therefore, sucks up other genres – tragedy, comedy, romance – and re-memorizes or re-articulates them. Although realism and classical Hollywood narrative have been placed in historical opposition to melodrama, which arose in the nineteenth century out of melodramatic theatre, cinema soon loses its character as 'cinema of attractions' and goes on to have a celebrated career institutionalized as classical, realist, narrative cinema. Realism is then seen to displace melodrama into more marginal genres such as women's film. Gledhill argues persuasively that this is not so and that, in fact, realism and melodrama are much more implicated within each other. Indeed this opposition is under revision, with retrospective historicist analysis restoring the label of melodrama to male action genres.

The boundary disputes between realism and melodrama are situated at the origin of cinema and are also associated with the idea of a modernist break with preceding traditions at the beginning of the twentieth century. The history of melodrama contests this idea of a modernist break. It also suggests that the division between narrative and the body (or the imaginary and real), characterizing both classical, realist film narrative and Freudian psychoanalysis can be re-read as a hysterical melodramatic mode. If this is so, we have also to look at the supposed origins of classical film culture in the nineteenth-century novel or play. Literary classics such as Shakespeare were circulated within nineteenth-century melodramas. Just as Mikhail Bakhtin's *The Dialogic Imagination* (1981) suggests that the novel reproduces all other forms of writing and speech, so Gledhill argues that melodrama does the same in a reverse orbit, drawing high culture and arts into its domain and producing them for a mainstream audience. Linda Williams also argues for melodrama as an organizing mode of American cinema, because its central component is that of the virtuous victim, the staging and retrieval of this victim's virtue and the sympathy elicited from the audience.[24] Like Gledhill, Williams contests the hegemony of classical realist narrative and contends that melodrama is not a peripheral genre of excess, 'or an aberration, but is what most often typifies popular American narrative in literature, stage, film and television'.[25]

These ideas support my claim that the Oedipal narrative is in fact a hysterical and phenomenological crisis of embodiment, that is, melodramatically split. However, the difference with melodrama is that we can see much more easily its operative, mobile tension between a private and social imaginary, whereas with the Oedipal myth we are left with a private imaginary masquerading as the socio-symbolic, projecting all other difference onto an abject space of the real. Gledhill notes how Steven Neale's 1980 monograph *Genre* maps classic narrative as the dominant organizing genre in film, but Richard Maltby, analysing data from the Production Code Administration in the 1940s, finds nearly a third of its submissions classified as melodrama.[26] Linda Williams also collects evidence from the American Film Institute catalogues that reveal a burgeoning persistence of melodramatic genres throughout the twentieth century.[27] To understand this continuation of melodrama, Gledhill suggests, we have to cast it as a historically variable imagination or imaginary. She is drawing on Castoriadis's notion of a social imaginary, here, but as Castoriadis's work also informs the theory of a bodily imaginary, we can also posit the mode of melodramatic imagination that Gledhill flags up as a historically situated, social *and* private imaginary.[28]

Peter Brooks makes the link between melodrama and psychoanalysis, arguing for the repression of the hysterical body under a realist secular ideology of individualism which returns as an excess to disturb the realist 'ego' of identity. Following Gledhill and Williams, we can also understand melodrama not as a displaced excess but as an organizing hysterical imaginary. Brooks stresses that the popular oppositions and stark contrasts within melodrama show how aesthetics and sensation come together to provide a moral occult, an ethically bounded individualistic society. Both Thomas Elsaesser and Ben Singer demonstrate the differing ways melodrama reveals the experience and polarizations of city life under capitalism and modernity, the divisions of class, sexuality and economics and the accompanying shock and dangers of living in this newly technologized, urban world.[29] The sensationalism of melodrama travels from life to film, and Ben Singer convincingly shows how stage melodrama never ended with the arrival of the cinema; it simply crossed over.

Gledhill traces the history of cinema and melodrama in two gender- and class-differentiated traditions: 'fairground with parlour entertainment, a "cinema of attractions" with a cinema of narrative fiction'.[30] Rather than the hegemony of realism over melodrama, we have to see both of them within a dialectical relationship which moves in relation to cultural value. Realism can be understood as a modality 'that makes a claim on the real' within the contested stakes of established and marginal groups.[31] This shifting relationship between realism and melodrama reveals how imaginary and real oscillate within a situated history of dominant and emergent communities. The Oedipal, sexual difference narrative which is equated with classical realist narrative represses hysteria and melodrama in terms of bourgeois individualism, identified within the Victorian age as separate private and public spheres. However, on another level, hysteria is also the organizing force of the Oedipal imaginary: a melodramatic imaginary which fixes and splits off sexual difference in a phenomenological understanding of modernity. This splitting between imaginary and real is not immutable. It is both historically fixed and mobile. Gledhill notes the evolving historical moments in the twentieth century, where successive movements of the working class, feminism and civil rights produce a reflexivity that influences media-mediated culture; a struggle then ensues to 'redefine cultural verisimilitude under the banner of realism'.[32] Melodrama has to recognize these changing definitions of the real, and has to shift accordingly, so allowing mobility between imaginary and real, dominant and subordinate.

If sexual difference can be seen as a fixed defence against the mobile performativity of realism and melodrama, then we have to look at the historical persistence of hysteria. Like melodrama, hysteria was located everywhere in Victorian England, and like the disappearance of melodrama, within the supposed organizing mode of realism in the twentieth century, so hysteria also 'disappeared', particularly from clinical diagnosis within the twentieth century, only to make its comeback in trauma theories and academic debates.[33] Hysteria has historically, like melodrama, been cast as a female character; the original or archetypal hysteria is supposed to be the girl's early identification with the mother. But as Juliet Mitchell has shown, Freud's own hysteria, particularly in relation to 'brothers' such as Fliess and Jung, disappeared (became 'normalized') in his theory of the Oedipal complex, whereupon, 'hysteria is returned to women'.[34] Hysteria's propensity to migrate into other constituent forms such as borderline states, eating disorders, multiple personality, etc. is matched by its mobility between genders. Hysterical features originally demarcated as feminine have migrated to masculinity in relation to soldiers of the twentieth century's world wars, and more latterly those exposed to Gulf War syndrome. Where gender exists so we find hysteria. And like melodrama, hysteria becomes epitomized in the most extreme polarizations of gender – its melancholic best, but also its undoing.

For Peter Brooks melodrama reflects hysteria as a mode of excess to a dominant Oedipal norm of realism and individualistic ideology. However, if hysteria is not the repressed 'other' of Oedipal sexuality, but its dominant organizing force, then what does that make melodrama? Linda Williams argues that melodrama cannot be viewed as an excess, but as a typification of American popular narrative in literature, film and television, a narrative that is immersed in questions of morality and value. She writes that melodrama

> is the best example of American culture's (often hypocritical) attempt to construct itself as the locus of innocence and virtue. If we want to confront the centrality of melodrama to American moving-picture culture, we must first turn to the most basic forms of melodrama, and not as many feminist critics – myself included – have previously done, to a ghetto subgenre of 'women's films'. Rather, we must seek out the dominant features of an American melodramatic mode.[35]

Williams and Gledhill argue for melodrama as an organizing modality; Rick Altman stresses the showmanship and display operative in melodrama that cannot be subsumed under a classical model; Elsaesser in turn suggests that melodrama is a mode of experience. Melodrama can, then, be seen as a bodily imaginary of modernity that moves between social and private worlds. Likened to Tom Gunning's cinema of attractions, this bodily imaginary cannot, as Williams points out, be repressed and subsumed under dominant notions of classical film. Melodrama is not, as Brooks and Altman propose, merely an excess that disturbs the hegemonic realist norm.

In his analysis of early melodramatic film Ben Singer has also criticized Bordwell's claim of the dominance of classical film style. Singer mobilizes a convincing account of melodrama as a specific and historical genre that links with key modernity themes of urbanization, the sensory shock of new technologies and the cultural splitting and mobility of forms of class and gender. Singer advocates melodrama as a key historical genre, but this does not, as he admits, exclude Williams's broader sweep of suggesting melodrama as an inclusive mode.

Key points

- Linda Williams and Christine Gledhill argue for melodrama as an organizing mode of American cinema.
- Realism and melodrama have been historically represented in terms of a narrative of Oedipal repression. However, we can also see them organized as a hysterical imaginary of modernity.

Melodramatic racial double or fix?

But is melodrama simply hysterical? Can it never move into an arena where the capacity for memory can be revived or found? To explore how it can dramatize a more cultural re-memory of the real we have to examine what is meant by a melodramatic imaginary – not just show how it doubles as classical realist film, but also understand how it can work with more realist film forms to challenge and move dominant hegemonic performances of the imaginary. The concept of doubling is central to melodrama and it is also central to the idea of a situated phenomenological imaginary. Doubling can be distinguished from splitting in the sense that splitting is always a hysterical projection onto the other's imaginary and involves a mono-imaginary, whereas doubling can creatively work to acknowledge the presence of (at least) two imaginaries.

At the beginning of the twentieth century W.E.B. Dubois named a double consciousness of black people: a performance that recognized an alignment or mimicry with a dominant white imaginary, but also at the same time a subversive distance and difference. Judith Mayne observes how this black performativity can be attributed to both actors and spectators of film and is very different from the textual codes of 1970s film theory. Of course, this moves the debate from an ideal subject or textual spectator to one that is by definition not ideal and therefore subsumed by the textual ideology: a performance that is also able to resist and perform differently.[36]

We can link this understanding of doubleness and splitting to melodrama. In *Playing the Race Card*, Linda Williams maps how American mass culture has 'talked to itself' through melodrama and the 'enduring dilemma of race'.[37] She reads the history of race relations in America as a melodramatic mode where 'moral legitimacy', to use Brook's term, is rendered 'through the spectacle of racialized bodily suffering'.[38]

Iconography of the suffering black male body and the threatened white female body (by a hyper-sexualized black male) has persisted in American culture. Williams begins her book from the perspective of her own raced and gendered anger and confusion at the outcome of the O.J. Simpson trial. Analysing her own psychic and emotional response makes Williams investigate its roots within a history of racial victims and villains in American culture, traced back to Harriet Beecher Stowe's *Uncle Tom's Cabin*. A negrophilic 'Tom' tradition where Afro-Americans are the objects of racial sympathy and its opposite an 'anti-Tom' tradition of negrophobic racism, exemplified by Griffith's *Birth of a Nation*, are both reflected in contemporary culture. They reappear in modern court dramas and films of the 1990s. Unable to limit her study of melodrama to films as originally intended, Williams is forced to recognize the dialectical interplay of racial melodramatic Tom sentiment and anti-Tom sentiment, which has suffused the history of American mass popular culture and entertainment. By addressing melodrama as part of a national American imaginary and a multimedia form, *Playing the Race Card* traces a drama of victimization and villification that straddles one hundred and fifty years of American history, traversing literature, film, theatre and television.

Although neither a masculine nor feminine form, racial melodrama is structured through markers of gender and sexual difference. So within *Uncle Tom's Cabin* and the Tom tradition the black man is portrayed as obliging, feminine and castrated. According to a modern black male consciousness, this docile character is robbed of his freedom, dignity and masculine sex. Tom and anti-Tom traditions are dialectically integrated within a gendered, heterosexual norm. This dialectic of sexual and racial difference becomes reinstated in the negrophobic tradition. For example, in Griffith's *Birth of a Nation* the black man is portrayed as an animalistic oversexed masculine predator of the ultra-feminine white woman: the white dress that never needs washing. We can see, here, how Oedipal sexual difference works at the level of race, by projecting onto black people an abject otherness. The Tom character or hero is acceptable, can legitimately be sympathized with, because he is castrated, whereas the anti-Tom, anti-hero, has to be removed because he operates as a phallic threat to white male ownership.

These are Oedipal binaries, but they are also hysterical ones, riven with all the idealization, denigration, jealousy and feelings of displacement that accompany the hysterical position. In the melodrama of the Tom and the anti-Tom tradition, innocence and virtue are restored through the suffering of the black man or the white woman, although this virtue is a pre-Oedipal innocence that relegates the victim to the status of a protected child, in relation to an Oedipal law which is inevitably phallic, white and colonial. As the history of

Fig. 8   Anti-Tom stereotype of Gus lynched by the Ku Klux Klan. From *The Birth of a Nation* (1915), directed by D.W. Griffith. © Epic / The Kobal Collection

slavery shows, it is only the white woman who can still lay claim to this innocence, as Tom's innocence is predicated on his condition as a slave. Emancipation from slavery and equal rights for the black man runs in contradiction to Tom's servile and castrated nature. Williams describes how the melodramatic traditions of Tom and anti-Tom are completely entangled. So, in the Rodney King trial we see a black man beaten by racist police, eliciting in Tom tradition a white sympathy for the beaten black man. However this sympathy does nothing to change the law, which ultimately upholds the negrophobia of the anti-Tom tradition by finding the police officers innocent.

Williams describes the O.J. Simpson trial in similar dialectical terms, noting her own sympathy for Nicole Simpson and the negrophobic tradition that it feeds into. Signalling the famous blackening of O.J.'s mug-shot, Williams shows how the racist framing of O.J. by the police as threatening and predatory to the innocent white woman is indelibly linked to the black jury's verdict of not guilty. In a sense, then, this trial was never and could never be just about the murder of a woman by her husband, because gender difference is always structured through race and vice versa. Williams's reading of the history of race relations in America is also a reading of the Oedipal imaginary that doubles as melodrama.

Mimicry and a deconstruction of the colonial imaginary

Black sexuality is hystericized in mainstream Hollywood films, the hysterical projection and splitting of a white, phallic imaginary in terms of sexual difference. The black body is thus the abject and castrated carnality upon which the Oedipal white subject is constructed. Franz Fanon is perhaps the most famous psychoanalyst to explore these issues in his seminal text *Black Skin, White Masks*.[39] Homi Bhabha has incorporated Fanon in terms of postcolonial studies, in order to explore the operation of colonial discourse in terms of conscious mechanisms of knowlege and power, but also in relation to the ambivalent flux of unconscious fantasy and desire.[40] Bhabha objects to simplistic ideas of colonial stereotypes that offer only one unitary point of identification; for him the stereotype is always a fundamentally contradictory mode of representation, 'as anxious as it is assertive'.[41]

Bhabha argues that aggression and narcissism construct dominant colonial stereotypes of the 'other'. The colonial stereotype symbolically and narcissistically disavows the other's difference, at the same time aggressively recognizing the unconscious lack that the other represents. In this way the stereotype is both fixed and a fantasy, becoming part of an institutionalized discourse of racism, inherited colonialism, but at the same time reactivating a more immediate desire. The racist stereotype becomes fixed as 'the same old stories', for instance the negro's animality. But at the same time compulsive repetition of these tired and familiar caricatures brings the fantasy: these stories are always 'differently gratifying and terrifying each time'.[42] Mimicry is an important strategy and support for colonial power. Operative in stereotyping, mimicry enables the colonized subject to be identified as recognizably the same, but different: 'not quite/not white'.[43] Bhabha gives as an example of mimicry the Indian civil servant, educated in English, who reflects the colonizer but at the same time disturbs him through a representation that seems uncannily familiar and yet strange. The colonizer perceives a distorted image of himself: mimicry as 'resemblance and menace'.[44] His mastery is then undone, as the returning gaze of the other dismantles narcissistic illusions of sameness. Mimicry thus subjugates the colonial subject but at the same time irrevocably slips into a parody and mockery of the colonizer, displacing his authority and arousing his paranoia.[45]

We can understand the Tom and anti-Tom stereotypes that Williams describes in terms of Bhabha's notion of colonial mimicry, as both servility and menace. However, I would argue that the menace of this stereotype does nothing to dismantle the colonizer's power. Paranoia, after all, can be seen to drive much of modernism's cultural imperialism.[46] Bhabha's notion of mimicry is premissed on a Lacanian, Oedipal imaginary which separates imaginary from real, an assertion of separation which Fanon never explicitly makes. If we look again at Fanon's analysis of the black man as the white man's other, we can see he distinguishes it on an imaginary level. Whereas Bhabha seems to theorize the colonial relation between colonizer and subject in terms of a universal and split Lacanian imaginary, Fanon re-reads and investigates the Lacanian imaginary ascribing *different* notions of the imaginary to the white and the black psyche:

> When one has grasped the mechanism described by Lacan, one can have no further doubt that the real Other for the white man is and will continue to be the black man. And conversely. Only for the white man the Other is perceived on the level of the body image, absolutely as the not-self, that is, the unidentifiable, the inassimilable. For the black man, as we have shown, historical and economic realities come into the picture.[47]

How, then, can we find an alternative to this colonial imaginary? If the colonial mimicry that Bhabha traces can be seen as a hysterical and melancholic mimesis, then the black man's resistance can only be in terms of a different imaginary. A cultural re-memory of tradition, then, which will mimetically embody the colonial subject's desire, rather than leaving him to subtend, in an abject state, his master's narcissism.

Racist mimicry and a double, black mimesis

I intend, therefore, to utilize these two readings of mimicry and mimesis in terms of a historical and racial melodramatic imaginary. Williams's work, as we have seen, describes a dominant, colonial melodramatic modality as mimicry. Other film scholars have focused on melodrama's subversive qualities, although these are seen as emanating from an independent tradition of films rather than the Hollywood mainstream. Oscar Micheaux's films have been taken up by Jane Gaines and Ron Green in an attempt to locate a position of cultural resistance to the racist mimicry and hysterical stereotypes that are mythologized in *Birth of a Nation*.[48] Central to Gaines's and Green's argument is the work of W.E.B. Dubois and his evocation of a double black consciousness. Dubois can be seen in many ways to anticipate Fanon's more psychoanalytic ideas, in his promotion of the two-ness of black identity, an idea that has also been recently revived by Cornel West in a definition of the Afro-American intellectual. For Dubois, this double consciousness referred to the sensation of 'always looking at oneself through the eyes of others, of measuring one's soul through the eyes of others, of measuring one's soul by the tape of a world that looks on in amused contempt and pity'.[49] The idea, then, is that the black man sees the world simultaneously through a white imaginary and also through his own Afro-American one. Dubois observes this as problematic, dividing the black man from himself: 'One ever feels his twoness', he writes, 'an American, a Negro; two souls, two thoughts, two unreconciled strivings; two warring ideals in one dark body, whose dogged strength alone keeps it from being torn asunder.'[50] But, as Ron Green suggests, we don't have to view this doubleness negatively. In his view, the films of Oscar Micheaux demonstrate this aesthetic twoness through style and their disruption of a classical continuity of editing. Thomas Cripps, the film historian of race movies, sees Micheaux's black double aesthetic as a retrograde step, and argues instead for the integration of black movies into Hollywood.[51] Challenging Cripps, Green states that black independent film-makers like Micheaux are vital precisely because they show the struggle of twoness that occurs through the process of Afro-American assimilation. In contrast, Hollywood merely returns images of black identity as those 'same old stories'.

Jane Gaines suggests that despite the bourgeois individualism of Micheaux's films, which depict black people through white eyes, his double aesthetic is also subversive. Micheaux's *La Negra*, the only surviving reproduction of the original *Within our Gates*, is the antithesis of *Birth of a Nation*. Released in 1919, four years after *Birth of a Nation*, *Within our Gates* raised so much racial fear and tension that it was effectively banned and kept off the screen. Gaines reads *La Negra* as a political response to the racism in *Birth*. Through parallel editing and narrative coincidence *La Negra* melodramatically presents the white mob, lynching and burning an innocent black family. This narrative is cross-cut with scenes that depict a white patriarch attempting to rape a mulatto woman. He (the patriarch) is abruptly stopped by a birthmark on her breast, a mark that proves he is her father.

Gaines argues that the double play of the rape and the lynch mob historically connects race and gender, a doubling that emphasizes the economics of black bodies as property. *La Negra* thus critiques and rewrites the colonial discourse operating in *Birth* and the scene where the evil black man Gus is lynched for his attack on the 'dear' white sister. White, Oedipal, symbolic law is, thus, melodramatically revealed as the hysterical law of the mob.

Conclusion

Film critics have taken up this notion of black double consciousness in different ways. Judith Mayne argues for the doubleness intrinsic to black spectatorship and acting; bell hooks claims a space for an oppositional black spectator, who can refuse the racist imagery and imaginary of dominant Hollywood films.[52] Jacqueline Bobo in her famous reading of Spielberg's *The Colour Purple* shows how the film situates its racist, melodramatic presentation of the black man in true anti-Tom fashion, against the black women spectators who draw a more progressive reading of the film.[53] But if progressive readings of Hollywood melodrama are only drawn from 'real' spectators reading against the grain, then to escape from this popular and dominant white imaginary entails a breaking with the narrative structure and sentimental power of melodrama. Popular Hollywood melodrama performs the body, but as a hysterical form it repeats but cannot re-member itself differently. The final chapter will then explore a phenomenological aesthetics of film (between film and spectator) which performs the body but also culturally re-members it. To use Gaines's terms, the 'jury is still out' on melodrama. Maybe they are just waiting for a different, anti-Oedipal judge?

Key points

- W.E.B. Dubois named a double consciousness of black people.
- In *Playing the Race Card*, Linda Williams maps how American mass culture has 'talked to itself' through melodrama and the 'enduring dilemma of race'.
- The melodramatic Tom and anti-Tom stereotypes illustrate Bhabha's notion of colonial mimicry as both servility and menace.
- Melodramas by Oscar Micheaux locate a double black consciousness as resistance to the racist mimicry of *Birth of a Nation*.

8

Film Aesthetics and Cultural Re-Memory

This book has argued for film spectatorship as a phenomenological mimesis which moves between hysterical performance and a more cultural re-memory. Re-reading psychoanalysis through such a phenomenological lens situates Oedipal narrative and sexual difference as a hysterical imaginary, one that has been exemplified by Hollywood melodrama. This final chapter turns to a consideration of film aesthetics within a contemporary postmodern moment to explore how film spectatorship can move beyond hysterical melodrama to embody a more social and cultural mimesis. Since the advent of structuralism and post-structuralism, phenomenology as a theory of the subject and film spectatorship has been abandoned for its marking of a bounded and distinct subject of perception, as an active agent of history. Although, Merleau-Ponty's earlier work subscribes to such a delimited, social ontology of the look, his later work *The Visible and the Invisible* exchanges this emphasis on the gaze for a more sensual description of the transference where the fleshy, tactile interaction of bodies deconstructs any delineation of subject and object. Returning film spectatorship to a mimesis of such a sensual imaginary allows us to revisit a phenomenological film tradition, exploring the performance of the body and memory in relation to film aesthetics.

Schizophrenia and the death drive of aesthetics

The images of two aeroplanes flying into the twin towers of the World Trade Center on 11 September 2001 are unforgettable. In a complete reversal of Baudrillard's simulacrum and definition of the postmodern summed up by his statement that the first Gulf War was unreal, merely a television spectacle, the images of 11 September were a smashing of the real onto the symbolic erection of Western capitalism. The postmodern image is no longer one of a virtual imaginary, but of an explosion of the real. This explosion is read in differing ways by the West and the East. Whereas a dominant American and European white imaginary reads this explosion as a work of abject evil and terrorism, an evil that must be 'daisy-bombed' out of existence, the Islamic world sees things differently and wants to point out how the attack on the WTC and the Pentagon was an echo of America's own hypocritical foreign policy. While not excusing the act of terrorism, the Islamic world perceived the war against Afghanistan as proof that the Western world only sees things from its own, white dominant imaginary, projecting the abject powers of horror onto the real of the racially othered, who are consequently denied access to their own subjectivity and social imaginary.

In many ways the war between the West and Afghanistan was like a high-concept Spielberg blockbuster: a disaster melodrama. In the past, the pleasure and excitement of watching such movies has been our knowledge of the fetishization of the image (and our disavowal of these films as real). However, in the wake of 11 September such virtual imaginary film time is over. In a sense Western time was stopped, quite literally, with this image marking the end of the simulacrum – Baudrillard's endless virtual imaginary – and the return of the real, as it was crashed forcibly, exploded even, by the traumatic real of a human terrorist bomb. I want to consider the status of this image in relation to the contemporary postmodern moment, in relation to film and in relation to the discourse of psychoanalysis.

The image of the twin towers can be seen as psychotically hysterical, even schizophrenic. It is real, in terms of a Lacanian real, in other words, impossible, psychotic and traumatic. But it is also real historically, the impossible has happened, impossible evil (that is through the imaginary and territorial lens of Western democracy and capitalism), but also (unlike Lacan's real) completely representable. Fredric Jameson discusses late consumer capitalism and film as schizophrenic. For Jameson, history and time are lost, schizophrenically scrambled to yield a nostalgic, perpetual present or style. Postmodern films reveal this style as melancholic but also as pastiche or dead mimicry: an imitation of styles. This imitation means on the one hand the failure of the 'art and the aesthetic, the failure of the new' where we are locked in the past, but – unable to access temporal continuity, or distinguish between past and present – we are locked in a schizophrenic isolation.[1] Like the schizophrenic, postmodernism

and film reiterate an intense but undifferentiated present, which nos-
talgically repeats a dead past (as the present), but can in actuality
access neither. Past and present cannot be connected and therefore
separated; consequently there is no projection into the future. Jameson
writes, 'If there is any realism left, it is a "realism" which springs from
the shock of grasping that confinement and of realizing that, for what-
ever peculiar reasons, we seem condemned to seek the historical past
through our own pop images and stereotypes about the past, which
itself remains forever out of reach.'[2]

Jameson understands this loss of time, history and memory, in a
Lacanian sense, as due to the failure of language. This loss of symbolic reality is a schizophrenic materialization and disconnection of
the signifier, where the world and image burn brightly and are hallucinatory with affect. But meaning is lost: 'the materiality of words
becomes obsessive, as in the case when children repeat a word over
and over again until its sense is lost and it becomes incomprehen-
sible incantation.'[3] For Jameson, the signifier has lost its signified
meaning to the extent that it becomes 'transformed into an image'.[4]
I want to ponder this understanding of the schizophrenic image and
indeed the linguistic, Lacanian framework that Jameson attaches it
to, as it seems to confuse several issues regarding the relationship
between history and madness, and the concomitant space-time
attributed to registers of the real, imaginary and symbolic.

The materiality of words becomes obsessive in the schizophrenic,
not simply because 'he' has lost 'normal' language, but because he
has lost his embodied sense of self in relation to the world, and cannot
therefore partake in an intersubjective meaning with the other. This
is why Lacan privileges the symbolic. For him it is only through the
social and linguistic Oedipal phallus that we can enter meaning and
culture. Jameson's postmodernism is paradoxically the mourning of
this Oedipal and linguistic differentiation, a mourning for the historical temporalities of modernism, without which we are left within
a melancholic mimicry of a deathly imaginary.

Louis A. Sass has recently reinterpreted schizophrenia not as
fusion, instinctual force or an excess of desiring bodily states associated with infancy, but as an increased hypersensitivity, characterized
by 'separation, restraint and propensity for introspection'.[5] For Sass,
the schizophrenic is a kind of deathly living, but this is a death of the
physical and emotional 'appetites', rather than rationality. In Sass's
view this alienation and disassociation from the body is a condition
of modernity, an alienation to which Merleau-Ponty's work responds
with an attempt to bring reflection back in touch with the senses, to
reach a *sur-réflexion*, where reflection does not destroy the thingness

of being and perception.[6] This *sur-réflexion* would not forget the pre-reflective body of experience, so although reflection is important, subjectivity is also on one level non-reflexive. Postmodernism, in the shape of Derrida and the deconstructionists, takes hyper-reflexivity to a level which in Sass's view mirrors the schizophrenic experience. Postmodernism is, therefore, hyper-reflexive and hyper-modern.

Sass's view of modernity fits with the argument in this book that the Oedipal is a hysterical, phenomenological defence and splitting, from the body, which if taken to extremes becomes mad or schizophrenic. Oedipus is the neurotic's flight from madness and disintegration, but it is not a higher form of sublimation or mediation; rather, as Reich understood, it is a kind of armour of splitting or disassociation that we all are familiar with. Only in its pathological form, as complete withdrawal from the world, does this disassociation manifest as psychosis. Sexual difference is the defence against dissolution, a splitting most obviously mapped in hysterical conditions. Within this phenomenological understanding of psychoanalysis in relation to modernism and postmodernism, hysterical Oedipal splitting (inherent to modernism) becomes more exaggerated within the postmodern condition, an ontological fragmentation that presents more frequently in contemporary mental disorders.

In an interesting and much-ignored book by Foucault entitled *Mental Illness and Psychology*, republished it is rumoured against his wishes in 1976, Foucault explores a phenomenological understanding of psychoanalysis, madness and mental illness.[7] What is so fascinating about this ignored book is that it completely overturns a binary that pits Freud against Foucault, for in this exploration of mental illness Foucault does not dismiss psychoanalysis; he re-finds it on a phenomenological level. Space-time distortion and an inability to have intersubjective relationships, defines, in Foucault's view, the mentally ill. Without intersubjective relationships, where an embodied relationship to the world is lost and the body itself is experienced as dead, the schizophrenic retreats more and more into a hyper-reflexivity, into a language which is nonsensical because there is no shared meaning. This, then, is the meaning of the disconnected signifiers, the bizarre and intense images of the schizophrenic. These images are full of affect; the body enacts a kind of artificial, exaggerated performance of the body, precisely because it is not felt to exist. Splitting is a way of fleeing reality. Hence, the Oedipal complex, hysteria, and schizophrenia are all forms of defence that have been historically constructed against an impending dissolution of our embodied relationship to the world. The move from so-called master narratives of Oedipal modernism to postmodern schizophrenia can be understood phenomenologically as a matter of degree of dis-association between the mind and the body. Schizophrenia is then simply a grotesque mirror held up to the Oedipal neurotic of what he might become if 'his' fetishized, sexualized defence (against what is essentially a crisis of embodiment) slips, and he, like the psychotic, dissolves into purely imaginary existence, carried away from a living engagement with the world.

Let us go back to the image of the twin towers, the image of the Western imaginary being crashed into and exploded by an abject real, the 'powers of horror' literalized by the terrorist/human bomb. In Iri-garay's account of a more embodied imaginary she critiques the estab-lished emphasis on knowledge, language and interpretation in the analytic encounter, because this linguistic deconstruction does not allow for creativity and imaginative painting. Such an Oedipal inter-pretative analysis has a 'negative' view of memory, and does not see memory as a place of embodied ground and territory from which the patient can use perception, imagination and the senses to be recreative.[8] Luce Irigaray suggests an aesthetics of the image, that is painted within the transference connecting imaginary and real through an imaginative perception, that 'spatialises perception' and 'makes time simultaneous'.[9] This painting, which connects past, present and future, is an opening of space-time for the patient in an intersubjective relation with the therapist and the world. Dreaming is also the work of this imaginative painting, but dreams, as Irigaray says, both 'hint at this and hide it', which is why the work has to be continued in the analytic session. If interpretation is not accompanied by this imaginative painting of the senses, then the imaginary is purely located as a mental counterpart and goes to war with the real. As we have seen, this is the dilemma of the hysteric, but in more severe cases this war between imaginary and real ends in psychosis.

Hence the image of the twin towers can be seen as hysterical and schizophrenic, the white Western, Oedipal imaginary, as a symbol of world capitalism, at war with the abject real of the human terrorist bomb, a horrible symbolic echo of America's foreign policy coming home to roost. The abject real of Bin Laden is portrayed as a racial-ized and sexualized, evil *'femme fatale'*. But just as the symbolic leaders of America and Britain cannot recognize another political imaginary, not having the imagination with which to paint it but remaining in a privatized Oedipal imaginary which is in actuality hysterically masquerading as a global symbolic, so, the ground and territory, which could be imaginatively restored to the Third World (through fairer trade regulations, etc.) is instead blown up and destroyed. Space-time is perverted; in New York time literally stopped, and spatial perception is traumatically demolished. Instead of a fluidity of space-time where the connections between past and present can be made through a creative memory, there is an hysterical absence of memory and in its place the dead mimicry of nostalgic forms, an imaginary severed from the real of history that merely repeats its old language, the same old colonial stories and racist stereotypes. This postmodern imaginary can deconstruct the terror of the twin towers through and onto the figure of Bin Laden, as a fanatic, a fundamentalist, the image of world evil. But the West's refusal to recognize its own projection of the abject real onto a third world, thus returned in an attack which mirrors our current global and colonial violence, led America and Britain, without any sense of the madness involved, to drop bombs and food parcels simultaneously on Afghanistan.[10]

The postmodern 'real' image of the twin towers as schizophrenic and hysterical is somehow much more reminiscent of Deleuze and Guattari's desiring machines and flows than it is of Lacan's notions of structure and lack. But the real that is terrifyingly returned with this 'real' image is not positive in any sense. There is nothing to be gained from the liberation of desire within society, if it is not mediated by a more social imaginary. Without a socially mediating imaginary, our primitive, narcissistic desires are purely destructive. But as Cornelius Castoriadis suggests, the quelling of our dreaming, imaginative, more private imaginary in the name of rationalism is equally monstrous as it kills 'what makes us human'.[11]

We can, then, distinguish a dialectical movement within postmodernism between first, Jameson's nostalgic, melancholic mimicry, a dominant Oedipal imaginary, and second, a more embodied imaginary which can culturally remember the real. Within postmodern film theory, Jameson's nostalgic melancholia combines with Guy Debord's society of the spectacle, David Harvey's time-space compression and Jean Baudrillard's simulacrum as confirmation that the real of history is lost, transformed into the Lacanian and schizophrenic traumatic body of the real. This disconnected, postmodern real comes to exist as image, hyper-reality, virtuality and the replicant. The crashing of the abject real into this simulacrum or screen image on 11 September has been anticipated by Hollywood many times. However, there is an obvious difference between watching films such as *True Lies* and *Airforce One* before 11 September and afterwards. Part of the voyeuristic pleasure of watching sensationalistic, Hollywood blockbusters is our disavowal of the historical real we mimetically dream in relation to these imaginary worlds. The pleasure we get from such encounters is both hysterical and affectual.

Steven Shaviro has written a compelling account of the material and affectual perception involved in cinema viewing.[12] Confronting the Lacanian, psychoanalytic tradition which foregrounds the castration, lack and symbolic pleasure in spectatorship, Shaviro highlights the embodied, sensual relationship to the cinematic image. Images are not explained through language and representation but through the demand they elicit, and the corporeal and tactile vision they bring into being. Cinematic images are a simulacrum, a mimetic repetitive and material replay between copy and original, until, as Deleuze and Guattari suggest, the real is carried 'to the point where it is effectively produced'.[13]

For Shaviro, cinematic images pull us into a masochistic, repetitive immediacy of the real: a passive and violent engagement with the filmic image, which dissolves constructs of subjectivity and perception. Such mimetic participation is not a phenomenological apprehension of the film object, because for Shaviro, film images are the traces of the real which explode aesthetic distance, affirm 'raw sensation' and root perception in the fragmented, agitated desire of the body. He writes, 'film hyperbolically aggravates vision, pushing it to an extreme point of implosion and self-annihilation'.[14]

Shaviro follows Deleuze and Leo Bersani in presenting desire and cinema viewing as a masochistic, anarchic force which extinguishes vision and representation. So, this is the fascination of the horror and the pornography film, a fascination with the image where the body of the spectator becomes masochistically shattered with excitement and fear. Shaviro cites as examples of this abject real, Carol Clover's work on the masochistic spectatorship of horror films, Buñuel's *Un Chien Andalou*, with its famous scene of a razor slicing an eyeball, and Andy Warhol's films. Such violent affectual immediacy, Shaviro proposes, is what Benjamin calls the 'disintegration of the aura in the experience of shock'.[15]

But Benjamin did not just theorize the dissolution of the aura; he also conceptualized its transformation, a re-memory of the real via the profane illumination of the image. Although Shaviro, like Deleuze and Guattari, sees the embodied and schizophrenic real as a revolutionary alternative to the Oedipal, I contend that this masochistic and mimetic form of violent abjection can certainly epitomize the thrill and the pleasure at stake in watching horror movies or sensational Hollywood films. It can also be used to understand the manipulation of audiences by dominant ideology. But what cannot be explained is how this mimetic masochism of the real becomes mediated aesthetically within an intersubjective relation. Indeed, because this anarchic revolution of the real dissolves all infrastructure, myth and the imaginary, then what we are left with is pure unfettered desire, not just the death drive of aesthetics, but the death of all sublimation.

This death drive or 'indifferent' aesthetics is illustrated most powerfully, in Shaviro's view, by Andy Warhol's films, especially his late ones. Criticized, for capitulating to crass commercialism, Warhol's films are exploitative and pornographic, shattering aura and violating the boundaries between avant-garde and commercial cinema, between self-reflexivity and vulgar narrative. Warhol's films depict a repetitive and fascinated voyeurism, to the point where mastery and all anchor points are lost. This is nothing less than the exposition of the emptiness and commodified construction of the personality. Like his famous interminable series of Campbell's soup labels, Warhol repeats images until they become emptied of 'pathos, meaning and memory'. Identity disappears in an abject repetition of the same, becoming simply an inert image of the real.[16] For Shaviro, it is no surprise that Warhol's films (films which cannot be distinguished as either complicit or resistant – they are in fact both) end up in limited circulation within the pornography market itself. The political implications of Warhol's film's are, that like pornographic films in general, they 'extinguish critical consciousness' and so render 'the mechanisms of power explicit'.[17]

Warhol's films, like those of the surrealists before him, can be seen as an aestheticization and politicization of a Freudian death drive, elevated to an exposition and critique of the forces of power and the culture industries in society. But the risk is, as Warhol's work makes so clear, that this critique is rendered useless as it becomes commodified by the deathly real it both celebrates and exposes.

There is much in Shaviro's analysis and indeed in Deleuze and Guattari's *Anti-Oedipus* which is persuasive, especially their critique of the Oedipal, heterosexual symbolic as a defensive neurotic structure that blocks more fluid connections between embodied desire and the social. Nevertheless, their uncompromising evacuation of the imaginary and celebration of the abject real might reveal Oedipal symbolic law as a hysterical force, but do little to offer an alternative. And it is in this sense that I want to critique the 'so-called' revolutionary status of the abject, schizophrenic body. As Shaviro shows us, the shattering of our identity and aura when watching film is a violent over-presence, that also marks complete alienation. I want to explore how film can figure a more embodied aesthetics that utilizes memory, rather than renders it meaningless. Such a filmic aesthetic might, possibly, explode or terminate vision and representation in the abjection of the body, but it will also re-memorize it tactically through an intersubjective relation.

Key points

- Fredric Jameson argues that late consumer capitalism and film are schizophrenic.
- We can distinguish a dialectical movement within postmodernism and film between first, Jameson's nostalgic, dead mimicry, and second, a more resistant imaginary based on cultural re-memory.

Phenomenology and film aesthetics

To understand fully the hysterical and cultural memory implicit within the filmic image, we have, I suggest, to return to a tradition of phenomenological film theory. Phenomenology can offer, as Vivian Sobchack has documented, an intersubjective model of film spectatorship as an alternative to the Lacanian split subject. In Lacanian theory the spectator or subject is always lost in the imaginary space of the other. Utilizing Merleau-Ponty's embodied narrative of perception, Sobchack describes the intersubjective movement between film text and viewer as one of temporal experience. Occupying a privileged moment of modernism, film, in Sobchack's view, captures the embodied presence of spectators. Whereas photography is locked into the empirical truths of realism and video represents the virtual non-presence of a postmodern age, film is exemplary in beckoning the spectator into the temporal flows of lived time.[18] As chapter 3 discussed, this reading traps the modernist cinema spectator in an idealistic space of embodied presence. Cinema spectatorship can alternatively be understood as a mimesis, which performs and reiterates the body within lived time and out of it. As such, film spectatorship moves between presence and absence, but as I intend to argue the lived time of cinematic presence is predicated on its loss. Psychoanalysis and Walter Benjamin inform us that psychic embodiment within lived time is only possible once the body of the mother and the historical object can be experienced as both lost and re-membered.

In *The Crisis of Political Modernism: Criticism and Ideology in Contemporary Film Theory* (1988), David Rodowick has documented the aesthetics of film history in terms of what he calls 'political modernism'. This aesthetic history of film follows a tradition of formalism and is associated with the European avant-garde film movements of the 1960s and 1970s. Political modernism understands spectatorship as a textual aesthetic, where both the aesthetics of the

film and the spectator's response are constructed through the semiotic structures of the text, a semiotics which symbolically transcends
the body and the real.

However, a phenomenological reading of film aesthetics as mimesis
can culturally re-member the aesthetic in terms of an embodied imaginary. Such a mimesis characterizes Sobchack's intersubjective film
experience, but the premiss of this more embodied temporal presence
of film is also an acknowledgement of its loss. The hysteric loses
nothing; out of time and psychically out of 'her' body, she replays
spectatorship and subjectivity, symbiotically within the scene and
imaginary of the other. The paradox of this pure presence and performance of the body is that it is completely disembodied at a psychic
level. To articulate an alternative to this hysterical spectatorship
where its mimesis can become embodied and move between presence
and absence means adding a psychological notion of memory to phenomenological explanations of film experience.

Psychoanalysis and phenomenology have occupied opposite poles
of film theory. Formalist approaches to film have advocated the
semiotic psychology of the spectator, whereas a realist approach has
foregrounded a phenomenological apprehension of the filmic image.
Phenomenology has been a fairly constant presence in the tradition
of realist film theory, most notably in the works of André Bazin and
Siegfried Kracauer. Whereas Bazin was directly influenced by figures
such as Sartre, Merleau-Ponty and Henri Bergson, Kracauer's phenomenological influences are perhaps more indirectly traced through
the Marxism of the Frankfurt School, particularly through the work
of his colleague Walter Benjamin. Bazin's emphasis on deep focus in
film, and the ontology of the filmic image, links with Kracauer's thesis
of how films capture the materiality of physical reality. The phenomenology of both these film thinkers has often been overlooked in
favour of a generalized bias against them for simplistic notions of
film as a window onto the world. However, both these writers agree
not just on the materiality of the filmic image and its ability to capture
and re-present the natural world, but also propose a psychology of
embodied vision.

This argument was taken up directly by Amédée Ayfre, a student
of Merleau-Ponty's who subsequently applied his theory to film. Ayfre
and his friend Henri Agel, who continued Ayfre's work after his
death, can be characterized as film thinkers whose phenomenology
opposed semiotics and structuralism. Dudley Andrews notes that
although the philosophy of Merleau-Ponty, Heidegger, Sartre and
Dufrenne were all the rage in artistic and academic thinking during
the 1950s, film was sidelined and not taken seriously as a proper

theoretical area of study. Consequently the application of phenomenology to film was little explored.

Film studies really came into its own as an academic area of study
with the advent of structuralism and semiotics in the 1960s. This
structuralist tradition, exemplified by the work of Christian Metz,
was forcefully critical of phenomenological approaches to film for
their essentialism and humanism. There is truth to these criticisms,
particularly in relation to Henri Agel, who directly opposed semiotic
film theory on the grounds that the study of film should not begin
with its material and ideological conditions but with the essence of
the artwork itself. Ayfre did explore film experience from the point
of view of the auteur and the audience, but ignored the way in which
they are part of a linguistic system that mediates the world. Filmic
images were then seen as creative self-realization, an authenticity
which transcended author, audience and film as an ideological language.[19] We can see from this how phenomenological film theory was
rejected by structuralist film thinkers as essentialist, and how it was
seen as complicit with traditional theories of art and aesthetics that
simply shored up a positive ideology of bourgeois humanism.

Bazin's phenomenology

Bazin's and Kracauer's phenomenological realism has been fairly
universally dismissed since the advent of 1970s film theory, both for
its emphasis on literal mimesis and its advocation of the spatio-
temporal integrity of the shot, representing life as an ontological,
unmediated continuity. The deep-focus, long-take style of this realism
was ideally summed up for Bazin in, first, Lumière's films, then
Flaherty and Murnau's work, then Welles and finally with Italian
neo-realism. However, Bazin's phenomenological understanding of
the psychology and temporality of filmic image has been recently
revived by Phillip Rosen, who illustrates how a *psychological* mimesis
of the 'real' is inherent within Bazin's notion of spectatorship. Rosen
emphasizes two basic ontological themes in Bazin's work.[20] First, is
the indexical trace of the image which refers to a past moment of the
real, and second, the defensive position of the subject/spectator who
wards off the threat of death and time passing. Rosen is critical of
what he sees as the tendency in Bazin's thinking to prioritize 'change
mummified' or a timeless ontology of the image, over the more radical
historicity that is inherent in Bazin's understanding of the temporality
of the film image.

Bazin's theory of the 'mummy complex' is where the film spectator's subjective obsession in relation to the film image seeks to master and control time through a timeless ontology.[21] It is only in genuine realist film that this defensive ontology can be subverted, evoking a more fluid and evolving temporality.[22] Belief in the film image depends on prior knowledge of the spectator: the subject's prior knowledge of referential evidence (the real) in the production of the image. Bazin thus clearly delineates between two sorts of realism. The first realism occurs in films where the 'mummy complex' is dominant. Here, the 'real' is obsessively preserved and the gap between historical real and the signifying image maintained. The mythic representation of Stalin in Soviet cinema is a key example of this preservative realism where real historicity is in fact evacuated. Second, however, is the realism in films that Bazin values, because it *reduces* the gap between the referent and the film image. For example, in 'The Stylistics of Robert Bresson', Bazin praises Bresson's filmic adaptation of the novel *Diary of a Country Priest* precisely because the referent of the novel, as a prior 'reality' to the film, is acknowledged within the film. This respect for the material presence of the novel thus minimizes the gap between referent and sign, real and imaginary, allowing a more fluid flow of time that connects past and present and projects into the future. However, Bazin ultimately sides with the 'mummy complex' and privileges the preservative obsession as a universal trait in the film spectator. Rosen sees this as problematic – a suppressing of temporality and historicity, in favour of ontology.

Embodied memory and the filmic image

Films, for Bazin, might privilege ontology, but they don't just defend against time. The mimetic perception of film is also inseparable from memory. Laura Marks's recent book *The Skin of the Film: Intercultural Cinema, Embodiment and the Senses* argues that Merleau-Ponty's account of embodied experience can only be understood as perception if it is linked to memory.[23] Another way of thinking about this is to understand how a pure presence of hysterical projection into the filmic image is disembodied. As Bazin tells us, it is only a re-memory of the real or past referent which can truly embody the spectator within time. The philosopher most concerned with time and cinema is Gilles Deleuze.

Deleuze derives much of his philosophy of the cinema from the ideas of Henri Bergson. In *Matter and Memory* Bergson argues that there is continuity between consciousness, matter and time. And also for Deleuze there 'is no difference at all between images, things and motion'.[24] These thinkers do establish a distinction though, between the image 'matter' of the objective universal, which Bergson calls 'present Image', and our subjective, selective perception of that whole.[25] In this account, as David Rodowick points out, we move in perception not between subject and object but between a universal and a more selective embodied image perception, 'responding, on one level, to human needs and, on another, to human freedom'.[26]

For Deleuze, there are two basic images in cinema: the classical movement image, which refers to cinema up until the Second World War, and the time image relating to postwar cinema. In thinking about the movement image, Deleuze wants to investigate how subjectivity is constructed; how perception is subtracted from the universal flow of images. He identifies three 'moments'. First, the perception image which selects our spatial centre in relation to the whole. Second, the action image which organizes and masters a temporal horizon. Finally, the affection image which links the action image to lived embodied qualities and states. Drawing on Balázs's micro-physiognomics of the facial close-up, Deleuze shows how affection images translate embodied expression onto the face.[27]

The movement image organizes us spatially in time, so film frame follows film frame causally in relation to action. The time image, however, links us to a more mental image that frees time from causality. For example, the movement image is characteristic of classical Hollywood cinema: an action thriller, say, with a chase, followed by the hero's defeat of the bad guy, rescue of the heroine and resolution of the plot. In time-image cinema there is no such linearity and the action shot might be followed by different images of, say, contemplation or replay which break with the linear flow in a more autonomous way. Time-image cinema is then more characteristic of avant-garde film, where the thin optical nature of the image requires the viewer to complete the meaning of the image.

Deleuze attributes the time-image cinema to the rise of such film directors as Godard, Rossellini, Antonioni and to a postwar period. This post-colonial period is where the ruins of empire and reconstruction of cities introduced, for the first time, more marginal, intercultural spaces. Deleuze called these spaces 'any spaces whatsoever' and they are associated with a more direct perception of time. The 'affection' images released in relation to these time images are not immediately followed by action, as in the movement image, and so allow for an emotional or 'feeling' contemplation of the event. Whereas the movement image guarantees a kind of truth associated with the grand narratives of modernism, the time image suspends that truth, separating time from causality and exposing a *durée*, or duration, where the passing of time can be witnessed.

The time image and memory

The time image is, then, associated with a kind of dialectics of memory. Time is always split into two images, a virtual image representing official history such as historical texts or family photos, and an actual image, of an unofficial 'present that passes'. Actual images remember what is not recorded, or within language. These sensual, recollection images are the absences in the smiling family photos or, on a wider level, the oral histories that are passed on outside official representation.

Recollection and time images excavate the past for fragments of the real. These time images are thinner; they do not completely correspond to official perception and so invite a temporal dialectic for the spectator, who recreates the object within the wider systems of time with which it is caught up. This is reminiscent of Walter Benjamin's apprehension of the auratic object and the profane illumination, but there are several differences between Deleuze's and Bergson's ideas on memory and Benjamin's.

Bergson and Deleuze argue for a particular and individual recollection, whereas, for Benjamin, it is the collective which is awakened. Bergson, we recall, shows how perception is subtractive: we take from the whole according to our individual embodied needs and responses. But Bergson does not acknowledge the obstacles to memory and perception caused by trauma and the unconscious, whereas Benjamin accentuates the involuntary and material nature of memory. He emphasizes the shock of coming across an object or film image which dissolves official history, recreating the past in a material and contingent sense.

For Marks, the time image does not elaborate on the embodied nature of the viewer or the collective nature of memory – an inter-subjective relation the viewer either represses or integrates. She writes, 'To raise the stakes of the optical image, we might ask, what's the point of "finally SEEING" if there's nothing to see? What's the point of having our clichés and preconceptions blown by the intensity of the time-image experience if we have no subsequent course of action?'[28]

Marks wonders whether the time image might also connect to and claim a more collective unconscious. This is also Benjamin's sense of an image which can shockingly dissolve official memory, but then reconnect experience with a more social memory. We can't just wrest time from the movement image; we also have to reconnect the time image to the movement image so that new collective stories can be told. Deleuze, like Bergson, privileges an intellectual imagination that intervenes in memory. They both downplay the embodied nature of cinema viewing, or perception, although they both accept it as a basis. Bergson, moreover, separates memory into memory images that actively imagine and modifications of the body that habitually repeat.[29] Benjamin's optical unconscious, on the other hand, does not accept this hierarchy between a selective mental imagination and a more primordial embodied mimesis.

Laura Marks seeks to develop and bring together phenomenology and Deleuze's time image into a theory of haptical cinema where the embodied contemplation between viewer and film image does not objectify images. It co-exists among them, inhabiting a space that Trinh T. Minh-ha describes as being nearby.[30] Haptical images are time images needing to be fleshed out and recollected by the sensual viewer, but they also encourage a plurality of sensual responses often in combination with sound, camera movement and montage. These images encourage reflexivity about the photographic representation of the image: they play with light, focus, the graininess of the film. Thus haptic visuality wrests time and memory from narrative representation and causality, forcing our recollection of the auratic nature and the micro-physiognomics of the image.

Key points

- Phenomenology can offer an intersubjective model of film spectatorship as an alternative to the Lacanian split subject.
- A phenomenological reading of film aesthetics, as mimesis, can culturally remember the aesthetic in terms of an embodied imaginary.

Aesthetics and re-memory in the films of Lars von Trier

I want to conclude this chapter, and indeed the book, with a discussion and reading of Lars von Trier's films *Breaking the Waves* and *Dancer in the Dark*. Both films are examples of Deleuze's time-image cinema and Marks's haptical cinema with the filmic images needing to be fleshed out and recollected by the sensual viewer. In *Breaking the Waves*, these effects are achieved through the combination of a classically shot art-house realism, combined with melodrama. With *Dancer in the Dark* innovative avant-garde methods are combined with melodrama and a gothic rendition of the American musical. Both films are shot with a hand-held camera and the thinness of the images, foregrounded especially in the digitally filmed *Dancer in the Dark*, evoke a haptic visuality and a sense of the past. In *Breaking the Waves*, Lars von Trier achieves technological innovation and sophistication, distancing the spectator in true counter-cinema tradition, mixing 'a documentary style' realism with narrative. But the spectator is also drawn into a visceral embodied and emotional response to the images in the film.

Breaking the Waves is set in a remote village on the northwest coast of Scotland, and centres on the tragic story of Bess (Emily Watson) a young, excessively naive and psychotic woman, whose spiritual and erotic love for her new husband Jan (Stellan Skargard) is matched by a similarly intense passion for God. Bess's innocent and giving love is contrasted with the brutalizing Calvinistic faith of the patriarchal and religious community in which she lives, a community where God's word is a paternal law and where any 'sinners' who stray from that written law are consigned to Hell. Bess's marriage to an outsider from the oil rig is treated with suspicion. When Bess is asked what the outsiders can contribute to the community she replies 'their music'; but music, emotion and physical love are frowned on by this cold symbolic community. Their inhuman laws and repression of all sensual feelings and responses are contrasted with Bess's instability in not being able to contain her emotions.

When Jan has to return to work on the oil rig, Bess finds solace again in her conversations with her psychic double – God. These conversations are psychotically literalized, with Bess crouching in the church speaking in her own voice and then in a much deeper voice, a critical super-ego that oscillates between her mother telling her to endure and the paternal law of the church urging her obedience and self-restraint. But Bess cannot endure Jan's absence; as she says to her voices in the church, 'I can't wait'. Praying for his return, Bess then hears that Jan has had an accident and suffered injuries to his brain and spinal chord. She is convinced her prayers have caused Jan's accident. In hospital Jan is paralysed, fighting for his life, and as the fluid in his brain rises he urges Bess to have sexual encounters with other men. At first this seems an altruistic act to free her from his illness, but as the film progresses it turns into a form of control where Jan gains perverse pleasure from Bess's sordid sexual encounters with strangers. Bess initially refuses Jan's requests, but his insistence that

Fig. 9 Emily Watson as Bess in *Breaking the Waves* (1996), directed by Lars von Trier. © Zentropa / The Kobal Collection

he will die if he is unable to be a witness to Bess making love is met by Bess's own self-delusions that her actions determine Jan's fate.

The descent of Bess into self-degradation and humiliation is also a selfless and pure love for Jan. Although her actions are utterly repulsive to her, she believes they will save Jan's life. Bess is dearly loved by her sister-in-law and by Jan's doctor, who collude in trying to section her under the Mental Health Act. The religious community makes Bess an outcast. The local priest turns a blind eye when Bess is stoned by local children; even her mother locks her out. Bess's sacrifice culminates in her brutal murder by men she has offered to prostitute herself to on the ships, although their savagery seems provoked by her obvious innocence and unwillingness to carry out the sexual trading of her body.

Breaking the Waves is indebted to the 1928 classic, *The Passion of Joan of Arc*, by the Dane Carl Theodor Dreyer, and also shows marked affinities in style to Bazin's favoured realist film – Bresson's *Diary of a Country Priest*. But the film also has strong links to the work of the Danish film-maker Douglas Sirk, the famous director of melodrama in the 1950s. Indeed, the dialectic in the film is between a raw documentary and escalating melodrama, making up the narrative style. But counter-posed to the narrative is also a non-narrative perception carrying the painterly, landscape scenes and shots accompanied by 1970s music, which break up the narrative into eight successive chapter headings. Contradictory editing and camera styles move between narrative and non-narrative perceptions, highlighting the images in relation to a background of natural reality. The spectator is pulled into the scene, rather than the story. The hand-held camera style draws the spectator into a raw documentary feel of being there, and this is combined with tiny jump cuts across scenes which foreground a relationship with the image. Lars von Trier talks about the importance in his work of achieving a distance and objectivity as an editor.[31] Not present at the shoot, his editorial work is then managed through the monitor and the digital filmic images that result in thin, Deleuzian, optical time images, often bleached of colour.

These thin, haptical and sensual images allow a space for the spectator and encourage an embodied emotional response or projection into the cinematic image. Like Deleuze's affection/recollection images, they inhabit those 'any spaces whatsoever' enabling embodied recollection and re-memory. Reminiscent of Balázs's understanding of the mimesis in relation to a micro-physiognomics of the image, the close-up shots of Bess and her facial expressions provide an emotional mobility which subverts narrative flows. This mobility is present in Bess's constant turning to the camera, her different facial expressions when she is talking to God in the church or the following of her facial expressions as she makes loves and reaches orgasm with Jan. These close-ups are an example of Benjamin's optical unconscious, where cinematic technology can mimic a childhood mimesis. There is a close-up of Bess's face when she is masturbating the unknown man on the bus. It is a child's facial expression, screwing itself up to do something it hates. Bess runs off the bus and is sick on the mossy bank. As she looks up she sees a rabbit twitching its nose and sniffing. Bess mimics back, sniffing and twitching her nose in response and smiles. She then walks off down the road, apparently untroubled. This close-up says more than any narrative dialogue; it also completely re-reads the previous scene on the bus, because it establishes Bess's innocence, and it links the spectator with a more haptic 'childish' mimesis of her image. Divested of responsibility, Bess's purity and virtue are established as the degradation becomes attached to the spectators, the people on the bus and the community, who observe Bess, but do nothing to help. Another way of understanding this is to say that we are not linguistically castrated and voyeuristically separated from the filmic representation of Bess. We do not objectify the images of Bess; instead we inhabit a haptical or embodied space near her image, and experience what it is like nearby, for her.

Speaking of Lars von Trier's direction of the film, the actress Katrin Cartlidge, who plays the sister-in-law Dodo, discusses how with this film the technical innovation was used to advance a much more emotional, experiential sense. She quotes him as saying that he wanted the technical side to be 'as light as a feather'.[32] The work of the cinematic language is then to get out of the way, so that the emotional and mimetic relationship with the images can be established. *Breaking the Waves* establishes haptical viewing between spectator and image, and it also achieves through an optical unconscious a mimetic re-memory of auratic nature which in turn transforms our relation to cultural memory and history.

This brings me to a final discussion of psychoanalysis, aesthetics and postmodernism in relation to *Breaking the Waves*. On one level, this film is very postmodern; it plays with styles and jumbles past traditions. The theme of psychosis and the postmodernism are therefore central to this film, but in my reading it is an embodied imaginary, or the optical unconscious that culturally re-members the hysterical, Oedipal, melodrama. Psychosis is mapped in this film not as a subversive schizoanalysis of the real that shatters representation and tradition, but as the territory where a mimesis between melancholia and mourning are played out between spectator and text.

The film plays with meanings of power, madness and the relationship between the individual and the community. The melancholic religious fathers in this film are the social and symbolic carriers of language and the law, although they are also revealed as the pure hysterical masquerade of an Oedipal imaginary. Bess suffers from neurotic and psychotic episodes. But her psychosis is a response to the organized paternal religion and the Oedipal symbolic law of the community, which disallows an embodied, spiritual intersubjective relation with the other. Bess's psychosis is a mimesis that (like Benjamin's defensive mimesis against the shock and alienation of the body in the modern world) operates as a protective shield against the trauma inflicted by the hysterical patriarchs of the community, a society whose castrating laws literally cut themselves off from emotional response and music. It is this absence of a sensual underpinning to the symbolic that Bess struggles with as her imaginary and real worlds become disconnected. Happiness and healing come to Bess with the outsiders' music and with Jan, whose physical and spiritual love returns her to feelings of shared meaning and an embodied ground to her feelings and identity.

Injured, Jan's lack of emotional responsiveness through brain alteration matches the mentality of the village community whose hearts become like stone once Bess has strayed from the word and law of

God. Alienation from the social community and Jan leads Bess into an increasingly imaginary and delusional world. Hysterical madness or psychosis eventually links everyone in the film – the patriarchal elders, Bess and Jan – because feelings are disconnected from the self through religious tradition, mental illness or neurological damage.

In a sense, though, Bess is less of a psychotic, and more of a saint, in her belief in the redemptive (carnal and transcendental) love that can exist between people. As a 'Joan of Arc' figure she suffers for society's betrayal of its ideals. But what makes this film a work of cultural re-memory, rather than a hysterical melodrama, is the way the spectator contributes sensual, emotional experience to the filmic images. Escalating melodrama in this film is not repressed under linear narrative representation; rather it is used in conjunction with contrasting technical styles and camera/digital work to wrest time and memory from the image and to instil an embodied contemplation. The melodrama moves from cramped interior domestic settings, where feelings are intense and compressed, to the wild expression of emotion with nature: Bess screaming her unbearable loss of Jan into the stormy sea. If the melodrama grounds the narrative in reality and makes it believable and identifiable to the spectator, then the camera work in this film creates its sense of illusion as a painterly imaginary where haptic images emotionally and aesthetically move the spectator.

The images in *Breaking the Waves* are profane illuminations; they don't just make you feel, they force you to think. Opening up the spectator to the experience of loss and mourning, these images are an optical unconscious, producing cultural memory. This film achieves this sense of mourning in relation to the image through its violent juxtapositioning of the spectator vis-à-vis the image. One minute you are emotionally, violently and sensationally identified with the image, a mimesis of the real, as Shaviro describes, where image and aesthetic distance are shattered. But this over-presence is immediately followed by a distancing and an ideational contemplation of the image. Von Trier talks about his refusal to go on shoots, and the important objectivity that is gained editorially by acknowledging that it is windy and cold at the production end, but still remaining at a distance. This movement between feeling and thinking, presence and absence, is a powerful dialectic in sensually immersing the viewer, but also allowing a space of mental reflexivity.

In apparatus film theory, symbolic linguistic and semiotic castration between spectator and viewed creates a narrative representation and fiction which textually implicates the spectator. I have argued within this book for an Oedipal and hysterical identification with the filmic image, a melancholia where the spectator becomes lost in the hysterical imaginary of the other. This hysterical imaginary can characterize mainstream Hollywood films as a dominant and organizing modality of melodrama. However, in *Breaking the Waves*, this Oedipal melodrama becomes culturally re-membered through an optical unconscious. No dead mimicry of postmodern style, but a haunting work of art and cultural re-memory, this film becomes a practice of the embodied imaginary that is produced between spectator and text.

Dancer in the Dark won the Palme d'Or at the Cannes Film Festival and was a controversial choice, in that many critics had panned the film on the basis that the lead actress, the singer Bjork, could not act.[33] *Dancer in the Dark* brings together real and imaginary worlds through its genre mixing of the musical with a real documentary style. Indeed, Lars von Trier states that the musical and the realist documentary make up the two shapes to the film. However, these intertwined and dialogic 'shapes' are also organized through melodrama. A melodramatic modality thus organizes dialogic interchanges between genres, and between fictional and real worlds. We can see in relation to *Dancer in the Dark* how melodrama moves the spectator between the imaginary and real, both within the film's two styles of musical and documentary, and between the film and the real, or the history outside the film. Bjork is not just a would-be musical star in the film; she is a musical star in real life. Her melodramatic performance in the film can be linked to the acting out between her and von Trier at the film festival at Cannes. Here, Bjork is cast as being herself, thus portraying 'real' emotion rather than acting. Her 'melodramatic' falling out with von Trier surrounds the very issue of excessive emotionality. Von Trier states that Bjork's inability to act, her display of real emotion, was what made the film work, despite his 'reputed' antagonism towards her inability to act during shooting. However, if hysteria is an acting-out based on a disassociation from psychic embodiment, then, Bjork is, conversely blamed and the film praised for her *lack* of hysteria. The utter impossibility for Bjork of being anything other than herself is also her inability to act and be melodramatic.

The inter-textuality of *Dancer in the Dark* is also present in the inter-relationship between genre, Hollywood and American history. The traditional Hollywood musical works alongside American society in a binary doubling between work ethics and entertainment. However, the breakdown of barriers between art and life and the self-reflective inclusion of the 'internal audience' in the musical is ultimately conservative. Jane Fueur writes:

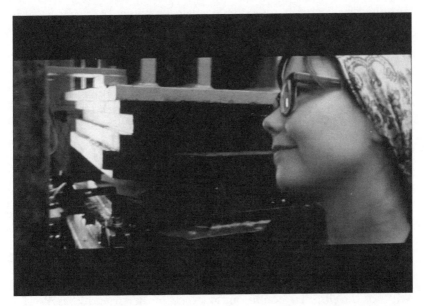

Fig. 10   Bjork as Selma in *Dancer in the Dark* (2000), directed by Lars von Trier. © Arte France / Blind Spot / Dinovi / The Kobal Collection

> all Hollywood films manipulated audience response, but the musical could incorporate that response in the film itself; all Hollywood films sought to be entertaining but the musical could incorporate the myth of entertainment into its aesthetic discourse.[34]

The musical then aesthetically manipulates the spectator into an ideal transcendence of social and economic concerns, masking its real enforcement of the reigning economic market.

Dancer in the Dark certainly plays with this American tradition of the musical and incorporates some of its characteristics. The film is highly stylized and manipulative of the audience, but it also evokes a phenomenological realism through various techniques. Lars von Trier talks about how he eschewed what would be the established way of making a musical, using one camera and a storyboard with a combination of tracking, dolly and crane shots.[35] Instead he used 'arthouse cinema' techniques of hand-held cameras and video to achieve a random live effect. In place of one camera and a storyboard, he instituted a hundred fixed cameras which enabled him to gain a looser, less controlled performance that resembled live theatre or television rather than film. *Dancer in the Dark* is set in America, although it is actually filmed in Sweden. Lars von Trier suggests it is a mythical America which is captured by the film, and it is interesting that the film also puts together the musical and the death penalty, a binary that comes out of the same moment of American history. Indeed, von Trier wants to accentuate the awfulness of the death penalty, its foreignness to Scandinavians, but also I suggest the barbarity that underlies America's and the 'free' West's liberal democracy. In trying to combine some of the darkness and tragedy of classical opera back into the musical, Lars von Trier introduces a realism that tempers its idealistic and escapist nature.

In *Dancer in the Dark*, Selma, a poor immigrant single mother, is working in a steel-plate factory in a small American town. Selma is going blind; her two passions are her son and love of musicals. The first roots her in a real world of deprivation and hardship; the second allows her to escape into an imaginary world of song and dance. Selma is eventually sacked for breaking the machine, caused by a combination of her blindness and her day-dreaming. Her hard-earned money that has been saved to pay for her son's eye operation, so he will not develop her condition, is stolen by her friendly landlord – Bill the police officer. A struggle ensues when Selma tries to retrieve the money and Bill is killed. Selma is subsequently tried for murder, found guilty and executed by hanging.

The utopian sensibility of *Dancer in the Dark* is embodied in Selma's dreaming and it takes off with the musical numbers.[36] However, these numbers connect with the real in two ways. First, they are actually written and performed by Bjork the real musical star; according to Lars von Trier, they actually tried to perform the numbers as live performances, but it was too difficult. Second, the songs take off from everyday life. Initially the film separates the musical from the narrative in a conventional realist style, where we find Selma dancing and singing in an amateur theatre performance of *The Sound of Music*, but a third of the way into the film, when Selma is working a night shift in the factory, the film suddenly becomes a musical. This take-off from the real into the imaginary world of the musical is triggered by Selma's dreaming. As she is an immigrant from Czechoslovakia, Selma's dreaming is a transcendental yearning for the American dream as embodied by the actual Hollywood musical, but like Benjamin's affectual shock, Selma's dreaming is also a time or recollection image found within the materialistic, repetitive actions of the factory machines. Lars von Trier states that the idea of making the musical erupt out of everyday objects was a trick to convey raw emotion, to block the transcendental tendency of music to escape from the real. The emotion in the film is also engineered through the use of melodrama, particularly Selma's blindness and her execution.

The scene of Selma's execution and the equally traumatic scene in *Breaking the Waves* where Bess sacrifices herself to the murderous men on the ship are almost unwatchable. Both scenes act as a traumatic shattering of the viewer's disavowal and aura, a deathly aesthetics, violent and voyeuristic, that breaks down the barriers between avant-garde and commercial cinema. However, as time images connected to movement images and narrative, they force us to remember not just the politics and history intrinsic to public execution and schizophrenia, but also our disavowal and responsibility as a community. The abject real of terror and violence that is bestowed on Selma and Bess as they are scapegoated in different ways outside the community forces us to acknowledge and remember our own hysterical projections. This moves them from a melodramatic mono-imaginary in the scene of the other to a more social acknowledgement of difference, a lived time of belonging, where real and imaginary worlds can be more creatively reconfigured.

Notes

INTRODUCTION

1 The phenomenology I utilize in this book is indebted to the work of
   Walter Benjamin, Maurice Merleau-Ponty, Luce Irigaray and R.D.
   Laing. As such, it does not follow the classical transcendental philosophy of Edmund Husserl, but offers a more materialist account of the
   lived experience of the body/mind. Historically, there is arguably a phenomenological reading of the unconscious in the work of early Freud,
   and Carl Jung. The phenomenology of a social unconscious returns in
   the Marxist writings of Walter Benjamin, Erich Fromm and Siegfried
   Kracauer. More recently, the phenomenological psychoanalysis of R.D.
   Laing and Luce Irigaray is indebted to the philosophy of Merleau-Ponty.
2 L. Kirby, *Parallel Tracks: The Railroad and Silent Cinema* (Exeter, University of Exeter Press, 1997), p. 50.
3 Uncle Josh was the famous rube in early film, featuring in
   Edison/Porter's *Uncle Josh at the Moving Picture Show*. L. Kirby, *Parallel Tracks*, p. 65.
4 W. Benjamin, 'The Work of Art in the Age of Mechanical Reproduction', *Illuminations*, edited and with an Introduction by Hannah
   Arendt, transl. Harry Zorn (London, Pimlico, 1999), p. 229.
5 T. Elsaesser, 'Cinema – The Irresponsible Signifier or "The Gamble with
   History": Film Theory or Cinema Theory', *New German Critique*, 40
   (winter 1987), p. 85.
6 D. Bordwell, *On the History of Film Style* (Cambridge, Harvard University Press, 1997).
7 B. Singer, 'Making Sense of the Modernity Thesis', in *Melodrama and
   Modernity* (New York, Columbia University Press, 2002), p. 111.
8 M. Taussig, *Mimesis and Alterity: A Particular History of the Senses*
   (London and New York, Routledge, 1993), p. 20.

9   R. Girard, *Things Hidden since the Foundation of the World*, transl. S. Bann (London, Athlone Press, 1987); J. Oughourlian, *The Puppet of Desire: The Psychology of Hysteria, Possession and Hypnosis*, transl. Eugene Webb (Stanford, Calif., Stanford University Press, 1991).

10 L. Williams, *Playing the Race Card: Melodrama of Black and White from Uncle Tom to O.J. Simpson* (Princeton, NJ, Princeton University Press, 2001); C. Gledhill, 'Rethinking Genre', in *Reinventing Film Studies*, C. Gledhill and L. Williams eds (London and New York, Arnold, 2000).

11 R. Bellour, 'Believing in Cinema', transl. Dana Polan, in *Psychoanalysis and Cinema*, E. Ann Kaplan ed. (London and New York, Routledge, 1990), p. 107.

12 F. Roustang, *How to Make a Paranoid Laugh, Or What is Psychoanalysis?*, transl. A.C. Vila (Philadelphia, University of Pennsylvania Press, 2000), p. 170.

13 C. Gledhill, 'The Melodramatic Field: An Investigation', in *Home is Where the Heart is: Studies in Melodrama and the Woman's Film*, C. Gledhill ed. (London, British Film Institute (B.F.I.), 1987), p. 27.

14 T. Elsaesser, 'Tales of Sound and Fury: Observations on the Family Melodrama', in *Home is Where the Heart is*.

15 Ibid., p. 49.

16 P. Brooks, *The Melodramatic Imagination: Balzac, Henry James, Melodrama and the Mode of Excess* (New Haven, Yale University Press, 1976), pp. 35–6.

17 L. Mulvey, ' "It will be a Magnificent Obsession" – the Melodrama's Role in the Development of Contemporary Film Theory', in *Melodrama: Stage, Picture, Screen*, J.S. Bratton, J. Cook and C. Gledhill eds (London, British Film Institute, 1994), pp. 121–34.

18 S. Freud, 'Five Lectures On Psychoanalysis', in *Two Short Accounts of Psychoanalysis*, J. Strachey transl. and ed. (London, Penguin, 1977), p. 40.

19 L. Mulvey, 'It will be a Magnificent Obsession', p. 127.

20 Ibid., p. 130.

21 E. Diamond, *Unmaking Mimesis* (London and New York, Routledge, 1997), p. 52.

22 Ibid., p. 5.

23 S. Freud, 'Some Character Types Met with in Psycho-analytic Work: Those Wrecked by Success II', in *The Standard Edition of the Complete Psychological Works of Sigmund Freud* (1953–74), James Strachey ed. and transl., vol. 14.

24 C.G. Jung, *The Theory of Psychoanalysis* (1913), in *Collected Works of C.G. Jung* (1893–1968), H. Read, M. Fordham and G. Adler eds, R.F.C. Hull transl. (London, Routledge, 1961), vol. 4, pp. 161–2.

25 S. Freud, *Mourning and Melancholia* (1917), in *Standard Edition*, vol. 14, p. 250.

26 Ibid., p. 240.

27 S. Buck-Morss, 'Dream World of a Mass Culture', in *The Dialectics of Seeing: Walter Benjamin and the Arcades Project* (Cambridge, Mass., MIT Press, 1991).

28 W. Benjamin, *Gerammelte Schriften*, Rolf Tiedemann and Hermann Schweppenhäuser eds, 7 vols (Frankfurt am Main, Suhrkamp, 1980–9), p. 576.

29 M. Cohen, *Profane Illuminations* (Berkeley, Los Angeles and London, University of California Press, 1993), p. 193.

30 W. Benjamin, 'The Work of Art in the Age of Mechanical Reproduction', in *Illuminations*, Hannah Arendt ed., Harry Zorn transl. (London, Pimlico, 1999).

31 W. Benjamin, 'A Small History of Photography' (1931), in *One Way Street and Other Writings*, Edmund Jephcott and Kingsley Shorter transl. (London and New York, Verso, 1998), p. 243.

32 Ibid., pp. 243–4.

33 Ibid., p. 229.

34 S. Kracauer, *Theory of Film: The Redemption of Physical Reality* (Oxford, Oxford University Press, 1960), p. 159.

35 Ibid., p. 165.

36 Ibid., p. 165.

37 Ibid., p. 166.

38 Kracauer's film theory has historically been classified as realist, and the more imaginative phenomenology of his work has been relatively ignored. The intersubjective and phenomenological film experience awarded to the spectator, in Kracauer's thinking, subverts the realist proposition that film can be passively apprehended as an objective reality that reflects the world.

39 L. Irigaray, 'Così Fan Tutti', in *This Sex Which is Not One*, C. Porter and C. Burke transl. (Ithaca, NY, Cornell University Press, 1985), pp. 86–7.

40 J. Rose, 'Feminine Sexuality', in *Sexuality in the Field of Vision* (London, Verso, 1986).

41 J. Lacan, 'The Mirror Stage as Formative of the Function of the I', Alan Sheridan transl., in *Ecrits: A Selection* (London, Tavistock, 1977).

42 M. Merleau-Ponty, 'The Child's Relation with Others', in *The Primacy of Perception*, J.M. Edie ed. (Evanston, Ill., Northwestern University Press, 1964), pp. 135–6.

43 V. Sobchack, 'Being with One's Own Eyes', in *The Address of the Eye: A Phenomenology of Film Experience* (Princeton, NJ, Princeton University Press, 1992), p. 121.

44 L. Irigaray, *An Ethics of Sexual Difference*, Carolyn Burke and Gillian C. Gill transl. (London, Athlone Press, 1993), p. 174.

45 See 'Postlacanian Feminism: Reading the Symbolic, Imaginary and Real', in *Arguing with the Phallus: Feminist, Queer and Postcolonial Theory* (London, Zed Books, 2000) where I discuss Irigaray's 'feminine', sexually symbolic *and* embodied imaginary.

46 L. Irigaray, 'Flesh Colors', in *Sexes and Genealogies*, G.C. Gill transl. (New York, Columbia University Press, 1993), p. 164.
47 Ibid., p. 155.
48 Symbiosis in my clinical experience is not an early developmental state, but a fantasy of oneness that is utilized as a defence against anxiety, pain and difference.
49 M. Merleau-Ponty, 'The Film and the New Psychology', in *Sense and Non-Sense*, H.L.D. and P.A. Dreyfus transl. (Evanston, Ill., Northwestern University Press, 1964).
50 Ibid., p. 52.
51 Ibid., p. 53.
52 Ibid., p. 58.
53 Ibid., p. 59.
54 V. Sobchack, *The Address of the Eye*, p. 165.
55 Ibid., p. 167.
56 Ibid., p. 168.
57 I cannot do justice to the complexity of Sobchack's work here and to the interesting implications her work also poses for the embodied relation between the film-maker and the film; see *The Address of the Eye*.
58 T. Elsaesser, 'The New, New Hollywood. Cinema. Beyond Distance and Proximity', in *Moving Images, Culture and the Mind*, Ib Bondebjerg ed. (Luton, University of Luton Press, 2000), p. 201.

INTRODUCTION TO PART I

1 L. Althusser, 'Ideology and Ideological State Apparatuses (Notes Toward an Investigation)', in *Lenin and Philosophy and Other Essays*, B. Brewster transl. (London and New York, Monthly Review Press, 1971).
2 For a detailed discussion of Althusser's and Barthes' influence on Apparatus theory see J. Mayne, *Cinema and Spectatorship* (London, Routledge, 1993).
3 J.L. Baudry, 'The Apparatus', J. Andrews and B. Augst transl., *Camera Obscura*, no. 1 (fall 1976), 104–6; C. Metz, *The Imaginary Signifier: Psychoanalysis and the Cinema*, C. Britton, A. Williams, B. Brewster and A. Guzzetti, transl. (Bloomington, Indiana University Press, 1977); L. Mulvey, 'Visual Pleasure and Narrative Cinema', *Screen*, vol. 16, no. 3 (autumn 1975), 6–18.
4 J. Lacan, 'The Mirror Stage as Formative of the Function of the I', *Ecrits: A Selection*, A. Sheridan ed. (London, Tavistock, 1977).
5 L. Mulvey, 'Visual Pleasure and Narrative Cinema', in *Feminism and Film Theory*, C. Penley ed. (London and New York, Routledge, 1988), p. 61.
6 T. Elsaesser, 'Tales of Sound and Fury: Observations on the Family Melodrama', in *Home is Where the Heart is*, C. Gledhill ed. (London, British Film Institute (B.F.I.), 1987); R. Altman, 'Dickens, Griffith and

Film Theory Today', in *Classical Hollywood Narrative: The Paradigm Wars*, J. Gaines ed. (Durham NC, and London, Duke University Press, 1992).

7   P. Brooks, *The Melodramatic Imagination: Balzac, Henry James, Melodrama and the Mode of Excess* (New Haven, NJ, Yale University Press, 1976); T. Elsaesser, 'Tales of Sound and Fury: Observations on the Family Melodrama'.

8   R. Altman, 'Dickens, Griffith and Film Theory Today'.

9   P. Brooks, *The Melodramatic Imagination*.

10 G. Nowell-Smith, 'Minnelli and Melodrama', in *Home is Where the Heart is*.

11 M. Borch-Jacobsen, *The Freudian Subject*, C. Porter transl. (Stanford, Calif., Stanford University Press, 1988), p. 28.

12 A. Bazin, *What is Cinema?*, H. Gray transl., 2 vols (Berkeley and Los Angeles, University of California Press, 1967).

13 C. McCabe, 'Realism and the Cinema: Notes on Some Brechtian Theses', in *Theoretical Essays* (Manchester, Manchester University Press, 1985).

14 D. Bordwell, J. Staiger and K. Thompson, *The Classical Hollywood Cinema: Film Style and the Mode of Production to 1960* (New York, Columbia University Press, 1985).

15 Ibid.

16 D. Bordwell, *Narration in the Fiction Film* (London, Methuen, 1985).

17 J. Mayne, *Cinema and Spectatorship*.

18 D. Bordwell, 'A Case for Cognitivism,' *Iris*, 9 (1989) 11–40.

19 J. Mayne, *Cinema and Spectatorship*, p. 59.

CHAPTER 1   SEXUAL DIFFERENCE, MELODRAMA AND FILM THEORY

1   M.A. Doanne, *The Desire to Desire: The Woman's Film of the 1940s* (Houndsmill and London, Macmillan, 1987).

2   M.A. Doanne, *Femmes Fatales: Feminism, Film Theory, Psychoanalysis* (London and New York, Routledge, 1991), p. 25.

3   Ibid., p. 26.

4   M. Safouan, 'Is the Oedipal Complex Universal?', B. Brewster transl., *M/F*, vol. 5/6, 1981, 84–5.

5   L. Irigaray, *This Sex Which is Not One*, C. Porter and C. Burke transl. (Ithica, NY, Cornell University Press, 1985).

6   L. Irigaray, 'The Power of Discourse', in *This Sex Which is Not One*, p. 78.

7   M.A. Doanne, 'The Shadow of Her Gaze', in *The Desire to Desire*.

8   L. Irigaray, 'Flesh Colors', in *Sexes and Genealogies*, G.C. Gill transl. (New York, Columbia University Press, 1993).

9   M. Hansen, *Babel and Babylon: Spectatorship in American Silent Film* (Cambridge, Mass. and London, Harvard University Press, 1994); D. Rodowick, *The Difficulty of Difference, Psychoanalysis, Sexual Differ-

ence and Film Theory (London and New York, Routledge, 1991); T. De Lauretis, *Technologies of Gender* (Bloomington, Indiana University Press, 1987).

10 L. Williams, 'Something Else Besides a Mother': *Stella Dallas* and the Maternal Melodrama', in *Home is Where the Heart is: Studies in Melodrama and the Woman's Film*, C. Gledhill ed. (London, British Film Institute (B.F.I.), 1987); T. Modleski, '*Loving with a Vengeance: Mass-Produced Fantasies for Women* (Hamden, Conn., Archon Books, 1982).

11 M.A. Doanne, 'The Shadow of Her Gaze', in *The Desire to Desire*.

12 L. Williams, 'Feminist Film Theory: *Mildred Pierce* and the Second World War', in *Female Spectators: Looking at Film and Television*, E.D. Pribram ed. (London, Verso, 1988), p. 76.

13 A. Walsh, *Women's Film and Female Experience, 1940–1950* (New York, Praeger, 1984).

14 P. Cook, 'Duplicity in Mildred Pierce', *Women in Film Noir*, E.A. Kaplan ed. (London, B.F.I., 1978).

15 L. Williams, in *Re-Vision: Essays in Feminist Film Criticism*, M.A. Doanne, P. Mellencamp and L. Williams eds (Frederick, Md., University Publications of America, 1983), p. 20.

16 M.A. Doanne, 'The Moving Image: Pathos and The Maternal' in *The Desire to Desire*, p. 81.

17 See chapters 4 and 5 on early film, where I bring a Marxist and psychoanalytic concept of the fetish together in an account of a disembodied and embodied mimesis.

18 T. De Lauretis, 'Oedipus Interruptus', *Wide Angle*, 7/1–2 (1985), 34–40.

19 T. Modleski, 'Time and Desire in the Women's Film', in *Home is Where the Heart is*, p. 327.

20 P. Brooks, *The Melodramatic Imagination*, p. 13.

21 L. Williams, *Playing the Race Card: Melodrama of Black and White from Uncle Tom to O.J. Simpson* (Princeton, NJ, Princeton University Press, 2001); C. Gledhill, 'Rethinking Genre', in *Reinventing Film Studies*, C. Gledhill and L. Williams eds (London, Arnold, 2000).

22 C.J. Clover, 'Her Body, Himself', in *Men, Women and Chainsaws: Gender in the Modern Horror Film* (London, B.F.I., 1992), pp. 21–65.

23 C. Battersby, *The Phenomenal Woman* (Cambridge, Polity, 1998).

24 See J. Laplanche and J.B. Pontalis and their reading of Freud's account of deferred action, or *Nachträlichkeit* in *The Language of Psychoanalysis*, D. Nicholson-Smith transl. (London, Karnac Books, 1988).

25 J. Benjamin, 'Sameness and Difference: Towards an "Over-inclusive" Theory of Gender Development', in *Psychoanalysis in Contexts*, A. Elliott and S. Frosh eds (London and New York, Routledge, 1985), p. 119.

26 J. Butler, *The Psychic Life of Power: Theories in Subjection* (Stanford, Calif., Stanford University Press, 1997), p. 146.

27 A. Phillips, 'Keeping it Moving', in J. Butler, *The Psychic Power of Life*, p. 153.

28 Ibid., p. 155.

29   J. Butler, *The Psychic Power of Life*, p. 165.

30   Ibid., p. 134.

31   S. Freud, 'Melancholia and Mourning' (1917), in *Standard Edition of the Complete Psychological Works of Sigmund Freud*, J. Strachey ed. and transl. (London, Hogarth Press, 1953–4), p. 250.

32   L. Bersani, *The Freudian Body: Psychoanalysis and Art* (New York, Columbia University Press, 1986).

33   M. Borch-Jacobsen, *The Freudian Subject*, C. Porter transl. (Stanford, Calif., Stanford University Press, 1988), p. 27.

34   L. Irigaray, 'The Gesture in Psychoanalysis', in *Sexes and Genealogies*, G.C. Gill transl. (New York, Columbia University Press, 1993).

35   W. Benjamin, 'On The Mimetic Faculty', in *Reflections: Essays, Aphorisms, Autobiographical Writings*, E. Jephcott transl. (New York, Schocken Books, 1978), p. 333.

36   Ibid.

37   W. Benjamin, 'The Work of Art in the Age of Mechanical Reproduction', in *Illuminations*, H. Arendt ed., H. Zorn transl. (London, Pimlico, 1999), pp. 229–30.

38   S. Buck-Morss, 'Dream World of a Mass Culture', in *The Dialectics of Seeing: Walter Benjamin and the Arcades Project* (Cambridge, Mass., MIT Press, 1991), p. 268.

39   S. Buck-Morss, 'Aesthetics and Anaesthetics: Walter Benjamin's Artwork Essay Reconsidered', *October*, 62 (autumn 1989), pp. 3–41.

40   R. Callois, 'Mimicry and Legendary Pychaesthenia', *October*, 31 (winter 1984), pp. 17–32.

41   See Lacan's discussion of Caillois and mimicry, which he uses as a basis for his thinking on the scopic gaze and the mirror stage. J. Lacan, *The Four Fundamental Concepts of Psychoanalysis*, J. Miller ed., A. Sheridan transl. (London, Hogarth Press, 1977). p. 73 and pp. 100–4.

42   J. Lacan, *The Four Fundamental Concepts*, p. 100.

43   This is why Lacan says heterosexuality is impossible, because men are always disavowing and fleeing the original relation to the mother, whereas women are always hysterically demanding.

44   L. Williams, *Playing the Race Card*; C. Gledhill, 'Rethinking Genre'.

CHAPTER 2   THE SEXUAL-DIFFERENCE SPECTATOR
IN WEIMAR CINEMA

1   See Peter Gay's discussion of this in 'The Community of Reason', in *Weimar Culture: The Outsider as Insider* (London, Secker, 1969), p. 35.

2   T. Elsaesser, *Weimar Cinema and After* (London and New York, Routledge, 2000), p. 545.

3   P. Petro, *Joyless Streets: Women and Melodramatic Representation in Weimar Germany* (Princeton, NJ, Princeton University Press, 1989), p. 69.

4 Ibid., p. 69.
5 Ibid., p. 158.
6 Ibid.
7 S. Kracauer, 'The Mass Ornament', *New German Critique*, 5 (spring, 1975), p. 70.
8 T. Elsaesser, 'The Irresponsible Signifier or "The Gamble with History": Film Theory or Cinema Theory?', *New German Critique*, 40 (winter 1987), pp. 65–91; H. Schlüpmann, 'Phenomenology of Film: On Siegfried Kracauer's Writes of the 1920s', *New German Critique*, 40 (winter 1987), pp. 97–115.
9 S. Kracauer, 'Cult of Distraction', in *The Mass Ornament: Weimer Essays*, T.Y. Levin transl. and ed. (Cambridge, Mass. and London, Harvard University Press, 1995), p. 326.
10 S. Kracauer, 'The Little Shopgirls Go to the Movies', in *The Mass Ornament*.
11 P. Petro, *Joyless Streets*, p. 68.
12 Ibid., p. 67.
13 S. Kracauer, 'The Little Shopgirls Go to the Movies', pp. 302–3.
14 P. Petro, 'Modernity and Mass Culture in Weimar: Contours of a Discourse on Sexuality in Early Theories of Perception and Representation', *New German Critique*, 40 (1987).
15 M.A. Doanne, *Femmes Fatales: Feminism, Film Theory, Psychoanalysis* (London and New York, Routledge, 1991).
16 D. Fuss, *Identification Papers* (London and New York, Routledge, 1995).
17 G. Koch, 'Surface and Self-Representation: "The Mass Ornament" and Die Angestellten', in *Siegfried Kracauer: An Introduction*, J. Gaines transl. (Princeton, NJ, Princeton University Press, 2000), pp. 26–48.
18 S. Freud, 'Le Bon's Description of the Group Mind' and 'Being in Love and Hypnosis' in 'Group Psychology' (1921), in vol.18 of *The Standard Edition of the Complete Psychological Works of Sigmund Freud*, J. Strachey trans. and ed., 24 vols (London, Hogarth Press, 1953–74).
19 S. Kracauer, *The Mass Ornament*, p. 78.
20 D.N. Rodowick, '*Last Things before the Last: Kracauer and History*', *New German Critique*, 41 (spring/summer 1987), pp. 109–39.
21 S. Kracauer, *The Mass Ornament*, p. 81.
22 Ibid., p. 77.
23 Ibid., p. 79.
24 G. Koch, *Siegfried Kracauer: An Introduction*, p. 37.
25 Mitchell's quite harsh attack on Reich and R.D. Laing in *Psychoanalysis and Feminism*, failed them for becoming psycho-political ideologists. By this, she meant that they bypassed Freud's radical concept of a *psychic* unconscious to collapse their work into ideological and experiential accounts of either the body or society. But Mitchell's defence of Freud via Lacan was perhaps also too resistant to the ways Reich and Laing insistently brought psychoanalysis back to the material conditions of the body and society, a materialism that has been sadly lacking in

the contemporary, high theories of Lacan. See J. Mitchell, *Psycho-analysis and Feminism* (London, Allen Lane, 1974).

26   E. Fromm, 'Freud's Theory of Dream Interpretation', in *Greatness and Limitations of Freud's Thought* (New York, Harper and Row, 1980), p. 97.

27   G. Koch, *Siegfried Kracauer: An Introduction*, p. 79.

28   T. Elsaesser, 'Cinema – The Irresponsible Signifier or "The Gamble with History": Film Theory or Cinema Theory?', *New German Critique*, 40 (winter 1987), p. 85.

29   G. Koch, *Siegfried Kracauer: An Introduction*, p. 80.

30   S. Kracauer, *From Caligari to Hitler* (Princeton, NJ, Princeton University Press, 1974), p. 7.

31   G. Koch, *Siegfried Kracauer: An Introduction*, p. 83.

32   K. Theweleit, *Male Fantasies*, S. Conway in collaboration with E. Carter and C. Turner transl. (Cambridge, Polity, 1987).

33   Ibid., p. xiv.

34   W. Reich, 'Interview with Kurt Eisler on behalf of the Sigmund Freud Archives, Oct. 18–20, 1952', in *Reich Speaks of Freud*, M. Higgins and C.M. Raphael eds. (New York, Noonday Press, 1968).

35   G. Deleuze and F. Guattari, *Anti-Oedipus: Capitalism and Schizophrenia*, preface by M. Foucault (London, Athlone Press, 1984).

36   Theweleit, *Male Fantasies*, p. 227.

37   Ibid., p. 225.

38   Ibid., p. 210.

39   T. Elsaesser, *Weimar Cinema and After*, p. 13.

40   Ibid.

41   Ibid., p. 70.

42   S. Kracauer, *From Caligari to Hitler*, p. 7.

43   L. Williams, 'When the Woman Looks', in *Re-vision: Essays in Feminist Film Criticism*, M.A. Doanne, P. Mellencamp and L. Williams eds (Frederick, Md., University Publications of America, 1983).

44   M. Hansen, 'The Mass Production of the Senses: Classical Cinema as Vernacular Modernism', in *Reinventing Film Studies*, C. Gledhill and L. Williams eds. (London, Arnold, 2000), p. 342.

45   The 'modernity thesis' was coined by David Bordwell in his book *On the History of Film Style*, referring to the body of work that links cinema to the sensory environment of modernity.

46   T. Elsaesser, 'Cinema – The Irresponsible Signifier or "The Gamble with History"', p. 67.

CHAPTER 3   FILM THEORY AND THE VISUAL BODY

1   L. Mulvey, 'Visual Pleasure and Narrative Cinema', in *Feminism and Film Theory*, C. Penley ed. (London, B.F.I., and New York, Routledge, 1988), pp. 57–68.

2   G. Deleuze and F. Guattari, *Anti-Oedipus: Capitalism and Schizophrenia*, preface by M. Foucault (London, Athlone Press, 1984).

3   J. Campbell, *Arguing with the Phallus: Feminist, Queer and Postcolonial Theory* (London, Zed Books, 2000).

4   L. Irigaray, 'The Poverty of Psychoanalysis', in *The Irigaray Reader*, M. Whitford ed. (Oxford, Blackwell, 1991), p. 98.

5   Ibid., p. 86.

6   L. Irigaray, 'Flesh colors', in *Sexes and Genealogies*, G.C. Gill transl. (New York, Columbia University Press, 1993), p. 155.

7   Ibid.

8   J. Mitchell, *Mad Men and Medusas: Reclaiming Hysteria* (New York, Basic Books, 2000).

9   S. Shaviro, *The Cinematic Body* (Minneapolis, University of Minnesota Press, 1993), pp. 8–17.

10 Ibid., p. 14.

11 Ibid., p. 15.

12 M. Merleau-Ponty, 'The Film and the New Psychology', in *Sense and Non-Sense*, H.L. Dreyfus and P.A. Dreyfus transl. (Evanston, Ill., Northwestern University Press, 1964).

13 J. Butler, *The Psychic Life of Power: Theories in Subjection* (Stanford, Calif., Stanford University Press, 1997).

14 J. Butler, 'The Lesbian Phallus' and 'Phantasmatic Identification', in *Bodies that Matter: On the Discursive Limits of 'Sex'* (New York and London, Routledge, 1993).

15 J. Butler, *Bodies that Matter*.

16 V. Sobchack, 'The Scene of the Screen: Envisioning Cinematic and Electronic Presence', *Film and Theory*, in R. Stam and T. Miller eds (Oxford, Blackwell, 2000), p. 77.

17 W. Benjamin, 'Surrealism', in *Reflections: Essays, Aphorisms, Autobiographical Writings*, E. Jephcott transl. (New York, Schocken Books, 1986), p. 191.

18 W. Benjamin, 'The Work of Art in the Age of Mechanical Reproduction', H. Arendt ed., H. Zorn transl. (London, Pimlico, 1999), p. 227.

19 Ibid., p. 226.

20 V. Walkerdine, 'Video Replay: Families, Films and Fantasy', in *Formations of Fantasy*, V. Burgin, J. Donald and C. Kaplan eds (London, Methuen, 1986), p. 168.

21 Ibid., p. 190.

22 J. Campbell and J. Harbord, 'Introduction', in *Temporalities: Autobiography in a Postmodern Age* (Manchester, University of Manchester Press, 2001), p. 7.

23 Here I am referring to the temptation that Lacan says the analyst must always refuse, to be the one that is certain and knows.

24 V. Walkerdine, 'Video Replay', p. 191.

25 K. Oliver, *Subjectivity without Subjects: From Abject Mothers to Desiring Fathers* (U.S.A. Rowman and Littlefield Publishers, 1998).

26 V. Sobchack, 'The Scene of the Screen', p. 72.

27 Ibid., pp. 76–7.
28 S. Kracauer, 'Photography', in *The Mass Ornament: Weimar Essays*, T.Y. Levin transl. and ed. (Cambridge, Mass. and London, Harvard University Press, 1995).
29 J. Spence and P. Holland eds, *Family Snaps: The Meaning of Domestic Photography* (London, Virago, 1991).

INTRODUCTION TO PART II

1 Ben Singer argues that the work of Guiliano Bruno, Leo Charney, Anne Friedberg, Tom Gunning, Miriam Hansen, Vanessa Schwartz and others makes up what amounts to a school of 'the modernity thesis', exploring the emergence of the sensory environment of cinema and modernity. See B. Singer, 'Making Sense of the Modernity Thesis', in *Melodrama and Modernity: Early Sensational Film and its Contexts* (New York, Columbia University Press, 2001), p. 102.
2 J. Crary, *Techniques of the Observer: On Vision and Modernity in the Nineteenth Century* (Cambridge, Mass., MIT Press, 1999).

CHAPTER 4   PERCEPTION AND EARLY FILM

1 M. Foucault, *The Order of Things* (New York, Vintage Books, 1970), p. 326.
2 Ibid.
3 See the argument between Jung and Freud on dreams, which I relate to a debate on the film hieroglyph in the next chapter.
4 See R.L. Gregory, *Concepts and Mechanisms of Perception* (London, Duckworth, 1974).
5 B. Balázs, *Theory of Film: Character and Growth of a New Art* (London, Dobson, 1953), p. 35.
6 Ibid.
7 B. Winston, *Technologies of Seeing: Photography, Cinematography and Television* (London, B.F.I, 1996), p. 23.
8 Ibid.
9 Winston quotes Benjamin remarking on the dioramas as 'the locus of the most perfect imitation of nature', p. 24.
10 Ibid., p. 25.
11 Ibid.
12 J. Crary, *Techniques of the Observer: On Vision and Modernity in the Nineteenth Century* (Cambridge, Mass., MIT Press, 1999).
13 J. Crary, 'Modernizing Vision', in *Viewing Positions: Ways of Seeing Film*, L. Williams ed. (New Brunswick, Rutgers University Press, 1994), p. 26.
14 Ibid.

15 J. Crary, *Techniques of the Observer*, p. 81.

16 Ibid., p. 132.

17 Ibid., p. 136.

18 Ibid.

19 K. Marx, *Karl Marx: Selected Writings*, D. McLellan ed. (Oxford, Oxford University Press, 1997), pp. 104–5.

20 Ibid., p. 92.

21 Ibid., p. 437.

22 C. Bernheimer and C. Kahane eds, *In Dora's Case* (London, Virago, 1985), p. 4.

23 M. Foucault, *The History of Sexuality Volume 1: An Introduction*, R. Hurley transl. (Harmondsworth, Penguin, 1976), p. 119.

24 E. Showalter, *Hystories: Hysterical Epidemics and Modern Culture* (London, Picador/Macmillan, 1997), p. 34.

25 Ibid., p. 35.

26 Ibid., pp. 34–6.

27 L. Cartwright, *Screening the Body: Tracing Medicine's Visual Culture* (Minneapolis, University of Minnesota Press, 1995).

28 Ibid., p. 2.

29 T. Gunning, 'The Cinema of Attractions: Early Film, its Spectator and the Avant-Garde', in *Early Cinema: Space, Frame, Narrative*, T. Elsaesser ed. (London, B.F.I., 1990).

30 M. Solmes and K.K. Kaplan-Solmes, *Clinical Studies in Neuro-Psychoanalysis* (London and New York, Karnac, 2000).

31 A.R. Damasio, *Descartes' Error: Emotion, Reason and the Human Brain* (New York, Grosset/Putnam, 1999).

32 A.R. Damasio, *The Feeling of What Happens: Body, Emotion and the Making of Consciousness* (London, Vintage, 2000).

33 S. Freud, *Studies in Hysteria* (1895), in *The Standard Edition of the Complete Psychological Works of Sigmund Freud*, J. Strachey transl. and ed., 24 vols. (London, Hogarth Press, 1953–74), vol. 2, p. 294.

34 C. Jung, *The Theory of Psychoanalysis* (1913), in *Collected Works of C.G. Jung* (1893–1968), H. Read, M. Fordham and G. Adler eds, R.F.C. Hull transl. (London, Routledge, 1961), vol. 4, p. 92.

35 Ibid., pp. 161–2.

36 Ibid., p. 112.

37 The Oedipal conflict for Jung, as for Lacan, is also symbolic, and is not defined as literal incestuous wishes of children. Whereas Lacan makes sexual difference a requisite of the symbolic, for Jung it is an imaginary complex that can be transformed into more intergenerational and his-torical symbols, through mediation of the archetypal image. Jung sees fantasies of incest clearly related not to infantile sexual wishes but to a symbolic and internal image of parental union. Jung's archetypal theory is problematic because its universal and biologistic basis leads back, as Frantz Fanon insists, not to history as difference, but to an essentialist account of white European colonialism. Nevertheless, for Jung, the route out of the Oedipal complex is not premised on the difficulty of

resolving sexual difference; rather it is based on the generational need to leave the family of sexual difference behind and replace it with a more historical (social and spiritual) mediation of the psyche.

38 C. Jung, *The Theory of Psychoanalysis* (1913), p. 109.
39 L. Williams, *Hard Core: Power, Pleasure and the 'Frenzy of the Visible'* (Berkeley and Los Angeles, University of California Press, 1989), p. 35.
40 Ibid., p. 46.
41 Ibid., p. 40.
42 Ibid., p. 43.
43 Ibid., p. 46.
44 M. Foucault, *The History of Sexuality Volume 1*, p. 55.
45 L. Cartwright, *Screening the Body*, p. 57.
46 Ibid., p. 60.
47 Ibid., p. 62.
48 Ibid., p. 79.
49 S. Freud, *Some Points for a Comparative Study of Organic and Hysterical Motor Paralyses*, in *Standard Edition*, vol. 1, pp. 168–9.
50 S. Freud, *Charcot*, in *Standard Edition*, vol. 3, p. 172.
51 S. Freud, *The Interpretation of Dreams* (1900), *SE* 4, p. 536.
52 L. Cartwright, *Screening the Body*, p. 8.
53 Ibid.

CHAPTER 5   EARLY FILM SPECTATORSHIP

1 C. Musser, *History of the American Cinema: The Emergence of Cinema, The American Screen to 1907* (New York, Charles Scribner's Sons, 1990), p. 19.
2 P. Gay, *Freud: A Life for Our Time* (London and Melbourne, J.M. Dent & Sons, 1988), p. 128.
3 S. Freud, *The Interpretation of Dreams: Studies in Hysteria* (1901), in *The Standard Edition of the Complete Psychological Works of Sigmund Freud*, J. Strachey transl. and ed. (London, Hogarth Press, 1953–74), vols 4 and 5.
4 S. Freud, *The Freud—Jung Letters: The Correspondence between Sigmund Freud and C.G. Jung*, W. McGuire ed. (London, Hogarth Press, 1974).
5 N. Burch, 'A Primitive Mode of Representation?', in *Early Cinema: Space, Frame Narrative*, T. Elsaesser ed. (London, British Film Institute, 1990).
6 T. Gunning, 'The Cinema of Attractions: Early Film, its Spectator and the Avant Garde', in *Early Cinema, Space, Frame and Narrative*, p. 57.
7 Ibid.
8 Ibid., p. 59.
9 T. Gunning, *D.W. Griffith and the Origins of American Narrative Film* (Champaign, University of Illinois Press, 1990), p. 4.
10 Ibid., p. 4.

11 B. Brewster and L. Jacob, *Theatre to Cinema: Stage Pictorialism and the Early Feature Film* (Oxford and New York, Oxford University Press, 1997), p. 215.
12 P. Gay, *Freud: A Life for Our Time*, p. 124.
13 Ibid., p. 125.
14 G. Koch, 'B. Balázs: The Physiognomy of Things', *New German Critique* (winter 1987), 40, pp. 115–47.
15 B. Balázs, *Theory of the Film: Character and Growth of a New Art* (London, Dennis Dobson, 1952), p. 48.
16 Ibid., p. 73.
17 See C. McCabe, 'Realism and the Cinema: Notes on Some Brechtian Theses', in *Theoretical Essays* (Manchester, Manchester University Press, 1985); R. Dyer, *Stars* (London, B.F.I., 1998).
18 This debate on identification will be further explored in my next chapter in relation to film spectatorship.
19 W. Benjamin, 'Image of Proust', 'On Some Motifs in Baudelaire' and 'The Work of Art in the Age of Mechanical Reproduction', in *Illuminations*, H. Arendt ed., H. Zorn transl. (London, Pimlico, 1970).
20 Ibid., p. 154.
21 Ibid., p. 157.
22 S. Kracauer, *Theory of Film: The Redemption of Physical Reality* (Oxford, Oxford University Press, 1960), p. 158.
23 S. Kracauer, 'Photography', in *The Mass Ornament: Weimar Essays*, T. Levin transl. (Cambridge, Mass. and London, Harvard University Press, 1995).
24 Ibid., p. 61.
25 M. Hansen, 'Introduction' to S. Kracauer, *Theory of Film*, p. xxvii.
26 S. Kracauer, *Theory of Film*, p. 306.
27 Ibid., p. 303.
28 M. Hansen, *Babel and Babylon: Spectatorship in American Silent Film* (Cambridge, Mass. and London, Harvard University Press, 1994).
29 Ibid., p. 130.
30 Maybe there is a need to reiterate at this point Juliet Mitchell's recent argument in *Mad Men and Medusas: Reclaiming Hysteria* (New York, Basic Books, 2000), where she states that the Oedipal and hysteric, especially in relation to Freud, are only fractionally separate.
31 P. Rosen, 'Entering History', in *Change Mummified: Cinema Historicity, Theory* (Minneapolis and London, University of Minnesota Press, 2001), p. 84.
32 *The Mother and the Law* is the title given by Griffith to a later edited film version of *Intolerance* in 1919.
33 M. Hansen, *Babel and Babylon*, p. 138.
34 M. Foucault, *The History of Sexuality Volume 1: An Introduction*, R. Hurley transl. (Harmondsworth, Penguin Books, 1976), p. 153.
35 Ibid., p. 205.
36 T.W. Adorno and M. Horkheimer, 'The Schema of Mass Culture', in *The Culture Industry: Selected Essays on Mass Culture*, J.M. Bernstein ed. (London, Routledge, 1991), p. 80.

37 P. Rosen. *Change Mummified*, p. 84.
38 M. Hansen. *Babel and Babylon*, p. 191.
39 S. Freud. *Interpretation of Dreams*, p. 457.
40 Jung continues, 'When I find sugar in urine, it is sugar and not a façade for albumen. What Freud called the "dream-façade" is the dream's obscurity, and this is really only a projection of our own lack of understanding', C. Jung, *The Practice of Psychotherapy*, in *The Collected Works*, vol. 16 (London, Routledge and Kegan Paul, 1954), p. 149.
41 R.D. Laing, *The Divided Self* (London, Penguin, 1990), p. 31.
42 H.D. writes, 'perhaps in that sense he was right (actually he was always right, though we sometimes translated our thoughts into different languages or mediums).' See 'Writing on the Wall', in *Tribute to Freud* (Manchester, Carcanet Press, 1970), p. 53.
43 Ibid., p. 45.
44 L. Marcus, *Close-Up 1927–1933: Cinema and Modernism*, J. Donald, A. Friedberg and L. Marcus eds (London, Cassell, 1998), pp. 99–100.
45 H.D., 'Conrad Veidt: The Student of Prague', in *Close-Up*, p. 123.
46 H.D. writes, 'So you see, I Sigmund Freud, myself standing here, a favourite and gifted, admit it, student of Dr. Charcot, in no way to all appearances deranged or essentially peculiar, true to my own orbit – *true to my own orbit?* true to my own orbit, my childhood fantasies of Hannibal, my identification with Hannibal, the Carthaginian (Jew, not Roman) – I Sigmund Freud, understand this Caesar. I, Hannibal', in 'Writing on the Wall', p. 85.
47 H.D., 'The Student of Prague', in *Close-Up*, p. 124.
48 See J. Harbord, *Film Cultures* (London, Thousand Oaks and New Delhi, Sage, 2002) for a discussion of modernism's relation between art and mass culture with regard to taste.
49 M. Hansen, *Babel and Babylon*, p. 193.
50 Ibid., p. 193.
51 J. Harbord, *Film Cultures* (London and New York, Sage, 2002).

INTRODUCTION TO PART III

1 M. Hansen, *Babel and Babylon: Spectatorship in American Silent Film* (Cambridge, Mass. and London, Harvard University Press, 1994), p. 101.
2 Ibid., pp. 12–13.
3 Ibid., p. 7.
4 Ibid.
5 Ibid., p. 110.
6 Ibid., p. 112.

CHAPTER 6   CULTURAL STUDIES, ETHNOGRAPHY AND THE
'REAL' FILM SPECTATOR

1   S. Radstone, 'Screening Trauma: Forrest Gump, Film and Memory', in *Memory and Methodology*, S. Radstone ed. (Oxford and New York, Berg, 2000); E. Showalter, *Hystories: Hysterical Epidemics and Modern Culture* (London, Picador, 1998).

2   E. Showalter, *Hystories*, p. 13. In much of what she says Showalter is right: hysteria is a cultural phenomenon, and conditions like M.E. and Gulf War syndrome have hysterical and psychological components to them. But then so do all illnesses, even heart disease and cancer, although the psychological aspects to these conditions are perhaps not as easy to verify. Although Showalter states that 'we can defend Freud's insights and try and restore confidence in serious psychotherapy', she takes issue with two therapists in the book who in her view tout trauma theory: the first is Juliet Herman, a Harvard professor who specializes in recovered memories of sexual abuse, and the second, Valerie Sinason, a consultant child psychotherapist at the Tavistock Clinic who has professionally staked her reputation on the realities of satanic ritual abuse. For Showalter, these therapists advance our modern culture's hysterical plague.

3   S. Radstone, 'Introduction', in *Memory and Methodology*, p. 11.

4   J. Harbord, *Film Cultures* (London, Thousand Oaks and New Delhi, Sage, 2002).

5   N. Couldry, *Inside Culture: Re-imagining the Method of Cultural Studies* (London, Thousand Oaks and New Delhi, Sage, 2000).

6   E. Showalter, *Hystories*.

7   R.D. Laing, *The Divided Self* (London, Penguin, 1969), p. 85.

8   J. Mitchell, *Mad Men and Medusas: Reclaiming Hysteria* (New York, Basic Books, 2000), p. 101.

9   C. Bollas, *Cracking Up: The Work of Unconscious Experience* (London, Routledge, 1995), p. 143.

10 Ibid.

11 M. Heidegger, *Being and Time* (Oxford, Blackwell, 1967).

12 Ibid.

13 W. Benjamin, 'On Some Motifs in Baudelaire', in *Illuminations*, H. Arendt ed., H. Zorn transl. (London, Pimlico, 1999), p. 155. Adam Phillips links this accidental rediscovery and re-memory of the past to the importance of contingency in the therapeutic situation. Life is not simply about having our desires or mourning our losses but opening ourselves up to a wider social environment of accidents and chance. Walter Benjamin sees the Marxist connotations of Proust's material apprehension of the image. If the past is found and remembered accidentally through encountering random material objects in everyday life, then the key to creative re-memory for the individual lies not just with personal dreams and desire, but with a wider historical collective.

Benjamin calls this embodied apprehension of the image which connects private and public a 'profane illumination'.

14 Ibid., p. 157.
15 See R.D. Laing, *The Divided Self.*
16 A. Gray, 'Learning From Experience: Cultural Studies and Feminism', in *Cultural Methodologies*, J. McGuigan ed. (London, Sage, 1997).
17 A. Kuhn, *Family Secrets: Acts of Memory and Imagination* (London, Verso, 1995); J. Stacey, *Star Gazing: Hollywood Cinema and Female Spectatorship* (London and New York, Routledge, 1994); V. Walkerdine, 'Video Replay: Families, Films and Fantasy', in *Formations of Fantasy*, V. Burgin, J. Donald and C. Kaplan eds (London, Methuen, 1986).
18 S. Moores, *Interpreting Audiences: The Ethnography of Media Consumption* (London, Thousand Oaks and New Delhi, Sage, 1993), p. 32.
19 S. Hall, 'Encoding/decoding', in *Culture, Media, Language*, S. Hall, D. Hobson, A. Lowe and P. Willis eds (Birmingham, Centre for Contemporary Cultural Studies, University of Birmingham, 1980).
20 C. Brunsdon and D. Morley, *Everyday Television: 'Nationwide'* (London, B.F.I., 1978); A. Gray, *Video Playtime: The Gendering of a Leisure Technology* (London, Routledge, 1992).
21 T. Modleski, *Loving with a Vengeance: Mass-Produced Fantasies for Women* (London, Methuen, 1982); J. Radway, *Reading the Romance: Women, Patriarchy and Popular Literature* (Chapel Hill and London, University of North Carolina Press, 1984).
22 I. Ang, *Watching Dallas: Soap Opera and the Melodramatic Imagination* (London, Methuen, 1985).
23 P. Scannell, *Radio, Television and Modern Life* (Oxford, Blackwell, 1996), p. 152.
24 Ibid., p. 13.
25 Ibid., p. 152.
26 Ibid., p. 174.
27 Scannell cites Barthes' evocation of the incommunicable self in *Camera Lucida* (1984) as an example of this 'ownmost' temporal identity.
28 M. Heidegger, *Being and Time*, p. 10.
29 Ibid., p. 173.
30 Scannell, *Radio, Television and Modern Life*, p. 177.
31 Ibid., p. 174.
32 R. Barthes, *Camera Lucida: Reflections on Photography* (New York, Hill and Wang, 1984).
33 Ibid., p. 91.
34 M. Heidegger, *Being and Time*, p. 176.
35 L. Mulvey, 'Afterthoughts on "Visual Pleasure and Narrative Cinema"', in *Feminism and Film Theory*, C. Penley ed. (New York, Routledge, and London, B.F.I., 1988).
36 J. Stacey, *Star Gazing*, p. 25.
37 I have utilized not just Irigaray's work, but also that of Diana Fuss, Judith Butler and Jessica Benjamin in a theorization of the bodily gay imaginary that situates a fluid and mimetic figuration of desire and

identification between women, a mimesis which oscillates between intersubjective recognition and more merged states of oneness (*Arguing with the Phallus*, 2000).

38 J. Stacey, *Star Gazing*, p. 28.
39 Ibid., p. 32.
40 Ibid., p. 63.
41 Ibid., p. 68.
42 Ibid., p. 139.
43 Diana Fuss refuses the Oedipal distinction between desire and identification, arguing that the female homosexual's turn to the mother 'suggests that the daughter must become her mother in order to have her' (*Identification Papers* (London and New York, Routledge, 1995), p. 67).
44 J. Stacey, *Star Gazing*, p. 135.
45 Ibid., p. 172.
46 A. Kuhn, *Family Secrets*, p. 5.
47 R. Barthes, *Camera Lucida*, p. 90.
48 Ibid., p. 78.
49 S. Hall, 'Encoding/Decoding', and 'Cultural Studies: Two Paradigms', *Media, Culture and Society*, vol. 2 (1980), pp. 52–72.

CHAPTER 7   STARS AND MELODRAMA

1 J. Mayne, *Cinema and Spectatorship* (London, Routledge, 1993).
2 R. Dyer, 'Introduction' to *Heavenly Bodies: Film Stars and Society* (Houndsmill, Macmillan, 1986), p. 8.
3 J. Mayne, *Cinema and Spectatorship* (London, Routledge, 1993), p. 138.
4 Ibid.; C. Williams, 'After the Classic, the Classical and Ideology: The Differences of Realism', in *Reinventing Film Studies*, C. Gledhill and L. Williams eds (London and New York, Arnold, 2000).
5 S. Cohan, 'Cary Grant in the Fifties: Indiscretions of the Bachelor's Masquerade', in *The Film Studies Reader*, J. Hollows, P. Hutchings and M. Jancovich eds (London, Arnold, 2000).
6 J. Fiske, 'The Cultural Economy of Fandom', in *The Adoring Audience: Fan Culture and Popular Media*, L. Lewis ed. (London, Routledge, 1992), p. 35.
7 Y. Tasker, *Spectacular Bodies* (London, Routledge, 1993), p. 74.
8 H. Jenkins, *Textual Poachers: Television Fans and Participatory Culture* (London and New York, Routledge, 1992).
9 H. Jenkins, 'Reception Theory and Audience Research: The Mystery of the Vampire's Kiss', in *Reinventing Film Studies*, C. Gledhill and L. Williams eds. (London, Arnold, and New York, Oxford University Press, 2000), p. 175.
10 C. Penley, 'Feminism, Psychoanalysis, and the Study of Popular Culture', in *Cultural Studies*, L. Grossberg, C. Nelson and P. Treichler eds (London and New York, Routledge, 1992), pp. 479–500.

11 J. Laplanche and J.B. Pontalis, 'Fantasy and the Origins of Sexuality' (1968), reprinted in *Formations of Fantasy*, V. Burgin, J. Donald and C. Kaplan eds (London, Methuen, 1986).

12 E. Cowie, *Fantasia*, MLF, 9, 1984.

13 R. Dyer, *Stars* (London, B.F.I., 1979).

14 C. Geraghty, 'Re-examining Stardom: Questions of Texts, Bodies and Performance', in *Reinventing Film Studies*, p. 190.

15 F. Roustang, *How to Make a Paranoid Laugh: Or What is Psycho-analysis?*, A.C. Vila transl. (Philadelphia, University of Pennsylvania Press, 1996).

16 C. Gledhill, 'Signs of Melodrama', in *Stardom: Industry of Desire*, C. Gledhill ed. (London, Routledge, 1991).

17 T. Elsaesser, 'Tales of Sound and Fury: Observations on the Family Melodrama', in *Home is Where the Heart is: Studies in Melodrama and the Woman's Film*, C. Gledhill ed. (London, B.F.I., 1987).

18 Ibid., p. 221.

19 R. Dyer, *Stars*, p. 225.

20 C. Geraghty, 'Re-examining Stardom', p. 193.

21 C. Counsell, *Signs of Performance* (London, Routledge, 1996), p. 198.

22 C. Geraghty, 'Re-examining Stardom', p. 193.

23 C. Gledhill, 'Rethinking Genre', in *Reinventing Film Studies*.

24 L. Williams, *Playing the Race Card: Melodrama of Black and White from Uncle Tom to O.J. Simpson* (Princeton, NJ, Princeton University Press, 2001).

25 Ibid.

26 R. Maltby, 'Genre', in *Hollywood Cinema: An Introduction* (Oxford, Blackwell, 1995), p. 111.

27 L. Williams, 'Melodrama Revised', in *Refiguring American Film Genres: Theory and History*, N. Browne ed. (Berkeley, Calif, University of California Press, 1998).

28 See J. Campbell, *Arguing with the Phallus: Feminist, Queer and Post-colonial Theory* (London, Zed Books, 2000) for an account of how Castoriadis's work informs the concept of a bodily imaginary.

29 T. Elsaesser, 'Tales of Sound and Fury: Observations on the Family Melodrama', in *Home is Where the Heart is*, C. Gledhill ed. (London, B.F.I., 1987); B. Singer, *Melodrama and Modernity: Early Sensational Film and its Contexts* (New York, Columbia University Press, 2001).

30 C. Gledhill, 'Rethinking Genre', in *Reinventing Film Studies*, p. 234.

31 C. Gledhill, 'Rethinking Genre', p. 235; T. Postlewait, 'From Melodrama to Realism: The Suspect History of American Drama', in *Melodrama: The Cultural Emergence of a Genre*, M. Hays and A. Nikolopoulou eds (New York, St Martin's Press, 1996).

32 C. Gledhill, 'Rethinking Genre', p. 236.

33 J. Mitchell, *Mad Men and Medusas: Reclaiming Hysteria* (New York, Basic Books, 2000).

34 Ibid., p. 79.

35 L. Williams, *Playing the Race Card*, p. 17.

36 J. Mayne, *Cinema and Spectatorship*, p. 155.
37 L. Williams, *Playing the Race Card*, p. xiv.
38 L. Williams, *Playing the Race Card*, p. xix.
39 F. Fanon, *Black Skin, White Masks* (London, Pluto, 1986), p. 104.
40 H. Bhabha, *The Location of Culture* (London and New York, Routledge, 1994).
41 Ibid., p. 70.
42 Ibid., p. 77.
43 Ibid., p. 92.
44 Ibid., p. 86.
45 Ibid., p. 89.
46 See David Trotter, *Paranoid Modernism*.
47 F. Fanon, *Black Skin, White Masks*, p. 161.
48 R. Green, ' "Twoness" in the Style of Oscar Micheaux', in *Black American Cinema*, M. Diawara ed. (London and New York, Routledge, 1993); J. Gaines, 'Fire and Desire: Race, Melodrama and Oscar Micheaux', in *Black American Cinema*.
49 W.E.B. Dubois, *The Souls of Black Folk* (London, Penguin, 1996), p. xxv, n. 47.
50 Ibid.
51 T. Cripps, 'Oscar Micheaux: The Story Continues', in *Black American Cinema*.
52 b. hooks, 'The Oppositional Gaze: Black Female Spectators', in *Black American Cinema*.
53 J. Bobo, 'Reading through the Text: The Black Women as Audience', in *Black American Cinema*.

CHAPTER 8   FILM AESTHETICS AND CULTURAL RE-MEMORY

1 F. Jameson, 'Postmodernism and Consumer Society', in *Postmodern Culture*, H. Foster ed. (London, Pluto, 1983), p. 116.
2 Ibid.
3 Ibid., p. 120.
4 Ibid.
5 L.A. Sass, *Madness and Modernism: Insanity in the Light of Modern Art, Literature, and Thought* (Cambridge, Mass. and London, Harvard University Press, 1992), p. 10.
6 Ibid., p. 346.
7 M. Foucault, *Mental Illness and Psychology* (London, Harper and Row, 1976).
8 L. Irigaray, 'Flesh Colors', in *Sexes and Genealogies*, G.C. Gill transl. (New York, Columbia University Press, 1993), p. 163.
9 Ibid., p. 155.
10 The so-called moral war against Iraq, led by the USA and the UK, also reflects such psychotic or hysterical disavowal, where Bush's and Blair's

moral and Oedipal crusade masquerades to cover over the difference of political discourses and imaginaries.

11   C. Castoriadis, 'Psychoanalysis and Politics', in *Speculations after Freud: Psychoanalysis, Philosophy and Culture*, S. Shamdasani and M. Muchöw eds (London and New York, Routledge, 1994), p. 4.

12   S. Shaviro, *The Cinematic Body* (Minneapolis, University of Minnesota Press, 1993).

13   Ibid., p. 18.

14   Ibid., p. 54.

15   Ibid., p. 46.

16   Ibid., p. 202.

17   Ibid., p. 238.

18   V. Sobchack, 'The Scene of the Screen: Envisioning Cinematic and Electronic Presence', in *Film and Theory: An Anthology*, R. Stam and T. Miller eds (Malden, Mass., and Oxford, Blackwell, 2000).

19   J.D. Andrew, 'The Challenge of Phenomenology: Amédée Ayfre and Henri Agel', in *The Major Film Theories* (London, Oxford and New York, Oxford University Press, 1976), p. 249.

20   P. Rosen, *Change Mummified: Cinema, Historicity, Theory* (Minneapolis and London, University of Minnesota Press, 2001).

21   The connection with Freud's analysis of the medusa's head in relation to the castration complex is duly noted here.

22   P. Rosen, *Change Mummified*, p. 17.

23   L. Marks, *The Skin of the Film: Intercultural Cinema, Embodiment and the Senses* (Durham, NC and London, Duke University Press, 2000).

24   G. Deleuze, *Cinema 1: The Movement-Image*, H. Tomlinson and B. Habberjam transl. (New York, Zone, 1986) p. 42.

25   H. Bergson, *Matter and Memory* (1911), N.N. Paul and W.S. Palmer transl. (New York, Zone, 1988).

26   D.N. Rodowick, *Gilles Deleuze's Time Machine* (Durham, NC, Duke University Press, 1997), p. 29.

27   G. Deleuze, *Cinema 1: The Movement-Image*.

28   L. Marks, 'The Memory of Images', in *The Skin of the Film*, p. 63.

29   H. Bergson, *Matter and Memory*.

30   L. Marks, 'The Memory of Touch', in *The Skin of the Film*, p. 164.

31   *Transformer* (Channel 4 documentary on Lars von Trier, 2001).

32   Ibid.

33   Indeed, it seems this was also the view of director Lars von Trier. Such was the antagonism between Bjork and von Trier that she refused to come on stage and accept the award with him.

34   J. Fueur, 'The Self-reflective Musical and the Myth of Entertainment', in *Genre: The Musical*, R. Altman ed. (London, Boston, Mass., and Henley, Routledge and Kegan Paul, 1981), p. 172.

35   L. von Trier, 'Interview with Lars von Trier', in *Dancer in the Dark* (London, Basingstoke and Oxford, Film Four Books, Macmillan, 2000).

36   Richard Dyer has revealed the utopian sensibility of musicals as an embodied non-representability that takes off from the narratives. This

analysis of the utopian and embodied nature of the musical is indebted to the work of Ernst Bloch, a Marxist critic from the Frankfurt School. Bloch understands Utopian longing and fulfilment to be constructed out of historical and temporal narrative moving towards an ultimate moment, together with a more spatial intersubjectivity, anticipating that moment with lyricism and a dramatic presentation of the 'not yet being'. See R. Dyer, 'Entertainment and Utopia', in *Genre: The Musical*, p. 189.

Index